Judging Children as Children

Michael A. Corriero

Judging Children as Children

A Proposal for a Juvenile Justice System

TEMPLE UNIVERSITY PRESS
PHILADELPHIA

Temple University Press
1601 North Broad Street
Philadelphia PA 19122
www.temple.edu/tempress

Text design by Kate Nichols

∞ The paper used in this publication meets the requirements of
the American National Standard for Information Sciences—Permanence
of Paper for Printed Library Materials, ANSI Z39.48-1992

Library of Congress Cataloging-in-Publication Data
Corriero, Michael A.
Judging children as children : a proposal for a juvenile justice system / Michael A.
Corriero.
    p. cm.   Includes bibliographical references and index.
    Contents: The proposition — The nature of adolescence — The criminal
responsibility of juveniles — Sentencing children tried in adult courts — Our hardest
to love children — Interactive justice — Fridays in the Youth Part / by Caroline Joy
DeBrovner — The experiment that failed — Creation of the Youth Part — The Youth
Part model — A model juvenile justice system — Juvenile justice policy reform.
    ISBN 1-59213-168-9 (cloth : alk. paper)
    1. Juvenile justice, Administration of—United States. 2. Juvenile corrections—United
States. I. Title.

KF9779.C67 2006
345.73`08—dc22   2005056048

Excerpt (p. 79) from "Another Brick in the Wall (Part 2)" Words and Music by George
Roger Waters (c) 1979 Roger Waters Music Overseas Ltd. Warner/Chappell Artemis
Music Ltd. All Rights Reserved. Used with Permission.

Excerpt (p. 79) from "Shame on a Nigga" Gary Grice/Clifford Smith/Corey
Woods/Dennis Coles/Jason Hunter/Lamont Hawkins/Russell T. Jones/Robert Diggs (c)
1993 BMG Songs, Inc. (ASCAP) /Careers-BMG Music Publishing, Inc. (BMI)/
Wu-Tang Publishing (BMI)/Ramecca Publishing (BMI) All rights on behalf of
Wu-Tang Publishing (BMI) and Ramecca Publishing (BMI) administered by
Careers-BMG Music Publishing, Inc. (BMI).

2 4 6 8 9 7 5 3 1

Contents

Preface

OR CENTURIES, philosophers have struggled to define justice, constantly seeking to improve the way humanity applies the concept. What is justice for children who violate the law? How should a just society judge young offenders? When is it proper to punish a child as a criminal? What form should the punishment take? And what justifies the practice? In *Judging Children as Children: A Proposal for a Juvenile Justice System,* I have attempted to address these issues in the context of our current national policy of trying children accused of crimes in adult courts. As the presiding judge of Manhattan's Youth Part since 1992, a special court in New York City which has the responsibility of resolving cases of children as young as 13 who are tried as adults, I have confronted the complex world of troubled children and children in trouble with the law. This book has grown out of that experience. I have attempted to present an accurate portrayal of certain consequences of the policy of trying children as adults as they have consistently and continuously been revealed to me. I hope the reader will conclude that this account is an honest appraisal of the issues presented by such a policy and that my recommendations for improving our juvenile justice system are reasonable, fair and attainable. I have provided models for application of my convictions and principles, and suggested how implementation of these models can be accomplished. New York City has been the laboratory for our work, but the issues I have encountered are present in all jurisdictions which seek to hold children criminally accountable in systems designed for adults. By no means do I believe I have the definitive solution to the problems presented by juveniles who commit crime, but I do believe that I have proposed a rational response to their behavior. I offer this work as proof that we can still be creative, compassionate and effective in seeking justice for children without compromising public safety.

Acknowledgments

THIS BOOK could not have been possible without the help of others. My first thanks go to my wife, Mary Ellen. Without her help, the production of this manuscript in a timely fashion and in a form acceptable to the publisher literally could not have been possible. Not only has she devoted her professional skills as a court reporter to the production of this work, but also she has been my muse, providing me with inspiration and encouragement. She has sacrificed many evenings, weekends, and holidays to help me with this project. She deserves my deepest gratitude.

Mollie Faber deserves special thanks for her dedication to the work of the Youth Part and the soundness of my judicial decisions. As my longtime trusted and gifted law clerk, Mollie's advice and counsel have been a source of solace for me in resolving the many difficult issues presented by the children who have appeared before us. Her encyclopedic knowledge of the Juvenile Offender Law has been invaluable. Mollie has been my first line of editorial criticism, reading every line, page and chapter of the manuscript, correcting my spelling, grammar, and syntax, and strengthening my legal analysis. We have one of those rare professional relationships created by a commonality of purpose resulting in an understanding and respect for each other's views.

Valerie Pels also deserves special thanks. She and Mollie shared responsibilities as my law clerk. Valerie has had extensive experience representing juveniles. Her sensitivity and awareness of the issues affecting children involved in the system greatly improved the quality and substance of my arguments.

My chambers staff also included Lisa Zimmerman, Ludwina Normil, and Sheridan Jack Browne, who served successively as my personal secretary, organizing our Friday calendar sessions and acting as our liaison with myriad alternative-to-incarceration programs and public agencies. I am grateful for their contribution to the work of the Youth Part.

I also would like to thank Alison Hamanjian and Kathleen Landaverde, who have recently joined my chambers staff, Alison as my law clerk and Kathy as my secretary. They have become indispensable to the work of the Youth Part.

Dr. Caroline Joy DeBrovner studiously observed the court for over three years and has contributed a significant chapter to this work. I am also indebted to her for her support and generosity in helping to establish the Youth Part library of books that we dispense to young people who come before the Youth Part.

A delightful group of college and law students helped with the tedious task of checking citations and authorities with camaraderie and aplomb. Jedd Bellman, Elizabeth O'Connor, Amanda Gail Gruber, Lindsay Jarusiewicz, Jodi Siegel, Diann Trainor, Robert Windsor, and Danielle Contillo are all deserving of thanks.

I would like to thank Temple University Press for appreciating the significance of the issues presented in this text, especially Janet M. Francendese, Editor-in-Chief, for her willingness to take a chance with a first-time author. Her thoughtful comments shaped and toned my presentation into a solid argument for reform. I also would like to thank her colleagues, Will Hammell, Matthew Kull, Ann-Marie Anderson, Gary Kramer, and Jennifer French, as well as my copy editor Laura Lawrie, for generously sharing their knowledge of the intricacies of publishing a work of this nature.

It is my hope that this book will memorialize the work of the Youth Part. I would be remiss if I didn't acknowledge those who worked in the Youth Part and contributed to whatever successes we may have achieved, the many lawyers—assistant district attorneys and defense counsel—who placed their trust in my judgment as to what was fair for victims and defendants. Among them is Nancy Ginsburg, of New York's Legal Aid Society, who was instrumental in the creation of the Juvenile Offender Unit, a special group of Legal Aid lawyers who work closely with social workers in the representation of juveniles in the Part. Recognition is also given to all the court representatives of the alternative-to-incarceration programs who have appeared in our Part. Special thanks to Nancy Bradley of We Care About You (WCAY), who was present at the inception of the Youth Part and set the standard to which all court representatives aspire. Angel Rodriquez, the director of The Andrew Glover Youth Program, has always been a loyal and outspoken supporter of the Youth Part concept. His program serves as a model to be emulated by all community-based programs.

The Youth Part courtroom is often filled with anxious members of the public, relatives of teen offenders, as well as victims, witnesses, lawyers, and police officers. The sensitive response of our courtroom personnel, court officers and court reporters enables us to address the complex issues presented by juvenile offender cases in a conscientious, dignified, and professional atmosphere. I am especially grateful to our court clerks, Patricia Laurie and Thelma Greenidge, whose sense of humor, professionalism, and dedication help us cope with the emotional impact of the human tragedies that unfold before us each day.

I owe an unrepayable debt of gratitude to the extraordinary adults, role models, family, friends, and teachers who have influenced my life. Of course, my first teachers were my late parents, Frank and Antoinette. Although they were not formally educated, they recognized the importance of offering me the best education that they could afford.

Finally, I would like to thank my daughters, Adriann and Jennifer, for allowing me to spend much of my spare time over the last two years researching and writing this book, a book that I hope will constitute a legacy for my grandchildren, Rebecca, Jessica, and Charles Joseph (CJ); a legacy of the value of a life devoted to seeking justice for children.

Prologue

S A TEENAGER growing up in Manhattan's Little Italy in the
1950s, I saw how easily a careless choice could draw one into
a situation that carried "the appearance of a culpability not
necessarily justified by the true facts."[1] Perceptions of such a childhood, to those who have not had a similar experience, may be shaped
by films such as *Mean Streets* or *A Bronx Tale*. To be sure, as children we encountered many crossroads, pinpoints in time where a
step to the right could lead to accomplishment and honor, a step to
the left trouble and tragedy. But I also remember Mulberry Street
as a place where America's promise could become a reality, a place
where with hard work, diligence, and the support of family a child
could fully realize his or her potential.

In the 1950s, Little Italy hadn't changed very much from the
early 1900s when Jacob Riis described the area as more like a sub-
urb of Naples than a part of America. My parents and I lived
across the street from the "Tombs," as the Manhattan House of
Detention was known. The Tombs was connected to and a part of the
Manhattan Criminal Court building. We lived in a three-room apartment on the top floor of a five-story tenement at the corner of Baxter

and White streets. My father did the work of a longshoreman at the Brooklyn Army Terminal, my mother was a seamstress in a factory on lower Broadway.

How I went from playing stickball against the walls of the Criminal Court building to presiding over cases as a judge in that very same building is a story more aptly reserved for a memoir than an academic argument against trying children as adults. Suffice it to say that my parents prepared me as best they could for those inevitable pinpoints in time when as a teenager I would be confronted with choices. Although they did not have a formal education, my parents saw the value of education as the only way to change the circumstances of life. As soon as I was old enough, they enrolled me in kindergarten at Transfiguration, a Maryknoll missionary school located on Mott Street which was then the heart of Chinatown, a few blocks from where we lived. I spent nine years with this group of Catholic missionaries. Despite their religious commitment, there was something about them—a worldliness in the best sense. I didn't realize it at the time, but most of the priests and nuns who taught us were only in their early 20s. They came to teach at the school to perfect their Chinese for service in China.

There were about 300 students at Transfiguration when I attended, about 30 in each class. The children and grandchildren of Italian immigrants were by far the majority of students in the 1940s and 1950s, although the number of Chinese students was growing. The school had been established in the early 1800s in the center of the city's poorest slums. It drew children from the old neighborhoods of the Five Points and Mulberry Bend, educating successive waves of Irish, Italian, and Chinese immigrants who sent there children their to learn English, religion and American principles. After Transfiguration, I attended Power Memorial Academy. I was now in the hands, literally, of the Irish Christian Brothers. Like the Maryknollers, they were strict disciplinarians; corporeal punishment was not unheard of nor condemned at the time, at least for the first two years of my attendance. Thereafter, the Brothers adopted a less physical but no less tormenting form of discipline—"detention"—an hour after school for every detention slip received during the day. An hour of silence seated, arms folded with your fellow miscreant classmates in the school lunchroom. Academically, the school provided a sound classical education: four years of Latin, literature, history, French, or Spanish. The Brothers insisted we attend a Catholic college. I enrolled in St. John's University. It was near to my home, just over the Brooklyn Bridge in downtown Brooklyn; it had a relatively small student body and it was the only coeducational Catholic college in the city. The law school was in the very same building as the undergraduate school. After receiving a liberal arts degree in social science, law school seemed like a natural and convenient transition.

I like to think that I had the benefit of two educations: one formal and traditional, the other taught by less conventionally distinguished educators but no less astute observers of the human condition—the Mulberry Street Boys. I learned firsthand about the concept of accomplice liability, circumstantial evidence, and the neighborhood's repulsion for informers. I have been able to put both educations to good use in my professional life. Both have helped me understand and cope with the challenges presented to me: first as an assistant district attorney in the Office of Frank Hogan in New York County from 1969 through 1973; and then as a criminal defense lawyer and as a judge since 1980 presiding in New York's criminal courts.

As a young prosecutor, I was frequently assigned to a special part of the Criminal Court—"Part 3."[2] This Part heard cases involving youths between the ages of 16 and 21. My experience in the Part helped shape and focus my interest in the way the law treated these offenders and ultimately helped me to develop the approach I have taken in the Youth Part. Working for "Mr. Hogan," as we respectfully and affectionately referred to him, was probably the most momentous event in my professional life. Frank Hogan was a legendary public servant renowned for his professionalism, independence and fearless integrity. His policy toward young offenders was especially significant to me. That policy was reflective of the conventional wisdom of the time; that courts and prosecutors had a special obligation to make sure that young people were treated fairly and effectively, recognizing that young offenders were malleable and could be positively influenced. The District Attorney's office worked closely with a special program called the Youth Counsel Bureau (YCB). The Youth Counsel Bureau had been established in 1941 by then District Attorney Thomas E. Dewey and expanded by Mr. Hogan, his successor. YCB worked closely with the judges presiding over the New York County Youth Part in identifying and counseling troubled youth when they first entered the system. The Bureau functioned as an independent and unofficial agency operating out of the District Attorney's office. It furnished, through referral to various private agencies, vocational guidance, psychiatric services, medical attention, and overall supervision. Its core principle was that proper guidance and assistance at a critical period in a youth's life might save him from a life of crime. As prosecutors, we were encouraged to send suitable youths to YCB. If they succeeded in the regimen provided by the Bureau, we were authorized to withdraw the charges against these youthful offenders.

In 1973 I left the District Attorney's office and specialized in the practice of criminal law. I represented many young offenders. One of the youngest was a 12-year-old boy accused of murder. Only after several meetings was I able to gain his trust and confidence. I learned that he was taking responsibility for the crime for an older boy who faced more severe punishment if charged because of his age. When he was arrested he did not deny the accusation—he was afraid of this boy and didn't want to be labeled a "rat." I was able to persuade him that there was a way to defend him without directly implicating the older boy but he had to trust me. What I had in mind was to have him take a lie detector test wherein he could freely express his innocence without specifically naming the actual perpetrator. The juvenile court prosecutor was receptive to my proposal. She apparently had doubts about the credibility of her only witness (who was actually the perpetrator of the crime). I suggested that she could select the polygraph expert who was to administer the test. She chose Detective Nat Laurendi of the New York County District Attorney's Squad, who had pioneered the use of the lie detector in criminal investigations for the DA's office. I knew Detective Laurendi and had worked with him when I was a DA. He was a skilled interrogator and I had confidence in his judgment. It took some time to explain the polygraph concept to my young client but he came to understand that the most important thing was to tell the truth. I reassured him that he would not be asked to name the person who committed the crime. He passed and the charges against him were eventually dismissed.

At first it appeared I had little in common with my youthful client, who was African-American and living in Harlem, but the similarities of growing up in neighborhoods such as Little Italy and Harlem proved greater than the dissimilarities; respect, honor, survival, all matters of great import to the street kids of both of those neighborhoods. Of course, there are significant differences between the neighborhood of my youth and the inner-city neighborhoods of today. Drugs, guns, and the breakdown of family cohesiveness render inner-city life for many children an experience that often leads to fear, futility, despair, and a sense of alienation and isolation.

In 1978 Ed Koch was elected Mayor of the City of New York. One of the centerpieces of his mayoralty was the establishment of an independent judicial screening committee whose responsibility was to search for and evaluate candidates for the Criminal Court. In May 1980 I was selected as one of his appointments to that court.

In 1982 and 1983 I was assigned to preside over one of the two remaining Youth Parts maintained in the New York City Criminal Courts. Youth Parts were gradually phased out and replaced by all-purpose Parts. By 1978 the only remaining Youth Parts were in Queens County. That assignment reinforced my belief in its value. The Queens Youth Part served as a focal point for myriad counseling programs available to young people. Many programs had court workers who attended sessions of the court each day. The mandate of the court, as I understood and applied it, required a judge to assume functions not customarily considered within the traditional realm of judicial responsibility. This included, for example, monitoring the progress of youths referred to counseling programs during the pendency of their cases and acquiring familiarity with the nature of these programs and their services. The proper functioning of the Part also depended upon the cooperation and support of the District Attorney. The Queens District Attorney's office, through the "Second Chance" program initiated by then District Attorney John J. Santucci, diverted many teenage defendants from the traditional process of the courts. In many respects, the Second Chance program was similar in function to that of the Youth Council Bureau. Defendants considered eligible for the Second Chance program had their cases adjourned for a lengthy period with the consent of the court. After satisfactorily completing counseling or community service their cases were adjourned in contemplation of dismissal or were dismissed.

In 1984, I was assigned to the Criminal Term of the Kings County Supreme Court. Shortly thereafter, I presided over my first "juvenile offender" murder case. A 13-year-old boy was accused of brutally murdering an elderly neighbor by stabbing her repeatedly with a screwdriver and then setting her body on fire. The boy was convicted and sentenced pursuant to the Juvenile Offender Law to an indeterminate term of nine years to life. The case highlighted the special problems of trying children as young as 13 in adult courts—the impact of their immaturity on the admissibility of incriminating statements, on their interaction with counsel and ultimately on their understanding of the consequences of their behavior.

In 1990 my concern for the issues presented to judges dealing with juvenile offender cases, led me to synthesize my thoughts in an article that I wrote for the New York Law Journal. It was entitled "Youth Parts: A Constructive Response to the Challenge of Youth Crime." The article traced the history of New York's special treatment of young offenders, describing the operation of the special Youth Parts that had existed in the adult courts, arguing that reestablishment of Youth Parts was even more crucial than ever, as the jurisdiction of the adult criminal courts was expanded in 1978 to include children as young as 13. I suggested that there were several advantages that could be realized in reestablishing such Parts: uniform treatment of teenage defendants; the concentration and integration of court and private agencies dealing with youths; and a greater diversion of teenage offenders to private agencies for supervision and counseling, thereby supplementing an already overworked and overburdened Probation Department.

The article set in motion a series of events that culminated in the creation of Manhattan's Youth Part in 1992. I have presided over that Part since its inception.

The Youth Part has become a catalyst for many projects involving at-risk children. The jurisprudential basis for the part has proven to be more than merely pragmatic. The court has served as a model for the mobilization and coordination of treatment and social services for children prosecuted in adult courts. Through the combined efforts of prosecutors, defense counsel, program representatives, and court personnel, children who might otherwise be incarcerated are instead under the supervision of the court and alternative-to-incarceration programs, continuing in school, living in their communities, earning diplomas, working, receiving counseling, and being held accountable for their actions in an attentive setting.

This special court has attracted the attention of social scientists, child advocates, criminologists, scholars, authors, the national and international press, criminal justice officials, and private foundations. The constant stream of Youth Part observers and the interest they having demonstrated in both the children and the process by which we adjudicate their cases is a powerful source of inspiration and encouragement. I hope this work will constitute a record of what we have tried to do and lead to reform of laws that are not responsive to the special issues created by prosecuting children as adults.

CHAPTER 1

_____

The Proposition

*As a judge, I cannot form conclusions in my own private
mind and stop there. I am obliged by my office to
express those conclusions in terms of action and by
official verdict.*
— BEN B. LINDSEY, JUDGE,
JUVENILE COURT OF DENVER, AUGUST 20 1925

L ORETTA, a 14-year-old African-American girl, was traveling
to school on the subway one morning with a classmate. Sitting across from them was another student also on her way to
school. The student was wearing an attractive pair of gold earrings.
Loretta's classmate, who was 15 years old, bigger than Loretta, and with
a reputation as a bully, noticed the earrings and decided that she was
going to have them. She stood up and walked over to the girl. Loretta
followed. "Give me your earrings," she demanded. The student ignored
her. She repeated the demand. The student tried to move away but
was blocked from doing so by Loretta. Again, the classmate menacingly
demanded the earrings. The student continued to ignore her. As the
train slowed to stop at a station, Loretta's classmate suddenly reached
down and ripped the earrings from the girl's pierced ears. As the doors
opened onto the subway station, they attempted to flee from the train.
Fortuitously, a policeman was standing on the platform. He saw the
young girl screaming and holding her ears. He stopped Loretta and her
classmate as they tried to run. Loretta was charged as an accomplice
in the robbery and prosecuted along with her classmate as an adult pursuant to New York's Juvenile Offender law.

When Loretta first appeared before me, I was told that she had never been in trouble before and that she was a talented dancer attending one of New York City's schools for the performing arts. I asked one of the court representatives from an alternative-to-incarceration program to interview Loretta who was being held in detention and tell me what she thought of her. A few days later the program representative returned to court. She told me that she wanted to work with Loretta but that Loretta had serious problems. She had asked Loretta a typical social worker question to get a sense of who she was and what her relationship to the community was: "Loretta, if you could change three things in your life, what would you change?" Loretta replied that she would change her country, her family, and her sex—her country because she believed America was a racist society; her family because her mother was a crack addict and she never knew her father; and her sex because she believed young women were vulnerable to physical and sexual abuse.

This book is about children like Loretta, whose response is indicative of the depth of issues many young offenders present. It is also about children like her classmate who all too readily choose violence as a means of getting what they want. It is the product of my effort to understand young offenders and the efficacy of laws enacted to address their delinquency and criminal behavior. My goal is to describe a humane and constructive policy of juvenile justice that will form the basis for a model of justice for minors—a model based on the true nature of adolescence and the realities faced by youth in 21st-century America.

Inscribed in marble over the Baxter Street entrance to the Manhattan Criminal Court building is Justinian's definition of justice— "Justice is the Firm and Continuous Desire to Render to Every Man His Due." The simplicity of this statement belies its complexity. As a judge, I am called upon to make this exacting evaluation virtually every day. Can we logically and justly equate a child's "due" with that of an adult's—equating a child's behavior and culpability with that of an adult?

Trying children as adults, instead of as children, is not just. Cicero said that true law, that is, a just law, is right reason in agreement with nature. Trying children in systems created for adults applying principles designed for adults is not right reason in agreement with nature. St. Augustine, Thomas Jefferson, Albert Einstein and many other philosophers, statesmen, and scientists believed in a law that transcended human law—the natural law. The proponents of natural law contend that effective laws reflect common sense and the natural order of things, whereas laws that do not accord with the immutable aspects of this universal law are invariably destined to undermine society's quest for progress, prosperity and peace. Manmade laws, which are generally imprecise tools for the regulation of human behavior, must be constantly reevaluated in light of common sense, reason, experience, and enlightened notions of human nature. Laws requiring automatic prosecution of children in adult courts are not merely imprecise tools purportedly designed to deter juvenile crime; they are largely ineffective because they do not recognize the natural developmental differences of children. In this text, the terms child and children are used in their broadest sense to include persons under 18 years of age. Legally, individuals are considered "minors" or "juveniles" in most states until they reach their 18th birthday.[1] There may be an element of controversy in the grouping of adolescents with children in terms of assessing criminal responsibility. Nevertheless, I contend that such a classification approximates more closely developmental reality.[2]

When we try children in adult courts, we do so as a result of flawed reasoning, penalizing them for not exercising that degree of judgment that we would expect of adults. Justice Anthony Kennedy in announcing the Supreme Court's decision in *Roper v. Simmons*[3] from the bench, a decision that held that executing juveniles under 18 was unconstitutional, stated: "From a moral standpoint, it would be misguided to equate the failings of a minor with those of an adult, for a greater possibility exists that a minor's character deficiencies will be reformed."[4] Anyone who has had the responsibility of raising teenagers or remembers what it was like to be an adolescent recognizes, for example, the powerful pull of peer pressure, yet we essentially penalize adolescents for not resisting negative peer pressure through the application of standards of culpability that we would expect to apply to adults. That is not to say that a 14-year-old cannot know or appreciate right from wrong, but how can we hold adolescents accountable as adults in adult courts for not exercising a level of maturity that they are not physically, emotionally or intellectually expected to possess? However, laws that require such an approach are presently the most commonly proposed method for addressing juvenile crime in America.

New York's Juvenile Offender Law and similar laws that mandate prosecution of children in adult courts without consideration of their individuality invariably inhibit a judge's discretion in granting such children a second chance. I have set out to write this book in order to persuasively argue that these laws should be repealed and replaced with more reasonable ones—laws that are flexible enough to recognize and accommodate the individuality and potential of children who engage in criminal behavior. Of course, not all of these children can be spared from imprisonment. Their crimes can be so horrendous and their lives so damaged that we have no recourse but to imprison them. But only a small number of youth prosecuted in the adult courts fall into this category.[5] Not to incarcerate these few would undermine confidence in our system of justice, and for the safety of society, such children must be confined for as long as is just.

At the turn of the 20th century, our juvenile justice process reflected a concept of childhood based on the notion that children are innocent, vulnerable, dependent, and incapable of making mature reasoned decisions.[6] As we enter the 21st century, after decades of disillusionment with the juvenile court process, the ideas and beliefs that had inspired the progressive and humane treatment of children, especially disadvantaged children, have been largely abandoned in terms of fixing criminal responsibility.

America and its children deserve a system of justice that not only holds children accountable for their behavior but also protects and nurtures those who can learn from their mistakes. James Hillman, author of *The Soul's Code*,[7] a book about the development of human personality, once told a television interviewer of an ancient African tradition wherein the elders of a village would look at a child as he or she entered the world and ask the question—"What is this child's destiny?" For them, the challenge was to discover that destiny and then to nurture it, to see to it that each child achieved his or her potential. In many ways, the challenge confronting the ancient elders is our challenge today. This challenge extends to all children, including those who violate society's rules. A juvenile justice process can play an important role in meeting the challenge of socializing our children, by viewing their transgressions as an opportunity to educate and socialize.

Early in my career as a judge while sentencing an old-timer, a seasoned petty thief with over 40 convictions, I asked him: "Is there no hope for you, no chance to rehabilitate you?" I took his response as sad, yet sage advice—"Judge, how can you 'rehabilitate' me when I have never been 'habilitated?'" I believe we have a moral obligation to socialize children, to supply them with the means and the opportunity to be contributing members of our society. Many of the children I see have not had a significant opportunity to be integrated into our society because of the dysfunctional circumstances into which they were born. In determining an appropriate sentence for juveniles tried as adults, we cannot ignore the social histories of children who have witnessed acts of violence, or been subjected to psychological and physical abuse which has literally transformed many of them from victims to victimizers. Justice presupposes that the party to be punished has an undiminished capacity to exert his free will to choose between right and wrong. This, in turn, presupposes that the party to be punished has a fair opportunity to learn and be exposed to acceptable standards of behavior. Setting aside issues of criminal responsibility for a moment and addressing a larger issue that emphasizes moral questions over empirical ones, how do you exact conformity with the moral code of a society when children have been born into and lived in situations where the fabric of normal, stable family life is nonexistent? Can it not be reasonably argued that such children never had an equal opportunity, compared with other adolescents, to learn a positive moral code from responsible adults? How do we expect children to act in conformity with social norms when they have never been integrated into society or socialized by those responsible for them? This does not make them any less dangerous, of course, but even when confinement of such children is the only option available, it should be designed to educate, discipline and counsel. In that way, childhood wounds can be addressed, perhaps even healed.

When I use the term rehabilitate, I do not mean in the sense of "curing" an illness or "changing" character. I view rehabilitation as engaging children in a process that assists them to "develop" character. Judges can play a significant role in that process, interacting with the children who come before them in such a way as to enable them to act as catalysts for change in a child's life. That is essentially what we try to do in the Youth Part. That is the challenge, as I see it, with respect to each child.

In recommending such an approach to the resolution of child offender cases, I am not unmindful of the public's concern for protection from violent youth. Focusing on the best interests of the child in this manner does not mean circumventing the best interests of society. The two interests are, for the most part, coextensive. What's good for the child in a democratic society is good for society as a whole. Nor does this focus neglect the interest of victims, who in many cases are unaware of the limitations of the criminal justice system as a source of solace and healing for them.

"Turning bad kids into good kids"—that is how a journalist friend once generously described my work. That, of course, is the underlying challenge for a juvenile justice system. My work in the Youth Part is not the process of an apologist for delinquent behavior nor is it an institutionalized form of letting young people "off." It does not excuse behavior or predetermine outcomes. It does, however, involve an understanding of the vicissitudes of childhood, especially those of children living in America's poorest communities.

In order to appreciate the nature of the court over which I preside and my experience, it is useful to begin with an explanation of the legal context within which children are prosecuted in New York's adult courts. In New York, children between the ages of 16 and 18 who are accused of a crime are subject to the exclusive jurisdiction of the adult criminal courts. They are prosecuted in the same fashion as adults and are subject to the same sentencing. In certain instances, they may be spared the stigma of a criminal record and a more severe adult sentence by being declared a "Youthful Offender." Youthful Offender (YO) status may be granted after conviction, at the discretion of the judge.[8] Granting a youth YO status permits the court to impose a nonincarceratory sentence, such as probation.

Children under 16 years of age are subject to a two-tiered court structure:

1. 13-year-olds charged with murder and 14- and 15-year-olds charged with murder or other serious, violent crimes specifically enumerated as "juvenile offender" (JO) crimes by the legislature are automatically prosecuted in the adult criminal courts pursuant to the "Juvenile Offender Law."[9] Pursuant to that law, a youth convicted of a JO crime is subject to mandatory imprisonment and a felony record, unless granted Youthful Offender treatment;

2. Other children under 16 years of age who are alleged to have committed "non-JO" offenses (which are less serious than JO offenses) are prosecuted in the Family Court as juvenile delinquents.[10] The Family Court (juvenile court) is a court with broad authority over family matters such as custody, child abuse and juvenile delinquency. New York's juvenile justice system thus encompasses two separate courts—an adult criminal court and a juvenile court, each with distinct and separate jurisdiction.

Before the enactment of New York's "JO" Law in 1978, all children under 16 years of age, regardless of the offense charged were subject to the exclusive jurisdiction of the Family Court where they could be "placed" in New York State's Office of Children and Family Services youth detention facilities, separate from adults, for no more than five years, or until they reached 21 years of age. This proved to be a mistake. New York should have had a "safety valve" in place that would have permitted certain children's cases to be tried in the adult court—children who were determined to be a significant danger to the public, as demonstrated by their offense and their past delinquent behavior.

In 1978, the legislature had an opportunity to remedy the situation, but instead of providing the juvenile court with the authority to transfer violent and dangerous juveniles to the adult court where they would presumably be exposed to lengthier periods of confinement, the legislature chose to authorize the wholesale transfer of an entire category of children to the adult court simply on the basis of age and arrest for a JO offense, without regard to the individuality or potential of the child.[11] Critics described the Juvenile Offender Law at the time of its enactment as the nation's harshest and most regressive juvenile law.[12] As a result of the enactment of the Juvenile Offender Law, for the first time in 76 years children as young as 13 were to be tried in the adult Criminal Court subject to mandatory imprisonment and a felony conviction unless granted, at the discretion of a judge, the legal equivalent of a second chance, Youthful Offender status.

In enacting the Juvenile Offender law, New York's legislature did not provide the adult court with any additional resources to deal with the special needs of these children. The adult courts were expected to resolve the cases of this new category of offender with existing resources. In effect, the legislature simply delivered these children to the steps of the adult courthouse. In the Manhattan courts, a juvenile offender's case was randomly assigned to any one of approximately 50 judges sitting in the adult court Criminal Term. These courts were not equipped to deal with the needs of young children. Cases took longer to proceed to trial than in Family Court,[13] generally resulting in less swift accountability, overcrowding at temporary detention centers, and escalating costs of detention. The creation of the Youth Part was designed to focus attention and scarce resources on these children by hearing their cases in one part before one judge. Its aim was to reduce the delays in juvenile offender cases, provide consistent sentencing, increase the number of children diverted away from costly incarceration, and reduce recidivism. The Youth Part was envisioned as a place where we would have an opportunity to reduce future crime rates. If we could help a teenager successfully address a drug problem, a drinking problem, return to school, find a rewarding job, or gain the maturity and tools to resist negative peer pressure, then perhaps we could prevent him from doing further harm to others as well as to himself. I wanted to work with these teenagers, once described as "our hardest to love children," because I felt that if I reached some of them and allowed them to earn the opportunity to turn their lives around, then I would be serving society to the best of my ability.

At the risk of oversimplifying our work, I can explain what I do in the Youth Part by reference to the 1993 film titled *A Bronx Tale*. Robert De Niro and Chazz Palmenteri starred in and produced this film. It is a movie about a boy growing up in an Italian-American neighborhood in the Bronx during the late 1950s and early 1960s. It explores the relationship of the boy with his father, friends and a gangster. The film captures many of the dark aspects and dilemmas of the child's experience: the tension between a neighborhood boy's sense of loyalty to his friends and what he believes is right; the conflict between his admiration for a hard-working father and his fascination with a smooth-talking hood.

A pivotal scene in the movie takes place when the 16-year-old boy nicknamed "C" is walking in the neighborhood, when a car full of his friends pulls up to the curb. "Hey, C, come on, get in the car." He jumps into the car—squeezes into the back seat, a friend on each side. He looks down and sees a box of Molotov cocktails at his feet. One friend sitting in the front seat brandishes a gun—C realizes that they are on their way to an adjoining neighborhood to settle a score.

As C sits in the car we hear him saying to himself, "I don't want to be here." "I don't want to do this. This is wrong." C is in turmoil. He feels he can't say or do anything. If he tells his friends, "Stop, I don't want any part of this, this is wrong," he believes he will lose their respect and their friendship. Just then the car is cut off by another car. The other protagonist in the movie, "Sonny," a local "wiseguy" (a gangster), who took a paternal interest in C, reaches into the car and pulls him out. His friends drive off to tragedy.

In the Youth Part, we metaphorically reach into that car and pull out a teenager like C. That's the child we're looking for—the child who may be in turmoil and because of peer pressure can't extricate himself from a situation; the child who is caught up in events perhaps initiated by others, but who doesn't yet possess the self-confidence or maturity to walk away, the child who feels he can't say, "Stop, that's wrong."

Prosecutors think there are fewer of those children in the car than I do. Defense attorneys think there are more of them. I try to strike a balance. How I strike that balance depends on my assessment of the individual culpability of the offender and the youth's potential to conform his behavior to the requirements of society.

Our challenge is to first "identify" those children who can be afforded an opportunity to prove that they deserve a second chance. We rely on the device of a "deferred sentence" to give certain youths a chance to earn probation and YO status by successfully completing an alternative-to-incarceration program. The process and methodology we use to determine these issues will be more fully discussed in subsequent chapters.

I would describe the Youth Part as a court designed to facilitate the identification of a corrigible youth from an incorrigible one, an apparatus that helps identify those youths who can demonstrate that they are capable of overcoming their problems without compromising public safety. The process of identifying the "malleable" child is essential to the fair and effective operation of any juvenile justice system. I have attempted to innovatively implement the Juvenile Offender law, to develop creative and imaginative dispositions for those children whom I believe can be safely channeled out of the system; children whose background and behavior are judged suitable for placement in alternative-to-incarceration programs. But this has been a daunting task. I have been engaged in a constant struggle to recognize the value of each child within a legal framework created by the Juvenile Offender law that essentially ignores their developmental differences and unique needs.

As of this writing, I have resolved the cases of over 1,200 children prosecuted pursuant to the Juvenile Offender Law, children accused of such crimes as murder, kidnapping, rape, robbery, and assault. I also have resolved cases of their older codefendants, bringing the total number of cases I have adjudicated involving teenagers into the thousands. I have reviewed the probation and mental health reports of these children. These reports have provided me with insight into their lives. I have sentenced 13-, 14-, and 15-year-olds to life in prison for murder and other young offenders to indeterminate sentences of confinement for serious crimes. I also have given many children a second chance, an opportunity to demonstrate that they can learn from their mistakes and become law-abiding citizens. I have released from detention approximately 65% of the juvenile offenders who have come before me and placed them into community-based alternative-to-incarceration programs and residential counseling programs, carefully monitoring their progress. The overwhelming majority of these children given a second chance and an opportunity to earn statutory youthful offender status, which permits them to avoid mandatory imprisonment and a criminal record, have successfully completed the programs.

I am reluctant to claim success for the Youth Part solely through statistical evaluations that ignore the human dimension of our work. I believe we have sufficiently demonstrated the success of the Youth Part process by developing ways to make it possible for young offenders to prove they are willing to change their behavior, within the framework of a law that carries a presumptive punitive response to their transgressions. In an effort to assuage those who would go no further in accepting our proposals without some statistical proof or validation of our efforts, the following discussion is submitted with a caution that the studies referred to can only provide at best indirect validation for our approach.

In 1996, New York's Legal Aid Society created a special team of lawyers and social workers to represent juveniles who appear in the Youth Part and other criminal courts in New York County. The goal of the team was to improve the representation of these offenders by proposing dispositions tailored to the juvenile's specific needs. This was to be accomplished through the preparation of detailed presentencing reports furnished to the court recommending, when appropriate, alternative community-based sentencing options. In 2004, a study was commissioned by the Society to evaluate the effectiveness of its approach.[14] Ninety-seven juvenile offender cases processed in Manhattan since 1996 were examined. The study revealed that 83%

of those juvenile offenders received Youthful Offender status or had their cases dismissed and thus exited the system without a criminal record.[15]

In terms of recidivism, the study noted that the Society's examination of the Office of Court Administration's records for the year 1999/2000 revealed a 30% recidivism rate for those juvenile offenders. Ten percent of their convictions were for felonies, 29% were for misdemeanors, and 63% were for violations (rounded numbers).[16] The report did not indicate how many of those juveniles actually appeared before me in the Youth Part. The cases of 13-, 14-, and 15-year-olds charged as juvenile offenders are initially processed in the lower Criminal Court before transfer to the Youth Part. Only the cases of juveniles who are indicted appear in the Youth Part. Consequently, it is difficult to determine how many of the 97 cases were actually processed in the Youth Part. However, the report, in my view, suggests that a process such as the Youth Part that incorporates and accommodates specialized representation of juvenile offenders with reliance on alternative-to-incarcerations programs, together with judicial supervision can improve the efficiency and outcome of cases involving children adjudicated in the adult court.

This conclusion is further evidenced by examining the recidivism rates of youths placed in alternative sentencing programs. The Youth Part relies heavily on private nonprofit community-based and residential alternative-to-incarceration programs. These organizations are a proving ground for many youth who are being considered for Youthful Offender treatment. They provide an array of services to these adolescents, including assessment, court and community advocacy, and intensive case management. One of these programs, The Center for Alternative Sentencing and Employment Services (CASES), recently initiated a recidivism analysis to document the lasting benefits of their program. The study revealed that 80% of those tracked over a two-year period since their graduation from the program had no new criminal convictions.[17]

Similarly, records kept by the Youth Advocacy Project, a program that specifically targets 13-, 14-, and 15-year-olds tried as juvenile offenders in the adult court, and that is also heavily relied on in the

Youth Part, reveal that on average 80% of youths referred to the program are not rearrested during the course of the program.[18]

The import of these findings is significant when compared to the outcomes for other court-involved youth. According to the Correctional Association of New York, 70% of the 16- to 18-year-olds arrested in New York City and sent to a city jail will be returned to jail within a year of their release.[19] In 1999 the New York State Division of Criminal Justice Services studied juveniles sentenced to the custody of the New York State Office of Children and Family Services (the agency responsible for custody of juvenile delinquents and juvenile offenders sentenced to imprisonment) and found that 75% were rearrested and 62% reconvicted within three years of their release.[20]

The outcomes presented in these studies indicate, albeit indirectly, the comparative benefits of providing juvenile offenders with the support and resources utilized in the Youth Part; although one study suggested that recreation of youth parts within the criminal court was simply a reform of degree rather than kind.[21] That study examined outcomes and sentences in juvenile offender cases for a two-year period (July 1994–June 1995 and July 1995–June 1996), and found that, even though more juvenile offenders processed in youth parts were granted Youthful Offender status than in other nonspecialized courts, incarceration rates were essentially the same.[22] This study, however, did not focus solely on Manhattan's Youth Part, it included dispositions in the City's other youth parts (by 1994 Youth Parts also were established in Bronx, Brooklyn and Queens counties).

Similarly, a report that focused on rearrest rates rather than conviction rates concluded that differences in the court processing of juvenile offenders in Manhattan and Queens (the report observed that Queens County relied less on placement and supervision of juveniles in ATI programs) did not affect the proportion of juveniles who were rearrested.[23] This report acknowledges, however, that the most severe rearrest charges in Manhattan were "significantly more likely" to be for nonviolent controlled substance charges, whereas the most severe rearrest charge was "significantly more likely" to be murder or attempted murder for those juveniles prosecuted in Queens.[24]

The report found that one out of every ten Queens juveniles of the sample cases examined who was rearrested was charged with murder or attempted murder compared to 1 out of every 100 rearrested Manhattan juveniles.[25]

As I noted earlier, it is difficult to quantify the human dimension of our work. It cannot be judged solely on the basis of statistical analysis. I believe that the Youth Part approach with its reliance on ATI programs is more effective than simplistic notions of automatic and mandatory incarceration. This is particularly true when we consider that the vast majority of children prosecuted as adults in New York and throughout the nation will return to society at a relatively young age despite their sentences. Indeed, this approach is made even more compelling since young people who have been incarcerated are far more likely to commit new crimes on their release than those who are placed in strict, effective alternative-to-incarceration programs.[26]

In addition to helping children live better lives, reliance on alternative-to-incarceration programs also save significant taxpayer dollars. In New York, the cost per annum to maintain a juvenile in a detention center is approximately $135,000.[27] The cost per annum for placement of a juvenile in an alternative-to-incarceration program is approximately $13,000.[28]

If we agree that children are malleable, that they have the capacity to change their behavior, then we can construct a juvenile justice system that encompasses within its parameters, a child's ability to change. That system would incorporate the predominant mode of prosecuting children for delinquent behavior, which existed in the United States almost from the inception of the juvenile court movement in the early 1900s. That early system favored the prosecution of children in separate juvenile courts, courts that would ideally have the authority, resources, and support to place and link children with appropriate support programs to service their special needs. That system also had a built-in "safety-valve," that is, the authority of juvenile court judges to exercise their discretion to "transfer" certain children to the adult criminal courts, but only after an individualized assessment of each child's crime, potential, and culpability. This judicial waiver or transfer system was gradually eroded in the latter part of the 20th century, resulting in the wholesale movement of young offenders into the adult system without such a hearing.

Since 1978, virtually every state in the United States modified its laws addressing the violence of offenders under 18 years of age.[29] Policy makers at the state and federal level have responded to the threat of juvenile crime by imposing tougher sanctions on juveniles and facilitating the movement of younger children into the adult system.[30] Many of these reforms have largely ignored the basic developmental differences between children and adults, and they have significantly restricted flexibility and systemic discretion in adjudicating children's cases.

In the chapters ahead, I will demonstrate that proposals to try more children automatically as adults, mandating imprisonment, and curtailing judicial discretion are at odds with human nature and sound social and economic policy. These laws should be repealed and replaced with laws that recognize the nature and capacity of children by requiring an individualized due process hearing for each child subject to prosecution as an adult. I will set forth a plan for change and illustrate precisely how this change can be realized. I propose that all jurisdictions create a "Youth Part" within their adult criminal courts modeled on Manhattan's special court to address issues created by the prosecution of juveniles in adult court systems. Chapter 9, "Creation of the Youth Part," and Chapter 10, "The Youth Part Model," provide a blueprint for replication. Although these proposals are specifically referenced to Manhattan's Youth Part, adoption of the strategy, process, personnel needs, and technology recommended to improve the youth part, with suitable modifications to accommodate the circumstances of individual jurisdictions, can enhance a court's capacity to isolate at-risk youth and to expeditiously identify those most likely to benefit from counseling.

A Youth Part under the leadership of a motivated judge, with the help of committed staff, cognizant of the concerns of the victim and society, can transcend the often impersonal court bureaucracy and connect with a youth, his family, his neighborhood, and the community. It is not a panacea but a creative response to the inflexibility of automatic transfer laws. It can serve as a vehicle through which imaginative and innovative ideas can be implemented; a court where the atmosphere is such that the presiding judge would be able to recognize and respond effectively to the "salvageable" youth. I recognize that my reference to a judicial assessment of "salvageability" risks being misconstrued as an arrogant assumption of authority not warranted in a due process judicial context. That is not my intention. The word salvageable is a strong word. By using it, I mean to convey the reality that given the shortcomings of a system, which requires incarceration of juveniles in essentially nonrehabilitating institutions, judges, who have the responsibility of sentencing these offenders, are often left with no viable alternatives and, therefore, are confronted with decisions that may indeed affect the ability of such youths to live productive and law abiding lives. Consequently, when I use the word salvageable I use it in that context and, where appropriate, substitute the word "incorrigible," a description with less authoritarian connotation.

The Youth Part process is only one aspect of the reform I propose. Present trends in American juvenile justice must be reversed and replaced with a model juvenile justice system that realistically responds to a child's criminal behavior without foreclosing such child's chance for a promising future. The United States "juvenile justice system" is not a single integrated system but an amalgam of 51 institutions, composed of each state and the federal government. Regional differences exist with respect to the threshold age of criminal responsibility and the appropriate discipline of children. The system I propose is sufficiently flexible to accommodate various local customs and values. I contend that the traditional juvenile court should be retained, but it should be true to its original conception as a social service provider and coordinator, a position supported by the American Bar Association's Juvenile Justice Standards. The model I present, which is more fully discussed in Chapter 11, incorporates four broad core principles of sound juvenile justice policy: precise identification of violent juveniles; dispositions that serve to educate and prepare children to become contributing members of society; flexibility in judicial decision making; and a process of decriminalizing the acts of juveniles who can demonstrate their willingness to conform their behavior to societal standards.

Although this text will explore the development of the law, it is not intended to be a legal nor scientific treatise. I have discussed some scientific literature from the discipline of developmental psychology to the extent that I thought necessary to present my thesis. As a judge, I believe I have been applying a commonsense approach to juvenile offending. This approach appears to be consistent with scientifically established principles of adolescence. I have not written this manuscript from the perspective of a social scientist. It is the accumulated experience of a judge who, for over 25 years, has had the responsibility of sentencing many young offenders. I would rather leave the science to the scientists.

The overarching objectives of this book will be to reaffirm the concept that children are developmentally different from adults, that a judge can be a formidable force in shaping the lives of the children who appear before him or her, and that recognition of these developmental differences, coupled with effective interactive techniques between a judge and child, will improve the quality of justice for children.

Dr. Caroline Joy DeBrovner, an assistant professor at Pace University in the Department of Criminal Justice and Sociology, has attended Friday (calendar day) sessions for over three years. She has contributed a chapter focusing on sociological theories of behavior modification as they relate to my interaction with the juveniles who appear in the part. Her chapter is intended to provide the reader with examples of the principles necessary to replicate the youth part process, especially the concept of interactive justice. The value of her chapter is in her ability to document the power and intensity of a relationship between a judge and juvenile. Dr. DeBrovner is of the opinion that although a judge's personality, life history, and charisma can make the difference between a good judge and a truly effective judge, she believes that she has been able to document the potentially replicable methods/strategies that we employ in interacting with the young people in the Youth Part. Her goal is to document that when judges are dealing with young children/adolescent offenders, properly offering the "carrot" is just as important as wielding the "stick." She describes examples of how a judge can shape his interaction with the youth that appear before him as a means of deterrence, rehabilitation, and education and how a judge can adopt strategies that enable a child to develop character and change behavior over time. As a result, the interactive technique that I discuss in Chapter 6, "Interactive Justice," is systematically explored by Dr. DeBrovner in her chapter.

I began with the story of Loretta to illustrate the dimension of the problems these young offenders present. The issue for me is, adapting a phrase that dramatically illustrates the consequences of decisions we are often compelled to make, are these youths just "dead kids walking" or are they children who have the capacity and potential to become contributing members of our society? How do you persuade a child like Loretta to believe that she has the power to change the circumstances of her life through the development of her talent?—that it is still possible for her to realize her dream of becoming a professional dancer, despite her problems? The relationship between the belief in the possibility of attaining one's dreams and crime is inescapable. There is an inverse relationship between belief and hope, on the one hand, and crime and violence, on the other. As belief and hope diminish, crime and violence increase. Despair in the lack of a future falls most heavily on the juvenile population of the inner city. It is expressed in such forms as "gangsta rap"—if you won't let me share in America's riches, I will take them. The frustration and bitterness so poignantly expressed by Loretta cannot be answered simply by resorting to the rhetoric of those who cry that today's youth have an equal opportunity to succeed just as we did. It is not that simple. The challenge posed by children like Loretta requires a rejuvenation of spirit, a concrete display of opportunity, and an absolute right to the best education available, so that these children will be prepared to embrace opportunity when it is presented.

We try to meet this challenge in the Youth Part. We ask children—no, we try to persuade them—to believe that they can accomplish their goals. We try to link them with services that will prepare them for the opportunity to succeed. We are not always successful, but the community expects us to make the effort and we attempt to do our part. Communication of these beliefs takes many forms in the Youth Part and is an integral part of our method. In the end, the Court's adjudication of a child as a "Youthful Offender"—literally granting the child a second chance, can be said to symbolically represent the elimination of barriers to a child's reentry into society.

The challenge I have set for myself in this book is to encourage the reader to appraise these children as they really are; to recognize that the decisions judges make, pursuant to laws requiring the automatic prosecution of children in adult courts, are life-altering for many of these children; to foster an understanding that how we treat these children will have an enduring impact on our own children and grandchildren. In the end, my philosophy is anchored to the belief that each child has value that we are obligated to recognize.

CHAPTER 2

The Nature of Adolescence

All I need is someone in the world
to lean on their shoulder and cry
someone to tell my secrets to without having to lie
someone that will make me feel good deep down inside
someone who would understand me and look in my soul
and see that I am more than just a fourteen-year-old.
—A JUVENILE OFFENDER

Remembrance

HOW MANY OF YOU have ever been fourteen? Let me see a show of hands." That is how I often facetiously begin a discussion with mature audiences on the relationship of adolescence to juvenile crime. The serious point of the question is to emphasize that offending and nonoffending teenagers, as well as adults, share at least one thing in common: the adolescent experience. Evoking the memory of our own adolescence is crucial to understanding the issues involved in judging the culpability of juveniles who commit crimes and determining the appropriate societal response to their behavior. The first step in capturing the nature of adolescence is to remember it. Not just the sweet memories made sweeter by the passage of time or the reminiscence of a time "free of responsibility" but also the feelings generated as much by failure as by success, by disappointment as well as gratification.

In order to make the journey from childhood to maturity, we all had to traverse the transitional adolescent period; a time when we saw ourselves evolving in size, strength, knowledge, and appreciation for what was right and what was wrong. For some, the journey has been much more difficult than for others.

Several years ago on network television, there was a popular series called *The Wonder Years*. It chronicled the boyhood adventures of "Kevin," its main character, growing up during the 1960s in America. The series format involved the voice-over of the adult Kevin who shared his reflections on his childhood exploits. At the end of each program, the adult Kevin would provide a moral. One evening I watched an episode in which Kevin, who had a secret crush on his neighbor and classmate "Winnie," was lamenting the fact he never asked Winnie for a date because he was afraid that his friends would ridicule him. The boys did not consider Winnie "attractive." (Of course, she grew up to be a beautiful and powerful business executive.) At the end of the episode, the adult Kevin posed the question:

But who are you at 14? Who are you at 14? You are what your friends think you are.

The idea that one's perception of self-worth as a teenager often does not come from within but from without, is an important observation on the nature of adolescence. It explains one of the major causes of juvenile criminal behavior—peer pressure. Key to resisting peer pressure is the capacity to believe in one's self, one's destiny. The strength of belief in the ability to realize one's dreams is directly related to a child's capacity to rely on that dream in order to resist choices that would compromise it.

Reflecting on our own adolescence provides us with examples of how adolescence affected our own behavior. Reflection is a useful exercise from which we can sort out the implications of judging juvenile behavior and assessing culpability. If we could, cognizant of our own adolescence, develop a method of measuring whether a child's conduct was reasonable, excusable or punishable, would we settle for a standard that relies simply on arbitrary age limits beyond which "childhood" is no longer legally recognized? Wouldn't we prefer a system of determining culpability that is based on a flexible assessment of an individual teenager's culpability rather than a standard of behavior designed for adults? Wouldn't we prefer a process of determining culpability that more clearly reflects the true nature of children rather than one based solely on arbitrary age parameters? Maturity is a process that develops over time rather than a precise, timed event. As such, at any given moment during a child's adolescence, we are witnessing an "evolving" appreciation of right and wrong, an "evolving" capacity to control one's impulses and resist peer pressure.

The argument for trying children as adults has formidable political appeal—but it does not have a sound basis in human nature or psychology. As Thomas Grisso and Laurence Steinberg point out in their groundbreaking research on the subject of competency of youth as trial defendants: "Adolescence—roughly the years between 10 and 17—is a time of rapid and dramatic change. These changes are highly variable, not only among different individuals, but along different dimensions within any given individual. One 15-year-old, for example, might be quite mature in appearance but emotionally still a child. Another may be intellectually ahead of his peers, but lag far behind in social skills. A teenager may act like an adult one day and be very impulsive the next, or be mature in one social setting and impulsive in another... It doesn't generally make sense to ask an adolescent to think or act like an adult, because he can't—any more than a six-year-old child can learn calculus."[1]

A Modern Psychological View of Youth

Adolescence was first recognized as a distinct developmental phase in modern psychology at the turn of the 20th century. It was classified as a transitional stage between childhood and adulthood brought on by the onset of puberty.[2]

Many scholars have researched the psychological effects of adolescence on criminal behavior. They have concluded that children, particularly those under 16 years of age, are developmentally different from adults—physically, intellectually, and emotionally. Notably, these differences result in an adolescent's diminished capacity to reason, that is, to know or appreciate the consequences of behavior or the wrongfulness of acts, a diminished capacity to control impulses and to resist peer pressure. Although these deficits do not make adolescents any less dangerous, experts have argued that they require a specifically defined manner of adjudication and scope of punishment.[3]

When teenagers commit criminal acts, gauging the level of their maturity is crucial in determining their culpability. I am proposing a system and method that will permit treatment of young offenders based on an individualized judicial assessment of their level of maturity and amenability to social service-oriented dispositions—a juvenile justice policy that treats adolescence as a distinct legal category.[4] Modern legal principles reflect the significance of the presence or absence of maturity. For example, in criminal law the presumptive absence of maturity, reflected in a chronological age, serves as a dividing line, separating criminal behavior from noncriminal behavior and as a factor mitigating the severity of punishment.

In various areas of the law, we have developed mechanisms to gauge the level of a child's maturity, that is, the ability to make reasoned judgments. For instance, in the area of abortion rights, judges in many states are required to conduct a "judicial by-pass" hearing to determine a teenager's capacity to knowingly and intelligently make a decision whether to have an abortion, independent of a parent's advice or consent. This proceeding is required in many states as a predicate to assigning adult status to a minor for the purpose of permitting the minor to make such a decision absent parental advice or consent. Under this approach, the boundary between childhood and adulthood is not a "legislatively mandated bright line; rather it is set by an individualized evaluation of the minor's maturity."[5] Closer to our context, the traditional juvenile court transfer or waiver hearing is another example of a mechanism that can be used to determine an individual child's level of maturity and amenability to social service dispositions.

Assessing a child's mental condition at the time of a crime presents a greater challenge than simply recreating the circumstances of the event. However, it is not a subject foreign to criminal jurisprudence. A judicial assessment of the level of a youth's maturity is

but become indignant if they think they are done a wrong. And though they love honor, they love victory more; for youth longs for superiority, and victory is a kind of superiority... And [they are] filled with good hopes; for like those drinking wine, the young are heated by their nature, and at the same time [they are filled with hopes] because of not yet having experienced much failure. And they live for the most part in hope; for hope is for the future, and memory is of what has gone by, but for the young the future is long and the past short; for in the dawn of life nothing can be remembered, and everything [can be] hoped for. And they are easily deceived for the reason given; for they easily hope for the best. And they are more courageous [than the other age groups]; for they are impulsive and filled with good hopes, of which the former quality makes them lack fear, and the latter makes them brave; for no one feels fear when angry, and to expect something good is a source of confidence. And they are sensitive to shame; for they have been educated only by convention and do not yet understand other fine things. And they are magnanimous; for they have not yet been worn down by life but are inexperienced with constraints, and to think oneself worthy of great things is magnanimity; and this is characteristic of a person of good hopes... For they live more by natural character than by calculation, and calculation concerns the advantageous, virtue the honorable. And more than other ages of life they are fond of friends and eager for companions, because they enjoy living with others and do not yet judge anything on the basis of advantage; thus, they do not judge friends that way. And all the mistakes they make are in the direction of excess and vehemence... ; for they do "everything too much": they love too much and hate too much and all other things similarly. And they think they know everything and strongly insist on it; for this is the cause of their doing everything too much. And the wrongs they commit come from insolence, not maliciousness. And they are inclined to pity, because of supposing [that] everybody is good or better than average... and they are fond of laughter and, as a result, witty; for wit is cultured insolence. Such, then, is the character of the young."[8]

Twenty-five-hundred years later, Aristotle's observations are still valid and valuable in understanding adolescence. An accurate understanding of the nature of adolescence is important in order to contextualize our work in the Youth Part and our recommendations to improve the juvenile justice system. In the treatise "American Youth Violence,"[9] Frank Zimring emphasizes a characteristic of adolescence that I often see in my courtroom. It is that at no other point in life is violence so common. It is, for most, the only time when one acts violently toward another. As Aristotle noted, the young are "quick tempered, and inclined to follow up their anger by action." The inclination to violence, therefore, should be understood as one aspect of the nature of adolescence. Of course, this does not mean that all adolescents are preordained to be violent, or that violence should ever be excused or go uncorrected and unpunished. However, the interplay between adolescence and violence does require a juvenile sentencing policy that is flexible enough to respond effectively to the context of its occurrence. Adolescence is also a time when peer pressure and "group standing" are significant factors underlying motivation for behavior. These aspects of adolescent behavior make the case for the exercise of discernment in determining the nature of an individual child's fault.

The Juvenile Nature of Juvenile Crime

I have found that there are three traits of teenagers that create fertile ground for juvenile offending that are consistent with Aristotle's observations: impulsivity, volatility, and collective adolescent behavior. I frequently see the consequences of these traits in the nature of juvenile crime. For instance, in one case, a 65-year-old widow who lived alone ordered several items from a local supermarket. Unable to carry the items home, the supermarket manager sent Robert, a 14-year-old who worked part-time as a delivery boy, to her apartment with her order. When the woman opened the door, she invited Robert in and told him to place the packages on her kitchen table. She then opened her purse to give him a tip. When Robert saw the number of bills in her wallet, he picked up a frying pan that was lying in her kitchen sink and hit her with it, grabbing her purse and running from the apartment. The widow, bruised and dazed, managed to call the police. Robert was quickly apprehended. His identity and home address were on file with his employer.

Shortly after Robert's first appearance before me, he pleaded guilty to robbery. During his plea allocution, I asked him, "Why did you do this? Didn't you realize you would be caught quickly?" He responded by telling me that he didn't know what came over him, but when he saw the money in the purse it was like he had an angel on one shoulder telling him to be good and a devil on the other. He listened to the devil.

In another case, Andrew, a 14-year-old boy, was arrested for attempting to smuggle a .38 caliber pistol into his school apparently to settle a score with another young man who insulted him in front of his girlfriend. When he was arraigned before me, his mother and a young boy who resembled the defendant were seated in the audience. The boy was Andrew's 11-year-old brother. When Andrew's case was called, I asked his mother to step up to the railing that separated the audience from the courtroom well. When she did so, the younger boy accompanied her. Her son Andrew was facing a mandatory sentence of imprisonment. The legislature had recently expanded the scope of the Juvenile Offender Law to encompass the crime of gun possession on school grounds. The amendment required mandatory imprisonment for that offense and imposed restrictions on granting Youthful Offender Treatment. I wanted his mother to understand that my options under the circumstances were very limited. She told me that she had five sons and that her two oldest sons also were in jail. The boy with her was her second youngest. I asked the boy what he thought of his brother and the situation. He said, "I look up to my brother as a role model, but he has to think before he acts." This young boy was apparently mature beyond his years and certainly more insightful than his brother. The mother was trying to raise these boys without a father.

I suggested that the mother call New York's Big Brothers Big Sisters for help. Perhaps, I thought, if this boy had a positive role model, a mentor, he could escape the destiny of his older siblings.

Impulsive behavior such as that described here results in rash decisions and reckless disregard of consequences. Aristotle observed that not only are the young impulsive, but also that they appear to be unable to control their impulses. He imparts a degree of involuntariness to their behavior. This assertion may actually reflect the powerful forces at work on the psyche of a youth. Nevertheless, it is not a view that society can or is willing to adopt as a matter of public policy. The occasion of the impulsive act, however, should be viewed as an opportunity to teach a child the value of self-control, a characteristic that can evolve.

"Self-control," as Professor Frank Zimring observes, "is the habit of behavior which can be developed over a period of time, a habit dependent on the experience of successfully exercising it. This particular type of maturity, like so many others, takes practice."[10]

Children and adolescents have had obviously less opportunity than adults to practice this habit of behavior. Therefore, it follows they have a diminished capacity to control their behavior. This does not excuse their impulsive acts but it does explain the foolish behavior of a Robert and the reckless behavior of an Andrew.

Volatility or quick temperedness as discussed earlier is also a form of impulsive behavior that often leads to violence. It results from a lack of mature coping skills, and an undeveloped self-image. When, for example, was the last time you were involved in a fistfight? For most, it was during our teenage years.

Collective adolescent behavior is the hallmark of juvenile crime. The desire for friendship, to belong, to be part of a group, to be accepted, is a powerful, if not dominant, adolescent trait. It heightens a child's vulnerability to peer pressure. The overwhelming majority of juveniles appearing before me are involved in group crimes. The group context of this behavior suggests that the motivation for criminal conduct often has less to do with, "I wanted the money" or "I wanted the jacket" and more to do with "what will my friends think of me if I'm not 'down' with the crime?"

The power of peer pressure on a child's decision to engage in criminal behavior is directly related to an adolescent's need to belong and be accepted by his peers. The consequence of "saying 'no' to negative peer pressure is not just withstanding the 'heat' of the moment," but it is also "coping with a sense of exclusion as others engage in the behavior and leave the adolescent increasingly alone... Further, the sense of exclusion remains whenever the group later recounts what happened. This feeling of loneliness then becomes persuasive and carries an easy solution. Go along with the crowd."[11] Consequently, a teenager may know right from wrong and, according to Professor Zimring, "... may even have developed a capacity to control his or her impulsiveness, if left alone to do so, but resisting temptation while alone is a different task from resisting the pressures to commit an offense when among adolescent peers who wish to misbehave..."[12] The ability to deflect or resist peer pressure is a useful tool that can help an adolescent avoid criminal behavior. Many youth lack the crucial skills to do so until maturity.

As a result of their propensity to socialize in groups and to act in groups, children rarely commit crimes alone. Because of the group nature of their behavior, involvement and culpability differ from participant to participant. This characteristic of juvenile crime, that is, its group context, requires a careful evaluation of a child's individual state of mind and extent of involvement in an underlying charge. Adolescents often seem to have their own conception of criminal responsibility when they act in groups. "Being there" for example, is often perceived as a circumstance that is sufficient for criminal liability. When a child offers to plead guilty, I often phrase an inquiry into the child's perception of culpability with the seemingly straightforward question: "What did you do to be guilty of this crime?" "I was there" is a common response. Of course, there is no crime of simply "being there." Mere presence at the scene of a crime does not in and of itself render one guilty of a crime. Action or acts, however slight, with the intent to further the crime, is necessary. Children or adolescents, because of their intellectual immaturity, often lack sufficient capacity to grasp the legal concept of accomplice liability, a principle central to understanding the group nature of juvenile crime.[13]

These characteristics—intellectual immaturity, impulsivity, volatility, and collective behavior—often result in what I call the juvenile nature of juvenile crime. The foolishness of their criminal acts sets young offenders apart from others and is apparent by the lack of sophistication in planning, executing, and covering up their criminal behavior. For example, one may justifiably believe, in light of the numerous cases involving food deliverymen, that these employees have one of the most dangerous occupations in New York City. A common scenario that we often encounter in the Youth Part is the crime of robbery, which typically involves a teenager calling a restaurant from his home, ordering food, and instructing the person to deliver the food to a particular address. When the delivery person enters the vestibule of the building to deliver the food, the youth who made the call as well as two or three of his friends are there, waiting for their victim. One of them threatens the delivery person with a knife, stick, or gun, another boy tells him to empty his pockets, another takes the food. The juveniles then run from the building and divide up the proceeds of their crime. The youth who made the call did not realize that the restaurant had caller-ID. In short order, the police arrive at the scene only to find the teens sitting on a park bench eating the stolen food. These youth now face as much as 10 years' imprisonment under New York's Juvenile Offender Law for their conduct.

Although the potentially negative traits of impulsivity, volatility, and collective adolescent behavior are potent traits in adolescence, we know by our own experience that our characters are not frozen forever by what we have done at 14 or 15 years of age. Naturally, we presume that children have the capacity to learn from their experiences, to move beyond the worst things that they have done. Isn't that precisely what growing up is all about?

In terms of constructing an effective sentencing policy for adolescents who commit crime, a quality of youth that must be considered is their "malleability" the recognition that because of their youth, adolescents are not wedded to their pasts. They are less committed to their misconduct and more adaptable to positive influence than most adults who commit crime. The adaptability of adolescents is also an aspect of youth that has support in recent research, which suggests that most criminal adolescent behavior is stage-related and disappears as a person grows older.[14] Recognition, therefore, that children are malleable, at least more malleable than adults, is a crucial element that must be integrated into a juvenile justice policy, in order that such a policy conform to human nature.

Finally, Aristotle gives us an illuminating glimpse into a salutary and encouraging aspect of youthfulness that can work in tandem with a child's malleability and that provides a strong basis for optimism in the ability to improve children's conduct. As Aristotle observed "[youth] live for the most part in hope; for hope is for the future and memory is of what has gone by, but for the young the future is long and the past short, for in the dawn of life nothing can be remembered and everything can be hoped for."[15]

Aristotle's eloquent description of the resiliency of youth, that is, their ability to positively adjust and be optimistic even in the face of significant trauma, both physical and emotional, is also a trait that I have observed in many of the young people who appear before me. Ancient Stoic philosophers asserted that we cannot help what happens to us but we can decide what our reaction to what happens to us will be. I saw this attribute in Alice. She was a 15-year-old Asian-American girl who was involved in a gang that kidnapped the son of a wealthy Chinese restaurant owner and attempted to extort a ransom. The owner of the restaurant contacted the police, who set a trap for the gang members and managed to free the storeowner's son unharmed. I learned that Alice was physically and emotionally abused as a child and ran away from her Chinese immigrant mother at 13 to live with the 19-year-old leader of the gang. Alice was ultimately conditionally released from detention to reside in a private residential psychiatric community and was periodically required to return to court so that her progress could be monitored. She was extremely intelligent and eager to display her progress in the community's school. Each time she appeared in court, she would bring her examination papers with her and I would review them. They were all excellent. She had straight As in all her courses. One day she showed me an exam that she had taken in Greek mythology. She had answered all but one question correctly. She had to consider whether the following statement was true or false: "Zeus created mankind, human beings, for the entertainment of the Gods, to be used as pawns or toys for their amusement." She answered "false". The correct answer is "true". According to Greek mythology Zeus and the other Gods did create human beings for their amusement. I believe she knew the answer was "true," and that her answer revealed more about her innate sense of optimism than her knowledge of Greek mythology; that she simply couldn't bring herself to believe, despite all that had happened to her, that beings in authority could be so cruel and uncaring.

The concept of children and adolescents as developing human beings draws both conceptually and historically from ancient ideas about the nature of youthful behavior as distinguished from adult behavior. Although children were not given special treatment for their bad acts in ancient courts, as society became more sophisticated and knowledgeable about human behavior and appropriate forms of punishment, it was gradually understood that distinctions were required based upon an individual's capacity to understand and to appreciate the harms caused by certain action. Thus, as the common law of England, the source for many of our legal concepts, evolved, rules were developed to help determine the level of maturity sufficient to hold children accountable. This discernment with respect to an individual's culpability based on a concept of psychological maturity was ultimately formalized in the legal principles of "infancy," "diminished capacity" and "proportionality."[16]

Because of the acknowledged developmental differences of children from adults, justice demands that they be treated in a manner consistent with those differences. A concept of justice based on fairness and "giving each person his due" cannot encompass a system that denies children full participation in civil society based on their immaturity and yet, at the same time, punishes them criminally despite their immaturity. Can we truly be a society committed to the idea of each person possessing inalienable rights if we fail to fully recognize the potential of each and every child in our society, especially those most vulnerable?

In creating a more just response to juvenile crime, we can start by considering a definition of adolescence proffered by Professor

Robert E. Shepherd Jr. of Virginia's T.C. Williams School of Law that succinctly acknowledges the interplay between adolescence and criminal behavior. He defines adolescence as "the psychosocial response to the profound biological changes of puberty within a social context."[17] This is the key to our approach in constructing an effective youth policy—the recognition that the experience of adolescence has a bearing on culpability, influencing behavioral choices, and that although the nonoffending teenager and the delinquent share the experience of adolescence, they often do so in vastly different social contexts.

CHAPTER 3

The Criminal Responsibility of Juveniles

When I was a child, I spoke as a child, I understood as a child, I thought as a child, but when I became a man, I put away childish things.
—1 Corinthians 13.11

B EFORE WE DISCUSS a juvenile sentencing policy that reflects the impact of adolescence on the prevalent social contexts within which juvenile offending frequently occurs, we must first consider the rationale for holding adolescents criminally responsible. In most states, in order to be criminally responsible, a juvenile/adolescent must reach a threshold age. The age of criminal responsibility varies from state to state. In New York it is as low as 13 for murder, 14 for other serious crimes. In Oklahoma, a child of 7 can be held criminally responsible provided the state can prove that, at the time of the act, the youth knew it was wrong. In Nevada the age of criminal responsibility is 8, Colorado 10, Oregon 12.[1] "23 states and the District of Columbia now have no minimum age at which children can be tried as adults for the most serious offenses. In the remaining 27 states, the minimum age ranges from 10 to 15. Today, an estimated 200,000 American youth under the age of 18 are tried as adults each year; about 12 percent of these are younger than 16."[2]

The ability or capacity of a child to form a criminal intent, that is, to knowingly recognize and appreciate that what one was doing was wrong is the critical issue that must be determined in imposing criminal responsibility on a juvenile or minor. Criminal responsibility is based on the theory that an individual is responsible for his actions and if he violates the law he should expect to be punished. The common law of England, from which we derive many of our legal concepts, is based on doctrines implicit in court decisions, customs, and usages rather than on codified written laws. Initially, the English courts drew no distinctions based on age with respect to criminal responsibility. Child and adult alike were subject to identical penalties. Gradually, the common law evolved to reflect a view of human nature that corresponded with ecclesiastical concepts, especially in the context of the capacity of an individual to commit sin.[3] Such moral responsibility was based on the knowledge of right and wrong and the ability to choose either course. The standard for criminal responsibility became not solely the act but the state of mind of the actor at the time of the conduct. Criminal responsibility was thus rooted in a view of human nature that holds that man is naturally endowed with a free will and the capacity to make reasoned choices. These two faculties gave man his autonomy and independence. The exercise of the will in a reasoned manner, therefore, renders human actions appropriate or culpable.

Holding youth criminally accountable for their behavior is ultimately a matter of degree. Aristotle, in discussing the nature of man, asserted that "For what each thing is when fully developed we call its nature."[4] Until a child becomes an adult he does not assume his true nature. His faculties of reason and liberty of choice are not yet fully developed. Therefore, we do not hold children of a certain age responsible for their acts because we believe they are not yet mature enough to make knowing decisions or to control their behavior. Every civilized society recognizes that without a level of maturity there can be no criminal responsibility. There are differences of opinion, however, as to what degree of immaturity precludes criminal guilt.

Historically, the relationship between immaturity and criminal responsibility was captured in the common law concept of infancy. By the Middle Ages, the courts had established seven years of age as the age of reason, following the lead of the ecclesiastical courts. The latter were cued by the Roman civil law, which established seven as the age of responsibility. For the church, it was the age of loss of innocence when a child could be guilty of sin. For the courts, it was the age of punishment when a child could be criminally liable for his behavior.

The infancy defense was adopted because judges concluded that criminal culpability necessitated sufficient maturity to act knowingly and intelligently. Where a youth's immaturity renders him unable to appreciate the likely consequences of his act or its wrongful nature, his conduct is not a product of meaningful choice and such an actor cannot be held criminally liable. Because of the difficulty in pinpointing the time at which an individual reached the age of reason—the threshold of criminal liability—the common law presumed that children between 7 and 14 years of age (14 being the age at which a male child was presumed to have attained puberty) did not possess sufficient intellectual capacity to engage in a process of right reasoning. This presumption could be rebutted by proof that a particular child under 14 in fact understood the nature and consequences of his acts. The rebuttable presumption was explained on the ground that some children matured more quickly than others. It also served an important public policy interest since it was believed that failure to punish particularly atrocious acts committed by children between the ages of 7 and 14 would encourage other children to commit similar acts with impunity. Consequently, the common law maxim developed that malice supplies the want of mature years. The more horrendous the crime, the more likely the child would be treated as an adult, recognizing that it does not necessarily follow that the more vicious or violent the conduct the more maturity the child possessed. In the final analysis, a child's infancy or immaturity, at times, yielded to the savagery of the act.

The process of determining maturity under the common law required judicial "consideration" of the level of a child's development, to determine whether a child under 14 possessed sufficient maturity to warrant punishment. In order to do this, the court delved into the state of mind of the offender. Did he possess a culpable state of mind when he acted? Factors evincing a child's awareness of the evil nature of his act were considered, such as a child's lying to cover up the deed, or hiding the fruits of the crime.

Before the founding of the juvenile court, the status of children in American courts was not so different from that of an adult. Children were tried in the same courts as adults. Although the common-law defense of infancy was available to children under 14 years of age, after conviction the treatment of children did not differ substantially from that of adults. Few sentencing options were available to judges other than hanging or imprisonment. Child murderers were hanged and child robbers imprisoned in proportion to the gravity of their crime and number of their offenses.[5] Little attention was paid to the individual characteristics of the young offender and little more was required of a judge other than impartiality and knowledge of the law. The process of law as it existed at the time, as well as the state of scientific and psychological knowledge concerning moral and intellectual development, did not support the proposition that children should be treated substantially different from adults. As society progressed and advances were achieved in understanding the psychology of human behavior, American courts began to integrate social and scientific developments. Courts began to focus on reform of the offender as well as avenging the offense. The founders and promoters of the juvenile court sought to incorporate this progress into a special tribunal for delinquent children.

The commonlaw rules were embraced by American judges because they were considered "consistent with the nature of man and the natural use of the faculties of intellect, will and his freedom to acquire the necessary knowledge to make the distinction between right and wrong. They were rules used to determine the ultimate fact of the ability of an individual to distinguish between right and wrong. The point in life when a person is capable of making the distinction may vary but once it is reached that person, whether he be an adult or a child, is capable of criminal intent."[6] The point at which the line between infancy and criminal responsibility, between the age of innocence and the age of reason should be drawn has long been debated. In the final analysis, it is resolved by public policy.[7] In explaining the concept of public policy and its seeming indifference to the plight of the individual, Oliver Wendell Holmes stated: "True explanation of the rule is the same as that which accounts for the law's indifference to a man's particular temperament, faculties and so forth. Public policy sacrifices the individual to the general good. It is more desirable to put an end to robbery and murder. It is no doubt true that there are many cases in which the criminal could not have known that he was breaking the law but to admit the excuse at all would be to encourage ignorance where the lawmaker has determined to make men know and obey. And justice to the individual is rightly outweighed by the larger interests on the other side of the scales."[8] Thus, the issue of when and how to hold children accountable, in the final analysis, is a question of public policy.

Laws that require the automatic prosecution of juveniles in adult court do not permit an individualized assessment of maturity before prosecution. Criminal responsibility is presumed as a matter of public policy. Even though current public policy has defined children as young as 13 as adults for prosecution purposes, a child does not become an adult simply on the basis of legislative fiat. The question remains: When do we cease thinking and understanding as a child? Does it happen all at once? If we travel from the state of New Jersey where the age of criminal responsibility is 18,[9] and cross the Hudson River to New York where the age of criminal responsibility is 13[10] for the crime of murder, do we suddenly acquire by that voyage the presumptive wisdom and judgment of an adult? Also, consider the anomaly that in New York a child of 13 can be considered criminally responsible for murder but not for robbery.[11]

The use of chronological age as the exclusive measure of criminal responsibility is in many ways arbitrary because children under the age of majority, 18 in most states, are deemed not to possess sufficient capacity to reason to the extent that they are not considered mature enough to enter into binding contracts; they are not considered sophisticated enough to vote or responsible enough to drive until 16, 17, or 18. Yet, today legislators and policy makers have determined that children as young as 13, 14, and 15 (and younger in some states), although not civilly liable for their choices or behavior, are criminally liable for certain conduct. A mere 25 years ago, most states treated children under 16 years of age as juvenile delinquents and not subject to the jurisdiction of adult criminal courts.

Age is merely a convenient approximation of maturity. Children at any given moment have actually three ages: a chronological age, the number of years the child has actually lived; an apparent biological age, the extent of the child's physical development; and an intellectual age, the level of intellectual maturity the child has attained. A child, therefore, can look 20 but actually be 14 and have the mental and emotional capacity of an 11-year-old. Whether a person has developed sufficient intelligence or maturity to understand the nature and consequences of his act is often extremely difficult to determine. Individuals who are emotionally and socially immature may be above the chronological cutoff age and, of course, there are young people below the chronological age who possess sufficient sophistication and understanding to appreciate the nature of their behavior.

Ascertaining maturity is often a matter of evaluating the nature of the crime, the manner in which it was committed, the degree of the offender's participation, prior delinquency record and the social history of the offender, including his school records and family relationships. How can we evaluate or measure a child's criminal culpability in determining criminal responsibility or appropriate sanctions? If we visualize a linear continuum of culpability corresponding to the intellectual growth of an infant, we would observe an initial point at which no liability exists because of infancy. This lack of responsibility continues through age seven. Further along the line there is a period of presumptive innocence that continues to the age of 14, corresponding to common law perceptions of responsibility; from 14 to 18, the age of majority, a period of diminished responsibility exists. Thus, as one progresses along the continuum the level of criminal responsibility increases until it fully vests in adulthood.

An assessment of maturity can best be accomplished through the mechanism of a judicial transfer hearing. In the model juvenile justice system I propose, no minor would be prosecuted in the adult court without a hearing, which includes a consideration of a youth's level of maturity. The advantage of such a strategy is that it provides an opportunity for exploration of the developmental differences of youth, it permits a suitable child to remain in the Family Court setting where more social services are available, and, at the same time, it permits the adult court to focus on violent juveniles. It also allows the courts to effectively utilize the one institution in our community uniquely qualified to identify violent and dangerous juveniles—the juvenile court. The judges of the juvenile court have seen many of these children as infants in neglect and abuse proceedings, as persons in need of supervision as they grew older, and as respondents in delinquency petitions before they reach their teens. By using the juvenile court as a screening device, only the most dangerous, incorrigible and violent juveniles would be prosecuted in the adult court. If the decision to transfer is informed, sensitive to the developmental needs of adolescents, and if adequate flexibility is given to the decision maker, the principle of isolating the violent and incorrigible child from the child that can be safely channeled out of the adult court system can be advanced. By enacting laws that serve that general purpose, local jurisdictions will be able to implement the policy of prosecuting in the adult court only those juveniles who are deemed dangerous.

For those children who meet the threshold of criminal responsibility, prosecution in adult courts would then be justified. However, the nation's interest in the protection of minors is not nullified simply because they are prosecuted in adult courts. Protection of the community from violent juveniles does not require abandonment of the goal of socialization of children who violate the law. In enacting laws requiring the prosecution of certain children in adult courts, state legislatures did not intend nor could they obliterate all distinctions between child and adult by such prosecution. Such differences are clearly recognized in decisions of the Supreme Court that reflect the traditional judicial concern for children, a concern based on the recognition that childhood is a time of human development often punctuated by mistakes in judgment. In *Belloti v. Baird*,[12] the Supreme Court in 1979 posited three reasons why children should be treated differently from adults: (1) their peculiar vulnerability; (2) their inability to make critical decisions in an informed, mature manner; and (3) the importance of a parent's role in child rearing.[13] In *Eddings v. Oklahoma*,[14] decided in 1982, the Supreme Court similarly stated: "Adolescents, particularly in the early, middle, and teen years, are more vulnerable, more impulsive, and less self-disciplined than adults. Crimes committed by youths may be just as harmful to victims as those committed by older persons, but they deserve less punishment because adolescents may have less capacity to control their conduct and to think in long-range terms than adults."[15] Viewed together, these cases reveal a judicial policy that recognizes that children are entitled to special care and protection because they are still developing physically, mentally, and emotionally; a policy that recognizes the diminished capacity and responsibility of children for their criminal behavior.

Even if a child has reached the age of statutory criminal responsibility and is thereby determined as a matter of law to have sufficient capacity to reason and to freely make choices, the overarching doctrine of proportionality requires punishment in just proportion to culpability. The basic premise of free will permits the criminal law to justify punishment as a deserved product, the just desserts of the individual's personal culpability. The same concept also permits the criminal law to vary the degree of punishment relative to the degree of blameworthiness of the offender in accordance with the principle of proportionality. Justinian's definition of justice, giving each person his due, requires the severity of criminal penalties to be proportional to the culpability of the offender and his offense. In the case of juveniles, behavioral scientists and child development specialists have argued that adolescents are developmentally different from adults in that they have a diminished capacity to resist the negative influence of their contemporaries, a diminished capacity to know right from wrong. Although they may meet the threshold for criminal liability, adolescence should be a mitigating factor in assessing punishment.

In determining the criminal responsibility of adolescents, therefore, we must recognize the peculiar traits of this stage of life that impact on a teenager's exercise of his free will. In the case of adolescents, this freedom is affected by several factors that diminish the adolescent's freedom of choice: peer pressure, poor impulse control, and lack of foresight. All affect the quality of choice and, therefore, although they do not excuse one from sanctions, they should mitigate punishment. Behavioral scientists who are conducting studies for the MacArthur Foundation's Research Network on Adolescent

Development and Juvenile Justice confirm that "the cognitive, emotional and social development of adolescents is incomplete and that, for instance, boys well into their teens have difficulty curbing their impulses, thinking through long-term consequences and... resisting the influence of others."[16]

Professor Elizabeth Scott summarized the findings of modern behavioral scientists with respect to the pertinent developmental factors affecting an adolescent's free will, that is, factors that contribute to immature judgment in ways that affect the manner in which an adolescent makes choices: "In general, youth are likely to have less knowledge and experience to draw on in making decisions than adults. Moreover, peer conformity is a powerful influence on adolescent behavior, and may lead teens to become involved in criminal activity to avoid social rejection... Adolescents also seem to perceive risks differently or less well than adults, and they are more inclined to engage in risky activities (smoking, drinking, unprotected sex, and delinquent behavior, for example). Finally, time perspective changes with maturity. As compared to adults, adolescents tend to focus more on immediate rather than long-term consequences" [footnotes omitted].[17] These adolescent characteristics would not ordinarily excuse one from liability, but they should be considered in mitigation of blameworthiness.

The criminal law, therefore, assumes that offenders must be able to make rational autonomous choices in order to be held criminally responsible. "The legitimacy of punishment is undermined if the decision is coerced, irrational, or based on lack of understanding about the full meaning of the choice."[18] I am not proposing that adolescent immaturity should excuse young offenders from all responsibility. Rather, it should support a standard of diminished responsibility once they are prosecuted in adult court. "A diminished responsibility standard recognizes that most young offenders are in a transitional developmental stage and calibrates criminal liability accordingly. Under such a regime, young offenders can be held accountable for the bad choices they make, without bearing the full cost of their mistakes."[19]

Professor Frank Zimring explains that "capacity in the common-law view of criminal responsibility was an all or nothing matter like legal insanity rather than a question of degree, yet the logic of diminished culpability argues that even after a youth possesses the minimum threshold of competence, this barely competent youth is not as culpable, and, therefore, not as deserving of a full measure of punishment as a fully qualified adult offender. Just as a psychiatric disorder of cognitive impairment that does not render a subject exempt from criminal law may still justly mitigate the punishment to be imposed, so a minimally competent adolescent does not deserve all of an adult's punishment for the same act."[20]

In addition to evaluating the traditional factors relevant to sentencing, in the Youth Part we routinely ask the court psychiatric clinic to interview young offenders to give us a sense of their intellectual and emotional capacity. All of this information demonstrates whether the offender has exhibited mature behavior in his home, neighborhood, and school, which in turn gives us some indication of his mental health and potential. There is, however, an important distinction that must be borne in mind when considering psychiatric profiles of offenders. There is debate within the legal and medical communities concerning the issue of criminal responsibility: "The law tells us that if we commit illegal acts, we must be punished. In doing so, it assumes that we have freely chosen to perform the act. Psychiatry does not make any such assumption about free will or choice. Psychiatric theory is determinant and assumes that behavior is caused, shaped or determined by prior events—either immediate events or those in the distant past—or by physiological states... For example, to the psychiatrist, an abused child is likely to become an abusive adult. He has learned from his parents that violent behavior is acceptable—he does not choose to abuse others. Or the psychiatrist may believe that chemical imbalances or chemical deficiencies within the brain will precipitate certain violent behaviors when certain external stimuli are present. In neither case could one be said to be 'responsible' for the violent action in the sense that one chose it, for one does not (at least within the ordinary meaning of the word) choose either one's parents or one's brain chemistry."[21] Despite the different perspective of psychiatry, as it relates to responsibility, psychiatric reports are relevant to decisions concerning treatability and suitability of the offender for sanctions other than imprisonment. These issues are complicated and exacerbated by the legislative requirement of trying children in adult courts. In the adult court, the level of a youth's maturity is relevant primarily in determining the nature of the sanction instead of as a defense to prosecution. In some instances, however, lack of maturity may be relevant in establishing that the offender, because of his extreme immaturity, was not able to form the culpable mental state necessary for the commission of the crime. Once culpability of a youth has been established, however, a judge should have the authority to craft a sanction that conforms to the offender's level of maturity and that enhances such a youth's potential to make a positive contribution to society.[22]

CHAPTER 4

Sentencing Children Tried
in Adult Courts

*The principal objective of policy in the adjudication and
sentencing of minors is to avoid damaging the young
person's development into an adulthood of full potential
and free choice. Thus, the label for this type of policy is
"room to reform."*

—FRANK ZIMRING

I N NEW YORK, virtually all children sentenced as juvenile offenders in the adult court, with the exception of those convicted of
murder, will return to society by the age of 21.[1] The pragmatic
realization that children convicted of serious crimes in the adult court
will return to society as relatively young men and women lends powerful support to the goal of rehabilitation as the dominant rationale
for juvenile sentences. For example, had I decided to deny Loretta
youthful offender treatment and sentence her to the maximum term
permissible for the crime of Robbery in the second degree under the
Juvenile Offender law (two and one-third to seven years), she would
return to society before she was 20 years of age with a felony conviction on her record. She would have experienced incarceration with
other children, many imprisoned for far more violent crimes. What
skills would Loretta have learned when institutionalized? Who would
be willing to hire her? How safe will we be from this child when she
is released? These are important questions that society must address
in developing a rational sentencing policy for children.

What are the chances that, after serving six or so years in prison,
Loretta will not commit any other offenses? Unfortunately, the

chances that she will not reoffend are poor. Statistics demonstrate that children like Loretta who have been incarcerated are far more likely to commit new crimes upon their release than those who are sentenced to strict, effective alternative programs that offer mentoring, socialization skills, anger management, mental health services, employment, and educational counseling.[2]

Recent estimates indicate that the average American citizen will live approximately 76 years.[3] Loretta would have a long life ahead of her as a convicted felon. Assuming Loretta reoffends, what would be the cost to society for her criminal behavior over her lifetime? According to Professor Mark A. Cohen, an economist at Vanderbilt University, preventing an "at risk youth" from turning into a juvenile delinquent and adult criminal will save society up to $2 million.[4] That figure is based on society's anticipated expenditures for a child who reoffends over the course of an average lifespan. The calculation includes the cost to society of repeated incarcerations because of recidivism; the cost to sustain such an individual on welfare during periods of nonincarceration; the cost of physical injury and property damage caused by his or her criminal conduct; the cost of health care, and the loss of tax revenues based on such an offender's diminished capacity to earn income.

At the beginning of the 20th century, the juvenile court was created as a social service designed to aid in the socialization of America's delinquent children. The century ended with a shift toward a more punitive approach to the same category of children who were once subject to the exclusive jurisdiction of the Juvenile Court. This change in public policy has occurred despite research, which demonstrates that punitive responses such as incarceration are more likely to lead to recidivism for young offenders than supervised involvement in responsible and responsive alternative-to-incarceration programs.[5] When young offenders are imprisoned, obviously they are unable to commit further crimes in the community. Once released from prison, however, New York State statistics reveal that over 60% reoffend within 36 months.[6] Even though incarceration is not likely to reform juvenile offenders, policy makers continue to focus on imprisonment by requiring more and more of America's teenagers to be prosecuted in adult courts—courts that are ill-equipped to deal with the special

developmental needs of such young offenders. When the Juvenile
Offender Law was enacted in New York, adult court judges were
expected to adjudicate the cases of these children with the same
resources as were available for adults.

I once sentenced a 15-year-old for a crime that involved significant and gratuitous violence. I imposed close to the maximum permissible sentence. All of the available information I had about the boy
led me to conclude that he was dangerous and without proper intervention would quickly reoffend on release. He had never lived in a
conventional home. He had been abandoned in a dumpster at birth
and spent the first 15 years of his life in one group home after another.
When I sentenced him, I made it clear that he should be given appropriate psychiatric care in the institution to which he was assigned. If
not, he would surely reoffend. At the time of sentence, his lawyer
made an application that the boy not have his hair cut when in prison,
for religious reasons. The boy had long hair, which he wore in braids.
The application was weak in terms of its being based on a religious
motive, but, nevertheless, I granted the application. Perhaps if I
showed this boy some slight grace, it might generate in him a sem-
blance of empathy for a society that he believed abandoned him. As
it turned out, he never got the treatment he needed and, approximately six months after his release from prison, he was arrested for
decapitating and dismembering an elderly man whose apartment he
had taken over and in which he was living. The crime was not discovered for several weeks until some of the body parts were found
in the vicinity of the apartment. The case received widespread pub-
licity because of its gruesomeness. On reading one of the newspaper
accounts, I recalled a statement he made in his probation report that
all he ever wanted was a home of his own. It appeared that now he
had killed to get one. A columnist who covered the story could find
but one thing to criticize—the fact that I had permitted the defendant to keep his dreadlocks. He missed, of course, the real story, that
the defendant had never received the psychiatric care that was
directed at the time of sentence.

To ignore the potential for rehabilitation of juvenile offenders,
even those incarcerated because of the seriousness of their crimes,

simply postpones temporarily their membership in the ranks of adult repeat offenders. I have had the responsibility of sentencing thousands of teenagers. I have had to decide who will be jailed and for how long, who should be saddled with a felony conviction for the rest of their lives and who spared a record. For most juvenile offenders, prosecution in the adult courts is their first encounter with the prospect of mandatory imprisonment and criminalization. The vast majority of juveniles and their families are not cognizant of the full consequences of such a prosecution. It is a momentous circumstance in the life of the teenager and his family. The responsibility of dealing effectively with juveniles when first encountered is highlighted by the remarks of a commentator who stated: "Every study that has ever been made indicates that if the known criminals between 16 and 21 years old—those young persons actually convicted and dealt with in the courts, had somehow been prevented by that conviction from continuing a course of crime, the country's total burden of offenses would be a small fraction of what it is."[7]

The collateral consequences of a felony conviction on a young offender are significant and have the potential of inhibiting rehabilitation and reintegration into society. A convicted felon is excluded from federally supported public housing; he is ineligible for student loans or other financial assistance if he was convicted of a drug-related offense; he loses his voting rights. In New York, an individual with a felony conviction cannot drive a taxi or work for the Transit Authority or many other public institutions.[8] Of course, there are valid reasons for these prohibitions, but when we consider the repercussions of felonization of 14-, 15-, and 16-year-olds, the courts must be cautious in condemnation.

Under our current system, incarceration, keeping the dangerous youth away from us for as long as is just is, at times, by default, the only option. Not to incarcerate juveniles who commit particularly heinous offenses would undermine society's faith in the system. However, if nothing has been done to change the course of an offender's life when he first encounters the criminal justice system, odds are he will continue to be a threat to society. Thus, from a purely pragmatic perspective, it is important to identify those young defendants for whom a window of opportunity exists to intervene to change their course.

In order to fulfill my responsibility to the public, I have found it necessary to develop a process that helps me to make that determination. I believe, as does Professor Zimring, that "when a young offender's need for protection, education and skill development can be accommodated without frustrating community security, there is a government obligation to do so."[9] The sentencing of juveniles in the adult court must have as its essential mission, therefore, the transformation of a young offender's behavior. Reform is the principal goal of a juvenile sentence. Assuming that reform is our goal, three questions would have to be posed before considering an appropriate sentence: First, does the juvenile represent a danger to society? Second, can he be rehabilitated—can he learn from his mistakes, does he have the capacity to develop his character? And, third, will he be amenable to a sentencing process structured to give him the opportunity to prove that he can behave appropriately in educational and other social settings? There are no precise answers to these questions—psychiatrists are not able to predict with certainty future behaviors, and neither can judges. But a judge is expected, because of his training and experience, to be a good judge of character.

My experience leads me to conclude that an appropriate sentence for a child convicted in the adult courts should strike a balance between protecting the public from violent juveniles and enhancing a child's ability to function as a law-abiding contributing member of society. This principle is based on a concept of justice that requires proportionate accountability of juvenile offenders, and a recognition of the characteristics of adolescence that require a teenage offender to be treated with special care, given an opportunity to change, and a chance to make a fresh start when consistent with protection of the public.

We view the prosecution of the offender in the adult courts as the beginning of a process of rehabilitation, as an opportunity for a young person to take stock of himself and make choices that lead to a future that will not be harmful to others. The philosophical underpinnings or the working principles of the Youth Part are that children by their nature are malleable; children learn appropriate behavior by the reactions of those responsible for them; and that discipline, to be effective, must be swift and measured to the offense. Over the last 20 years, a great deal has been learned about the nature of adolescence. Psychologists and behavioral scientists tell us that attitudes, behavior patterns, and even character are changeable but change becomes more difficult the older we become. Psychologists have discovered that there is a set of human strengths that can act as buffers against negative behaviors: courage, optimism, interpersonal skill, work ethic, hope, honesty, and perseverance.[10] Much of our efforts at prevention involve assisting youth to utilize these attributes when confronting the issues of their daily lives. In the Youth Part, we try to link youth with services that can develop these strengths.

Psychologists also tell us that children learn their moral code and adjust their behavior in response to a discrete system of reward and punishment. They learn a code of morality and develop a conscience through the reaction of their parents, teachers, and those responsible for their conduct.[11] Through a discrete system of reward and punishment, those responsible for children can teach them to adjust their behavior. The same approach can be applied in dealing with juvenile offenders.

Discipline and encouragement play an important role in a child's development. Children need discipline to learn and they need to be disciplined when they misbehave. I prefer the term "discipline" to punishment when discussing the consequences of juvenile criminal behavior because it more closely approximates the purpose of society's intervention. When children misbehave, we don't "punish" them to exact retribution. We discipline to educate; we seek socialization, not retaliation. Encouragement provides incentive to continue positive behavior. It creates a sense of well-being that focuses a child's efforts to learn, appreciate, and ultimately demonstrate appropriate conduct. Most criminal justice experts agree that, in terms of public protection and the rehabilitation of offenders, not only is the certainty of discipline crucial but also the immediacy of it. When dealing with children, it is imperative that they be disciplined for their transgressions as quickly as possible, so that they can relate their act to its consequence and develop a sense of the significance of their behavior.

Discipline delayed is tantamount to no discipline at all. More important, it loses its corrective significance and engenders resentment. It is therefore important to deal expeditiously with the cases of juvenile offenders because swift action increases the effectiveness of the court's intervention. If an accused juvenile offender is not guilty of the crime charged or guilty only of a lesser offense appropriate for disposition in a juvenile court, adjudicating the case quickly is critical. Juveniles arrested and prosecuted in adult courts are subject to bail requirements. Those unable to make bail are confined pending trial in institutions that do not provide continuity of education. Children confined even for a short time experience great difficulty returning to school. Even more traumatizing is the impact on the child's social development, as he is removed from his family at a crucial point. Juvenile courts such as New York's Family Court recognize the urgency in dealing with these cases. Strict time limits are imposed on prosecutors.[12] In the adult courts these time limits are generally not as stringent.[13]

In order to implement these concerns, we have structured the Youth Part process as a system of reward and punishment in the sense of providing encouragement and support when appropriate, as well as timely instilling discipline and exacting a cost for misbehavior when necessary. We do this chiefly through the device of deferring a youth's sentence for a sufficient period to enable the court to monitor a youth's performance in a treatment program. This permits a proportionate response by the court to any misbehavior during the monitoring process.

I believe we have had some measure of success in the Youth Part because we have integrated the principle of accountability with that of the recognition of the developmental differences of children.

We do this in stages: First, we gather as much information as is available about the youth. The Probation Department conducts a prepleading investigation (PPI) with the consent of the youth's attorney to document the youth's social history. A psychiatric report is also ordered with the consent of defense counsel for each youth (referred to as a 390 report because it is authorized pursuant to Section 390 of the Criminal Procedure Law). The Court has become a focal point for youth counseling and alternative-to-incarceration programs who assist in determining whether or not youths meet criteria for admission into those programs. Because all juvenile offenders appear in one part, many programs send court representatives to the Part daily and especially on "calendar" day (Friday) to help identify potentially suitable youths.

Second, after gathering this information, we assess the youth's background and involvement in the offense to determine his level of culpability. We make an effort to assess the offender's level of maturity. This assessment requires a comprehensive portrait of the offender; a portrait that is often supplemented by defense prepleading and sentence memoranda. It is important that the court be able to assemble as much information about the offender as is available. How has the child reacted in terms of demonstrating mature behavior in his home, neighborhood, school, and, if there was prior contact with the legal system, how has he performed under supervision? This information helps us to assess prospects for rehabilitation, illuminates the offender's risk potential, and informs the court of the persistency and intensity of the offender's violation of social norms. This information also can reveal an offender's capacity for and willingness to evaluate behavior choices. It may disclose patterns of criminal behavior and the offender's aptitude and willingness to change that pattern. In addition to concrete information from objective sources, we try to get to know the defendants and develop a rapport with them through periodic court appearances in court. We then make a determination as to whether we can give the defendant an opportunity to prove himself. If so, we identify an appropriate community-based program for the defendant.

Third, when a guilty plea is to be entered and the offender's background and involvement in the crime permit the court to consider an alternative to incarceration, a plea is structured to allow the court to test the child's willingness and ability to cooperate.

Essential tools in this process are: (1) the postponement of sentence after a plea; (2) the conditional nature of the sentence (conditioned on compliance with terms of a plea agreement usually requiring cooperation with an alternative-to-incarceration program); and (3) validation of the child's performance after plea. In order to validate the child's progress, the Court closely monitors performance in the program weekly by calls from court staff to the child's counselor, and approximately every three weeks when the child appears in the Youth Part for formal report. These contacts provide the Court with timely information and convey the Court's concern and interest in the child to the child. If the Court learns a defendant has violated the terms of the deferred sentence, the case is immediately advanced and the problem is addressed.

The question often asked is, How do I arrive at a specific sentence? Factors that must be considered in deciding on a sentence for juvenile offenders include respect for the suffering of the victim and the victim's family, maintenance of public confidence in the rule of law, and recognition of the state's responsibility to protect children and ensure their development. Determining an appropriate sentence also requires reflection on the facts of a case, the individualized circumstances of an offender, recommendations of prosecution and defense counsel. On such reflection, the outlines of a sentence usually crystallize from my accumulated experience in dealing with cases of this nature. I find it useful in this process to convene an in-chambers conference for most cases. The atmosphere of these conferences is informal but the objective is clear: What is the fairest disposition available for this offender and society?

In these conferences, the determination of whether to grant or deny Youthful Offender treatment is usually the first and most important decision we have to make. Although this determination may seem unique to New York, it is actually similar to the issue confronting judges in other jurisdictions who must determine whether a sentence is to be of a juvenile or adult nature. For example, in Michigan, as well as a number of other states where a form of "blended" sentencing has been adopted, judges sentencing juveniles tried in adult or juvenile courts have three options: A youth can be sentenced as an adult, with full adult penalties; as a juvenile; or subject to a conditional (blended) sentence. This last option involves initially sentencing a youth as an adult but delaying the implementation of the adult sentence pending placement of the youth in a juvenile facility. If at age 21 the child is not rehabilitated, the judge can then implement the adult sentence.[14] This is analogous to the Youthful Offender paradigm in New York. If Youthful Offender status is denied, the youth faces mandatory imprisonment under New York law (at least one to three years for robbery and all other juvenile offender crimes, except murder). In that case, there is no need to consider an alternative-to-incarceration program because there is no sentence alternative other than prison.

The factors that the court must consider in determining whether to grant or deny Youthful Offender treatment are crucial and ultimately center upon the prospects or potential of a youth for rehabilitation. In the context of Youth Part cases, when a conditional plea is deemed appropriate to give a youth an opportunity to prove that he's amenable to rehabilitation under the auspices of an ATI program, a temporary period of confinement is often made a part of the disposition. The duration of that temporary period of confinement is in certain cases based on a principled compromise. The term "principled compromise" implies that no interest is compromised without moral justification. Because the sentencing of juveniles is complex, a consensus as to what is considered a fair outcome is often all that is possible. This frequently unfolds in the context of an agreement between the prosecution and the defense under the guidance of the judge as to the appropriateness of granting Youthful Offender treatment.

The rationale for compromise is based on the realization that the determination to grant or deny a particular juvenile offender YO treatment is subject to appeal, either by the prosecutor if it is judged to be unreasonably granted, or by the defense if it is judged to be unreasonably withheld. Thus, the determination can be challenged as an abuse of discretion. The issue needs to be settled before an alternative program can be agreed on. If the district attorney is not in agreement as to the granting of YO treatment and the court proceeds to grant it over the objection of the prosecutor, a subsequent successful appeal by the prosecutor will require resentencing the juvenile to a mandatory period of imprisonment. In order to resolve this issue, a compromise reached between the position of the district attorney and the defense attorney, a compromise that often depends on an agreement as to the duration of temporary confinement before a youth is given an opportunity to earn YO status.

This process includes the systematic input of social workers, psychologists, psychiatrists, and other behavioral experts to help individualize sentences and to develop sentencing options in lieu of incarceration. At the core of the process is the conditional sentence that permits the court to assess a child's willingness and capacity to conform his conduct to acceptable standards of behavior. The conditional sentence allows a determination that is not limited to assessing a youth's past behavior as the basis for granting or denying Youthful Offender treatment. By deferring or postponing a decision to grant such relief, a judge can base his ultimate decision on a child's performance after Youth Part intervention.

The philosopher Michel Foucault, who traced the history of punishment and discipline in Western civilization in his landmark treatise *Discipline and Punish,* in a chapter entitled "The Means of Correct Training," said, "In discipline, punishment is only one element of a double system; gratification—punishment; and it is this system that operates in the process of training and correction. The teacher must avoid as much as possible the use of punishment; on the contrary, the teacher must endeavor to make rewards more frequent than penalties. The lazy being more encouraged by the desire to be rewarded in the same way as the diligent than by the fear of punishment; that is why it will be very beneficial, when the teacher is obliged to use punishment, to win the heart of the child, if he can, before doing so."[15]

Foucault began this seminal work by contrasting descriptions of a brutal torture and the oppressive freedomless regimen of prison life. According to Foucault, the transition in modern society from torture to imprisonment also was a transformation of the object of punishment from the "body" to the "soul." When Foucault refers to the soul, he is not referring to a religious concept. Unlike the soul represented by Christian theology, Foucault's soul is not born in sin and subject to punishment, but it is, rather, borne out of methods of discipline, supervision, and constraint. He demonstrates that the idea of "caging" a human being for a period of time is no more useful to society than the consequences of public exhibitions of brutal dismemberment of transgressors. He ultimately concludes that imprisonment is nothing more or involves nothing more than torturing the soul of the offender.

Notwithstanding Foucault's criticism of imprisonment or the goal of imprisonment as a means of transforming an individual's behavior, in my view, the cautious and precise use of incarceration or confinement may provide the opportunity to stir the "soul" of an individual, to reconsider choices. The use of temporary imprisonment as part of a process leading to the development of the soul is not unlike the development of "conscience," and it leads us to an examination of how our American juvenile justice system can best respond to juvenile offenders.

There are two important aspects of my view of punishment as it relates to adolescents; the first is getting their attention. In order to impress on children the consequences of their behavior, we must first command their attention—compel them to listen. In the Youth Part, we often accomplish this when necessary by resorting to the concept of a split sentence—some punishment in the form of incarceration, coupled with supervised freedom. The second aspect reflects the reality that we are sentencing children. In so doing, we also must recognize the powerful pull of our nurturing instincts. Frank Zimring articulates a valuable insight as to the predominant goal of a sentencing policy toward American children. He characterizes it by the terse phrase "Room to Reform." The heart of this approach is to afford children an opportunity to learn from their mistakes, when to do so would not pose an unjustifiable risk to society, so that as these children mature, they will not be precluded from becoming contributing members of our society.

"Corrective" imprisonment or split sentences should be used sparingly and only when necessary. The danger to be avoided is based on the advice I received from a program representative who had actually served significant time in prison. He said that whatever term I decided on, the duration of such term was pivotal. If it were too long, there was a real danger that the offender would become acclimated to prison life, learning to survive the brutality of confinement; if it were too short, the sentence would lose its terrifying effect. The key was to craft a sentence that had the right balance and was measured to the individual. Otherwise, the threat of imprisonment becomes meaningless as a deterrent.

I also would add to that advice that we should do all we can to avoid Foucault's searing criticism of the way in which punishment can be administered. "By the word punishment, one must understand everything that is capable of making children feel the offense they have committed, everything that is capable of humiliating them, or confusing them:… a certain coldness, a certain indifference, a question, a humiliation, a removal…"[16]

Of course, not all juvenile offenders must be imprisoned for their involvement in criminal behavior. But for those whose behavior warrant incarceration, we can consider the judicious use of imprisonment as an opportunity for education and reflection, which, when followed by supervised freedom in the community, can provide a valuable practical lesson to the offender. It is an extension of the idea that in isolation an offender will have the opportunity to develop conscience. Confinement in this context is considered one part of the process, securing the attention of the juvenile as a method of demonstrating the consequences of criminal behavior, especially in a setting such as New York, where imprisonment is mandatory unless a judge exercises discretion in granting Youthful Offender treatment.

In the Youth Part, we try to convey to the young offenders that we care about their future and that society and I, as the judge, have certain expectations; if they cannot live up to those expectations, there will be serious consequences. In many instances, this may be the first time that a defendant has experienced structure. Some respond very well. This approach is certainly not appropriate for every defendant; identifying those defendants for whom it has merit requires a thorough and careful analysis.

What is not traditional about this process is that it requires judges to supervise the coordination of the agencies providing services to the juvenile so that an integrated, supervised, and carefully monitored program is available to the offender. The theory on which this approach is based is that corrective treatment of a young person, with temporary incarceration when necessary, prevents recidivism more effectively than long-term imprisonment.

We have tried to create a process, to craft a sentence that impacts on the youth's response to challenges he faces in his environment. We recognize that our efforts to affect the child's environment are extremely limited, so we concentrate on his response to the conditions with which he is presented, to provide him with the means to constructively react to the adversities of his surroundings.

Alternative-to-incarceration programs are important interventions in that process. I consider them extensions of the court. They help juveniles gain insight and learn skills that will enable them to better manage their behavior. ATI programs, which are predominantly privately run community-based programs, have as their mission to provide the court with an alternative to a sentence of imprisonment. These programs provide educational and social training which encourage and guide positive behavior. They offer safeguards that can lend confidence to a judge's decision to release a youth who will then be afforded supervision and counseling. They offer a youth an opportunity to prove him- or herself and build a history of responsible behavior that would justify a judge's decision to grant a second chance. It is essential, however, that such programs accede to the monitoring process, that is, that they be responsive to the court.

The Youth Part's approach to sentencing does not ignore the necessity for the incarceration of dangerous juveniles, but it is designed to strengthen a suitable offender's resistance to negative behavior, to provide incentives for a youth to build skills and make productive choices. It emphasizes a positive approach in dealing with young offenders and sets up the objective of rehabilitation, development of character and giving the youth the tools to react constructively to negative pressure. In sum, we view contact with a child as an opportunity to positively influence behavior by guiding and rewarding the child who makes productive choices.

If the role of the judge dealing with juveniles is to facilitate a child's rehabilitation, then the judge should strive to take advantage of opportunities to educate the child to his responsibilities whenever possible. In an insightful editorial for the *New York Times*, Brent

Staples observed that the lack of educational programs in prison contributed significantly to recidivism.[17] He also asserted that the value
of prison education could extend well beyond job-preparedness:
"Reading, writing and thinking allow many ex-offenders to reflect on
their actions instead of living on impulse."[18] The idea that reading,
writing, and thinking is a prescription for rehabilitation is crucial in
considering methods of rehabilitation of juveniles before they are
subject to extensive imprisonment. Enabling children to reflect on
their choices instead of acting on impulse is an essential ingredient
in preventing juvenile crime. Because we view education as the heart
of rehabilitation, as the key to the transformational process, a core
question for me is whether a child is educable. Is he ready? Does he
possess the capacity to learn? Can we adequately address, through
counseling services, his intellectual and emotional issues? Not every
child comes to us in an educable condition or open to our process.
As a last resort, we must deprive these children of their liberty when
their crimes require. Less than a third of the children we see fall into
this category. For the others, we try to develop a disposition that
helps us to foster their educability.

The challenge we face in the juvenile and criminal justice system
is that of socializing children who commit criminal acts and integrating them back into our society. I believe the answer lies with education and in the development of a process of accountability. A judge is
in a unique position to address the ills affecting many of the children
who appear before him by using his authority to coordinate and
enforce sanctions. Ignoring these issues by simply imprisoning youth
merely delays their inevitable reentry into society, rarely cured of these
ills, rehabilitated or prepared to meet their obligations as citizens.

The philosopher Andre Compte-Sponville, in his book *A Small
Treatise on The Great Virtues,*[19] examines classical human values to
help us to understand what we should do, who we should be and
how we should live. He states: "… a principle of Kantian ethics is that
one cannot deduce what one should do from what is done. Yet the
child in his early years is obliged to do just that. And it is only in this
way that he becomes human. Kant himself concedes as much. 'Man
can only become man by education' he writes, 'he is merely what

education makes him and that process begins with discipline which changes animal nature into human nature.'"[20] If I conclude that a child has the capacity to learn then that is the first step in determining whether or not he can be offered a second chance.

The Youth Part's orientation is to look forward, to prepare the juvenile for the future. Once guilt has been established, the challenge is to craft and supervise an intervention that would change that child's future behavior. The main mechanism on which we rely is rigorous judicial monitoring of a defendant's participation in court-ordered programs. The role of the judge in the evaluation of a youth's progress is shaped by this mission. Implementation of the monitoring process requires interaction with a youth, dialogue, and the ability to listen. Through the monitoring process, we believe we can favorably influence a child's behavior.

Several years ago, I was invited to Israel by ELEM, an American/Israeli organization that funds, supports, and operates programs for at-risk children in Israel. ELEM was founded in 1982 by social workers, lawyers, and educators involved with America's juvenile justice system. They were joined by representatives from Israel's Family Court and Ministry of Welfare. A partnership emerged to develop and evaluate effective outreach, treatment, and rehabilitation programs in Israel for a rapidly rising population of alienated and poorly educated Israeli and Arab youth. ELEM's goals included the sharing and exchange of information about effective outreach and treatment methodologies between American and Israeli officials. The purpose of my visit was to evaluate ELEM's programs and offer suggestions for improvement if warranted. I took advantage of the opportunity to meet and talk with as many children as possible. On one occasion, we visited a crisis shelter in Tel Aviv called Machom Aher (A Safe Place). When we arrived, I was told we were just in time to witness a ceremony honoring "the most progressive child." This sounded rather political, I thought. I soon learned that this had nothing at all to do with politics. Instead, the award was to be given to the child who made the most progress from where he or she was when the child entered the program. That child was not always the best-behaved child but the one who showed the most relative improvement. This was an interesting way of looking at the behavior of children. I have taken a similar approach in evaluating the progress of children whom we have ordered to comply with alternative-to-incarceration programs. It is a realistic way to appraise the youth's prospects for rehabilitation and hope for a constructive life. This concept of rewarding or encouraging the progress of a child meant that you met the child where he or she was and you worked forward from that point.

Some may perceive the Youth Part approach as unduly protracted and less expedient than a prison sentence. If results be the important thing, however, then this method, despite its difficulty and whatever skill it requires, does restore, I submit, more offenders permanently to productive roles in society, whereas the methods associated with punitive sanctions primarily ostracize them. The majority of children given a second chance successfully complete an alternative-to-incarceration program while the overwhelming majority of juveniles sent to prison re-offend. If the purpose of our system of criminal jurisprudence and of our prisons is simply to punish, then they have succeeded. If, by contrast, the real purpose of our system of criminal jurisprudence is to rehabilitate and normalize behavior so that in the end offenders may be restored to society as law-abiding citizens, then we must make the effort at the first opportunity that is presented. We must understand the distinction between trying children as if they were adults and trying them in adult courts. The former implies inattention to the complexity of adolescent behavior, whereas the latter can combine the due process protections of the adult court with an appreciation of the developmental differences of adolescents.

If we accept that children are developmentally different than adults because of their lack of maturity, then we must give them room to reform. "At the heart of this process is a notion of adolescence as a period of learning by doing, when competence and decision-making can be achieved only by making decisions and making mistakes."[21] For this reason, adolescence is a period that is mistake prone by nature. The special challenge here is to create safeguards in the prosecution of children for their criminal behavior that reduce in an appropriate case the permanent costs of their mistakes.

As part of the 100th anniversary of the Juvenile Court of Cook County, Northwestern University's Children and Family Justice Center, in partnership with The Justice Policy Institute, published *Second Chances: 100 Years Of The Children's Court: Giving Kids a Chance to Make a Better Choice.*[22] The pamphlet chronicled the lives of successful men and women who had been given a chance to recover from their juvenile offenses. The list included a U.S. senator, a former deputy drug czar, a senior White House advisor, a renowned poet, the chief prosecutor of a large city, a member of President George H. W. Bush's honor guard, an Olympic gold medalist, a judge, and a TV reporter. These former delinquents told their stories. They stand as excellent examples of the value of a juvenile sentencing policy that recognizes adolescence as a period of learning by doing, when competence and productive choices can be achieved notwithstanding adolescent mistakes.

CHAPTER 5

Our Hardest-to-Love Children

In every child who is born, under no matter what circumstances, and of no matter what parents, the potentiality of the human race is born again.
—JAMES AGEE, *LET US NOW PRAISE FAMOUS MEN*

THANK YOU for helping us to better understand our hardest to love children." Those words were handwritten at the bottom of a letter I received after making a presentation to New York's Citizen's Committee for Children. Who are these children? What are they capable of? What challenges do they present?

Two boys, one 15, the other 18, startled a 31-year-old nurse's aide returning home from work one dark evening. The boys stepped from the shadows as the woman turned a corner a few blocks from her home. Surprised, she acknowledged the boys with a smile. "Where are you going, bitch?" was the response. As she turned, she was struck in the face with a baseball bat. Hurt and disoriented, she was pushed into the hallway of an abandoned building reeking from urine and littered with empty crack vials. One of the teenagers, the older of the two, threatened her with a knife while the other began to systematically beat her, almost ritually, as she described it. She pleaded with them to stop. She offered them her money. The younger man took her earrings and her money. But that didn't satisfy him. He then ordered her to remove her clothes. She hesitated but was struck again because she was not moving fast enough. She desperately tried to stall by taking her clothes off slowly, hoping that someone would rescue her. Again, she was struck. Finally, she was standing in front of them completely naked. The younger boy ordered her to turn around and bend over. Indignant, she'd had enough. She defiantly and courageously told them, "You better be prepared to kill me because I'm not going to let you do this to me." With that, the older boy, standing watch, said to the younger boy "Let's go. Let's go. We've done enough."

A 52-year-old man taking a leisurely stroll in Central Park on a beautiful Sunday afternoon saw a group of 10 or so teenagers walking toward him. As he passed through the group, he accidentally struck one of their shoulders. A young boy spun round, slammed him in the face, and punched him, knocking him down. As he lay helplessly on the ground, he heard the laughter of the group. Then someone from the crowd said, "He needs a cap in his ass." A 15-year-old girl walked over to him, took out a gun and shot him in the groin. The laughter continued as the group ran away, leaving him with a bullet permanently lodged near his urethra.

One cold winter morning, three young boys, friends, met at an old abandoned wire factory located in a rundown desolate area of New York City on the outskirts of one of the city's poorest neighborhoods. The abandoned factory was used as a clubhouse. Although three boys entered the factory that day, only two boys left. A year later, on another cold winter morning, a homeless man looking for shelter and a place to sleep stumbled over a black plastic bag at the bottom of an elevator shaft in that same abandoned factory. He pulled the bag from its place and was stunned by what he saw: a skeleton, grotesquely mangled, wearing a waist-length jacket draped around its upper torso, hands tied together with twine, cinderblocks covering the body, the pointed corner of one lodged in the skull. Two 15-year-old boys are eventually charged with murdering their 18-year-old friend, whom they had beaten and tortured before pushing him five stories to his death in that dark, dank elevator shaft.

In sentencing children found guilty of horrendous acts of violence, such as those described here, often there are no acceptable options other than incarceration. For the immediate safety of the community, such offenders need to be segregated from society.

However, children who murder, rape, and engage in such acts of extreme brutality are in fact a small percentage of the juveniles who are prosecuted in the adult courts.

The most common cases in the Youth Part are group robberies involving multiple defendants, possessing varying levels of maturity, different degrees of involvement and culpability. New York's Juvenile Offender Law brings before the court many youth who are swept into the adult system because of the broad definition of an offense; juveniles who play relatively minor or peripheral roles in otherwise serious and violent offenses. Because of the rigidity and overinclusiveness typical of laws requiring the prosecution of children as adults, involvement in a crime, even if only slightly more than mere presence, can have dire consequences for a juvenile, exposing a youth to mandatory imprisonment and a felony record. The case of 14-year-old James is illustrative. James and six of his high school classmates were passing through Grand Central Station after class one day when one of his fellow classmates, Thomas, decided to look for other students carrying the popular "Jansport" knapsack. Thomas was physically the biggest of the group and its apparent leader. A student carrying the fashionable knapsack was spotted walking alone. The group, including James, surrounded him and Thomas told the student, "Run up your bag." The student tried to walk away, but he was blocked by James and the others. Thomas then said, "Take off your bag or I'll cut you," simultaneously taking a box cutter from his pocket and menacingly displaying it to the student. The student then handed the knapsack over to Thomas. The group hurried away. A witness observing the incident stopped a police officer and informed him of what occurred, pointing out the group. A chase ensued. Other police joined in. James, Thomas, and two others were apprehended and arrested. They were all charged as juvenile offenders with the crime of robbery in the first degree.

Robbery in the first degree is defined in New York's Penal Law as follows: A person is guilty of robbery in the first degree when he forcibly steals property and when, in the course of the commission of the crime… he or another participant in the crime uses or threatens the immediate use of a dangerous instrument."[1] James and the other arrested youths were charged with "acting in concert" in the robbery. The significance of "acting in concert" in the commission of a crime is explained in Section 20 of New York's Penal Law (criminal liability for conduct of another), which states: When one person engages in conduct that constitutes an offense, another person is criminally liable for such conduct when, acting with the mental culpability required for the commission thereof, he solicits, requests, commands, importunes, or intentionally aids such person to engage in such conduct.

Thus, in the case here, each juvenile was considered as liable as his codefendants, no matter how minor his role may have been in the commission of the crime, provided he aided in the commission of the crime in some fashion. Equal liability under the law also means equal exposure to statutorily mandated punishment. The Juvenile Offender Law provides that if an age-eligible youth is guilty of robbery in the first degree, he faces an indeterminate range of imprisonment of a minimum period of one to three years and a maximum period of three and one-third years to ten years. Imprisonment is mandatory unless the presiding judge adjudicates the juvenile a "Youthful Offender." A Youthful Offender adjudication allows a judge to impose a nonincarceratory sentence of probation or a combination of imprisonment (not exceeding six months) and probation or imprisonment not exceeding one and one-third years to four years. Granting Youthful Offender status also relieves a youth of the stigma of a felony conviction.

Many of the offenders appearing in the Youth Part are like James, who, because of the concept of accomplice liability, are charged along with those who are more culpable. Although the idea to commit the crime was Thomas's and he alone possessed a weapon and threatened violence, James was charged under the theory that he was an accomplice; in other words, he made it possible for Thomas to commit the crime by blocking the victim's escape, knowing that Thomas intended to take the property. Consequently, as an accomplice James faced the same potential penalties as Thomas. James eventually pled guilty and on his successful completion of an alternative-to-incarceration program, he was granted Youthful Offender treatment with a sentence of probation, which resulted in his record of conviction being sealed.

In yet another case, Danny, a 14-year-old, traveled to Manhattan one day with a group of older boys from his Brooklyn neighborhood to settle a "beef." When he and the others reached their destination, a third-floor tenement apartment, one of the members of the group drew a gun and started firing into the apartment, causing its occupants to flee out a fire escape window. As the group, including Danny, ran down the stairs of the tenement, the police entered the building, and the older boy passed the gun to Danny. The police arrested the group and a .9-millimeter automatic handgun was found in Danny's sweatshirt pocket. Danny was charged with attempted murder under New York's Juvenile Offender Law. If convicted, Danny faced a mandatory term of imprisonment of a minimum of one to three years and a maximum of three and one-third to ten years. (The other members of the group also were charged with attempted murder.)

Danny had no prior record and was doing well in school. His statement to the police at the time of his arrest revealed that he was not aware that one of the older members of the group had a gun. He stated he was hanging out in a local park when the older boys and some others said they were going to Manhattan to "straighten out" some other kids for some vague reason. He tagged along with his friends. It was clear from the statement and other evidence that the older members of the group had used Danny as a "human holster" when the police approached, because he was the only juvenile.

A conference in my chambers was held in Danny's case. At the conference, both the district attorney and defense counsel agreed that Danny was not the shooter, although there was some evidence that he was aware that one of the group had a gun. The police investigation also revealed that, once at the location, Danny saw this individual fire the gun into the apartment, did nothing to prevent this from happening, did not leave, and may have helped to kick the door open before the gun was drawn and fired. It was the consensus of both counsel that in light of the defendant's relatively minimal involvement, his age, and lack of prior criminal record, he should be given an opportunity to avoid further incarceration subject to certain conditions. Danny was to plead guilty to burglary in the first degree. On his plea, he would be released from Spofford (a juvenile detention facility) to the custody of a nonresidential alternative-to-incarceration program with which he would have daily contact and that would provide appropriate counseling. He was to return to school and attend every day. If Danny cooperated with the program and successfully graduated, he would be sentenced to five years' probation and, at that time, declared a Youthful Offender, thereby avoiding a felony record. However, if he failed to cooperate with the program or attend school, or became involved in any other criminal behavior, he could be immediately remanded and subject to a sentence of a minimum of two years and a maximum of six years, a sentence that would result in a felony conviction. Danny was required to appear periodically in the Youth Part so that his behavior and progress could be monitored. After approximately one year, Danny successfully graduated from the program and was sentenced to a probationary period of five years and granted Youthful Offender treatment.

Perhaps the most difficult cases to resolve in the Youth Part are those involving children like Roberta and Maria. When Roberta was seven years old, she answered a knock on the door to her apartment. Her father, who was estranged from her mother, was standing at the door. "Go get your mother," he told the little girl. She walked into the kitchen, tugged at her mother's dress. "Mommy, daddy's at the door." Her mother walked to the door, Roberta trailing behind. As her mother approached the open door, her father doused her mother from head to toe with gasoline from a can he was hiding. He then ignited her clothing with a cigarette lighter setting her on fire. Roberta's mother survived but was horribly disfigured. Eight years later, Roberta, now 15, stands before me for putting a gun to a stranger's head and threatening to shoot him unless he turned over his money.

In Maria's case, when she was six years old, she was walking with her mother holding her mother's hand, when her father approached them on the street. Accusing her mother of having an affair with his best friend, he took out a knife, slashed the mother across the face, and then stabbed her repeatedly in the chest. She fell to the ground, dead, still holding Maria's hand. Eight years later, Maria appears before me for slashing the face of a rival girlfriend over a boy.

In the cases of Roberta and Maria, sentences were arrived at through a principled compromise that gave both of them a chance to earn Youthful Offender treatment. In Roberta's case, the same assistant district attorney who prosecuted her father for the attempted murder of her mother appeared in court to speak on her behalf. That prosecutor remembered her as the little girl who sat in his office as he interviewed her in preparation for the trial of her father. He remembered telling her mother that she should seek psychological counseling for herself and for her child, especially because her daughter felt responsible for what happened. The mother, overwhelmed with her own issues, was unable to get services for either of them. The seriousness of Roberta's case warranted that she remain incarcerated for a period of time. The specific duration of her confinement was arrived at as a result of a compromise. Because the prosecutor was willing to give Roberta a chance to avoid extended incarceration and a criminal record, an agreement was reached that could lead to Youthful Offender treatment and probation. Roberta was to be held in detention for eight months and then would be released to an ATI program where she would receive appropriate counseling, with the understanding that if she did not cooperate with the program she would be denied YO status and face mandatory imprisonment of as much as two to six years. Roberta fulfilled the terms of her agreement and was ultimately granted YO status and placed on probation. She completed her five-year probationary period without incident and became gainfully employed.

In Maria's case, I was reluctant to make a commitment as to a deferred sentence without the victim and the victim's family having an opportunity to express their concerns with respect to any prospective sentence. With the consent of the prosecutor and defense counsel, they were invited to a chamber's conference. I explained the sentencing options that were available to me. A conditional sentence was proposed, a sentence that would include a period of imprisonment but also would give Maria an opportunity to obtain appropriate psychiatric counseling. Maria was to remain in detention for one year and then released to an alternative-to-incarceration program for an additional year. If she successfully completed the counseling regimen of the program, she would then be sentenced to five years' probation and granted Youthful Offender treatment. If she violated the terms of the plea agreement, then she could be sentenced to as much as three to nine years in prison. The victim and the victim's family deemed the proposed disposition satisfactory.

Maria pled guilty pursuant to the agreement and was released from detention after a year. She received the necessary counseling and was eventually granted Youthful Offender treatment and sentenced to five years' probation. While on probation, she incurred several minor violations including smoking marijuana and missing a number of appointments. She also gave birth to a child. She eventually completed her probationary term without committing any further violent crimes.

I recognize that the use of detention in this fashion as part of a "split-sentence" resulting from a compromise between the prosecution and defense does not fit neatly into the theoretical conception of juvenile detention as temporary segregation pending disposition of a case. Nevertheless, the primary issue in the context of Roberta and Maria's cases was whether they should be given an opportunity to earn Youthful Offender status, an opportunity they would not otherwise have had but for the compromise worked out between the lawyers and the court. A determination to grant or deny Youthful Offender treatment is ordinarily based on the past behavior of a youth and the nature of the offense. In cases such as Roberta's and Maria's, it would have been difficult to grant them YO status without giving them an opportunity to demonstrate their willingness to address the issues that contributed to their criminal behavior. Thus, dispositions resulting from such a compromise often result in more juvenile offenders receiving Youthful Offender treatment than would otherwise have been considered eligible.

In determining the degree of culpability that we can justly place on the shoulders of children who commit violent acts, we must consider far more than the nature of the offense that brings them before the court. We must examine each child's individual circumstances and social history. The nature of the offense does not tell us all we need to know about the nature of the offender. We cannot be content to

merely impose what seems to be the "statutorily" appropriate punishment that is graduated solely according to the gravity of the crime.
The fact that Roberta held a gun to someone's head and that Maria
slashed the face of a girlfriend cannot in those cases be the end of our
inquiry. In constructing an appropriate response to the crimes of
Roberta and Maria, we must focus not only on what they did, but also
we must look deeper than the apparent immediate, obvious motives
of jealously, revenge, or profit.

It is not surprising that studies have found that children who have
witnessed violence manifest behavioral problems. In the late 1950s,
criminologists began examining the impact of juvenile crime on the
baby-boom generation to determine whether there was a link between
child maltreatment and delinquency. Two trends emerged from these
studies: "First, that there has been a steady increase in the incidence
of child maltreatment, child abuse and neglect; second, there has been
a steady increase in juvenile delinquency and violent crime."[2] The
relationship between maltreatment and delinquency seems so logical
that one would naturally conclude that a child who is the victim of maltreatment could easily become a delinquent adolescent. Empirical
research supports this commonsense assessment. Studies indicate that
maltreated children manifest more aggressive and problematic behavior than children who are not neglected. "A host of literature exists suggesting that maltreated children exhibit a higher proportion of inse-
cure attachments to their parents, tend to ignore or refuse maternal
discipline, exhibit more aggression toward peers and caregivers, are
more aggressive and significantly less compliant, possess poor impulse
control, are deficient in emotional development, particularly self-con-
cept and aggressiveness, present greater anxiety, frustration, and
aggression in cognitive problem-solving situations than nonmaltreated
children. Various researchers have suggested that maltreatment
teaches aggression as a means of solving problems, prevents children
from feeling empathy for others, is an affront to their sense of fairness,
destroys their sense of trust, diminishes their ability to cope with stress
and destroys the fabric that bonds them to family and community."[3]

Most of us have a sense of the psychological, physical, and social
profiles of the typical young offender. The government has long

known who the children most likely to commit criminal acts are and where they live. In 1967, a report prepared by the President's Commission on Law Enforcement and the Administration of Justice revealed that for over a century government officials have known that crime rates are higher for children living in impoverished areas.[4]

In his book *Crime in America* (1970), Ramsey Clark was even more specific: "We know where children most likely to commit crime live. We know how to find them. With a few instructions, even census takers can provide the names and addresses of at least those children who have no parents, have been beaten or abused, are not sent to school regularly, cannot read, or share a room with four people. Professionals can find 90 percent of the children likely to become delinquent."[5]

The overwhelming majority of children prosecuted as juvenile offenders in the Youth Part are African-American and Hispanic teenagers, predominantly male, although the proportion of females has risen. Generally, they are born into single-parent homes, most of them headed by young women; they live in the poorest urban neighborhoods. These children often describe a childhood characterized by trauma, separation, and loss; the lack of one consistent caretaker or positive role model; a neighborhood that is impoverished; a family of relatives who have been arrested and incarcerated, and others who suffer mental illness. The children I see often have been physically and emotionally abused, living lives punctuated by neglect and indifference. When they get sick, they go to a crowded hospital emergency room for basic care where they are simply one of many poor, sick people. When they go to school, they are just one of many children jammed into overcrowded, ill-equipped classrooms.

In attempting to paint a portrait of these children, I have described the nature of the violence of which they are capable in order to demonstrate how a child can be transformed into a dangerous human being. After more than a dozen years studying the probation reports of these children, I can almost recite their contents even without reading them. I invariably find several of the following factors:

- no father in the household;
- no regular attendance at school;
- mother unemployed, on welfare;
- mother recovering drug addict;
- father in jail;
- mother dead of AIDS;
- living with grandmother;
- grandmother, recovering alcoholic;
- living in foster care homes almost from birth;
- subject of neglect, abuse, or abandonment proceedings;
- prior family or juvenile court arrest;
- prior PINS (Person In Need of Supervision) petition;
- classified as special education student;
- abuses marijuana or alcohol;
- possible gang affiliation.

I have seen a child who has lived in 16 different foster homes before the age of 15; another child whose mother has lived in 12 different apartments, causing him to be enrolled in eight different schools before he was 14 years of age. I have seen children under 16 who have not attended school for extended periods of time; one 15-year-old child who was not enrolled in any school for two years before he was arrested on a charge of robbery. I have seen psychiatric reports detailing the precarious emotional and mental states of children who have personally witnessed the violent deaths of parents, relatives, and friends; children who have lived with a succession of men who have had relationships with their mothers, one child reporting at least six different men in his home before he reached the age of 14. I have seen children who have been raped, sexually abused, and physically assaulted by stepfathers; children who attempt or talk of suicide, like the teenager who reported she didn't know why her mother even had her and she wished she was dead, concluding that her mother gave birth to her only to use her as a baby-sitter for her siblings. I have seen children who have had to share a single bathroom with as many as 12 siblings. One lawyer told me that his client, a 14-year-old boy, was embarrassed to come to court because he only had one set of clothes, which he had worn repeatedly. This boy was both an orphan and homeless. In New York City, an average of 13,000 children spend their nights in homeless shelters with their families.[6] Consider the complications homelessness presents for school enrollment and normal social interaction by these children.

Bob Herbert, a *New York Times* columnist, described such children as "jobless and hopeless."[7] He said, "You see them in many parts of the city hanging out on frigid street corners, skylarking at the malls or bowling alleys, hustling for money wherever they can, drifting, in some cases, into the devastating clutches of drug-selling, gang membership, prostitution, and worse. In Chicago there are nearly 100,000 young people ages 16 to 24 who are out of work, out of school, and all but out of hope. In New York City there are more than 200,000. According to a new study by a team of researchers from Northeastern University in Boston, the nationwide figure of children who are not in school, not working is a staggering 5.5 million and growing. This army of uneducated, jobless young people, disconnected in most instances from society's mainstream, is restless and unhappy and poses a severe long-term threat to the nation's well-being on many fronts."[8]

Of course, not all children born into single-family households or impoverished conditions become delinquent or engage in violent behavior. As the Reverend Jesse Jackson, who himself was raised in a single-parent home, pointed out "… the best predictor of criminal behavior is not who heads the family but whether the custodial parent supervises the child, disciplines the child and builds a sense of cohesiveness and a strong sense of family. This is true whether the family is mother-headed, grandmother-headed or other relative or non-relative-headed."[9] I am not suggesting that the guardians of these children—mothers, fathers, grandparents—do not try to guide them, but their efforts are often stifled by the monumental task of trying to make a living in the face of debilitating poverty and in the shadow of constant temptation from drug dealers and gang members.

The manner and degree of punishment morally justifiable for children such as Loretta, James, Roberta, and Maria, and those whose backgrounds fit the profile of young offenders, has been the subject of much debate. All too often, the debate has been centered simply on whether these children are viewed as erring children or evil criminals. The issue for me is not that simple. It is not unusual to see a newspaper article reporting the plight of disadvantaged children, such as the increase in the number of children living in homeless shelters and another article that same day in that very newspaper referring to a gang of teenage "monsters" who beat an old man and stole his money. These stories demonstrate the two sides of the dilemma we face when we consider the issue of juvenile justice—recognizing the plight of disadvantaged children, on the one hand, and society's revulsion at the capacity of children for violence, on the other.

The demonization of children is an understandable visceral response to the nature of their violent behavior. It is often driven by sensational and extraordinary cases of violence. But when we consider the best way to deal with children like Loretta and James who face mandatory imprisonment and felonization for minimal involvement in a crime of violence, children like Roberta and Maria whose crimes, although serious and traumatizing to their victims, will ultimately result in their return to society at an early age, even if given lengthy prison sentences, it is, in my view, not useful to see them simply as evil. To hold that they are not evil is not to deny their dangerousness but to address the issues raised by their behavior as best we can; to ask not what made kids "monsters" but what made kids act like monsters.

If we start with the premise that these children are deserving of nothing but disconnection from the community, then there is really nothing we can do to cultivate their humanity. We face an ancient philosophical question: Are there individuals who are born evil "on whose nature," as Shakespeare said, "nurture could never stick"?[10] I prefer, at least in terms of constructing a system of punishment for juvenile offenders, to approach the issue from the point of view that children are born neither good nor evil but susceptible to many influences.

I refer to all of the juvenile offenders I see as "children" despite the violent nature of their crimes. I make no apologies for that reference. It is a matter of respect for the dignity of each person who appears before me. And because they are in fact minors, juveniles, youths, not to think of them as children is to avoid addressing the issues that affect their behavior. Labeling and treating them as evil or monsters skirts the issue and improperly relinquishes our responsibility. If these crimes are committed by aberrational devils, then not only are we not responsible for them, there is nothing we can do to prevent or alter their behavior. By my estimate, in 20% of the cases of children prosecuted as adults, the safest response is an indeterminate sentence to state prison. The 20% to which I am referring are those children whose problems and difficulties are so severe that we currently do not possess the mechanisms in terms of services and psychoanalytical therapy needed to adequately address their issues in a nonsecure setting. Therefore, in order to ensure that they get whatever services society can provide, they will have to be confined and segregated with the hope that they will ultimately address those issues that led to their criminal behavior and learn to conform to society's standards.

I believe that this is a morally appropriate justice system response to such children; a response that requires for the safety of society the segregation of such children for the purpose of providing whatever therapeutic services are available. It is unfortunate that many of our juvenile detention institutions do not or cannot provide adequate therapeutic services, but that does not mean that we can simply permit the release of such young offenders into the community simply because of their immaturity. The moral burden in such a context is on policy makers to insure that our institutions can provide sufficient therapeutic services. The remaining 80% of youth prosecuted in the adult court can benefit from alternative-to-incarceration programs, although some also will require a period of detention before being given an opportunity to earn a second chance.

I have always welcomed visitors to my courtroom. We have cultivated an open door policy. It is important to "see" these offenders. Their "childishness" is immediately apparent in their demeanor, mannerisms, speech, and interactions. They are invariably seen for what they are, not evil-looking superpredators, but children who unfortunately are capable of horrendous acts of violence; children nevertheless—our hardest-to-love children.

CHAPTER 6

Interactive Justice

*What we are engaged in here isn't a chance conversation
but a dialogue about the way we ought to live our lives.*
—SOCRATES

S OME TIME AGO, I began noticing more and more young people appearing in my courtroom with headphones around their
necks. Rap or hip-hop dominates the music industry today as
opposed to the rock-and-roll of my generation. My own experience
with this music was limited to chance encounters while I found myself
stopped at a red light. Suddenly my car would start to vibrate from
the loud pulsating sounds coming from a vehicle that pulled up next
to me. Curious about the music and its influence, I sought out my
nephew, Billy Grant, a precocious and musically talented young man.
He was able at a young age to read and play Mozart, Beethoven, and
other classical composers on the piano, yet he was a typical teenager
who knew and enjoyed the music of his generation. "Billy," I asked
him at a family gathering, "what is it about rap that the kids like?" "The
lyrics," he nonchalantly responded. "The lyrics!," I said, incredulously.
"Why? How can you say that? I can't get beyond the pounding repet-
itive beat." He went on to explain that "Method Man" was a particularly good lyricist. He told me that Method Man was a member of a
group called Wu Tang Clan. The group was comprised of kids who
grew up in the projects of Staten Island. Billy said that each member

of the group was a talented rapper. Still skeptical about the lyrical attraction, I asked for an example. He said, "Method Man"—"You can never capture / Method Man's stature / in rhyme or rapture."[1] "Why," I conceded, "that has depth, a certain appreciation for life."

A few weeks later, a young man entered my courtroom wearing a Walkman. When his case was called, he walked to the defendant's bench. In an officious tone, I asked him what he was listening to. He responded that he was listening to music. I asked him what kind of music. He told me he was listening to hip-hop, to a group called Wu-Tang Clan. I said, "Do you know Method Man?" He looked at me in astonishment. I said, "Do you know—and I began to recite 'you can never capture...'" I turned to the court reporter after completing the rhyme and asked if she recorded that. She likewise looked up at me in astonishment. I wanted to get a transcript of the minutes to show Billy how I had used what he had told me. I turned back to the defendant, who now looked at me as he had never done before. I could imagine him saying to himself, "What kind of a judge would take the time to learn a rhyme?" But that's the point. I wanted him to know I was interested in him and I was interested in what he was listening to.

After this incident, I sought out some other artists Billy appreciated. One group he particularly liked was Pink Floyd. You may remember the words of "The Wall." "Hey teacher, leave those kids alone / We don't need no education / We don't need no thought control / No dark sarcasm in the class room / Hey, teacher, leave those kids alone / because all in all / you're just another brick in the wall."[2]

To what wall was Pink Floyd referring? I believe it is the wall of communication, the barrier of communication between the generations. Pink Floyd was exploring the idea that as we become older we seem to forget what it was like to be a teenager. We become the teacher who talks at children rather than with them. Such was the realization I had speaking to Billy and watching the reaction of the young boy to whom I quoted Method Man. Music is one way to breach the wall between generations and music is also a way of learning more about what it's like to be a teenager today. Of course, I'm not suggesting that judges should be "rapping" in their courtrooms. The point is that if you want to influence the behavior of a child, you must find ways to relate your message that resonate with that child's experience, thereby gaining their trust and building on that trust so that they will listen and act on what you have to say.

The methods I am proposing are not meant for all judges, all circumstances, and all criminal cases. Some cases require the detached magisterial style and others do not. Not all judges would be comfortable communicating in the fashion that I'm suggesting with young offenders. Some are more reticent and reserved in their approach. Still others do not see interaction as part of their role. I submit, however, children's cases impose an obligation on the part of a judge to make the effort to forge a bond.

This notion of judicial responsibility may not fully correspond to the traditional view of a judge as a detached arbiter of facts who eschews personal contact with litigants. However appropriate that role is in civil cases that involve issues such as the interpretation of contracts or liability for negligent behavior, or for that matter criminal cases involving adults, such a role is usually not effective in resolving the cases of juveniles. Courts have a special responsibility to court-involved children.

The founders and promoters of the juvenile court envisioned a tribunal presided over by a judge sensitive to the vulnerability and developmental needs of children. They foresaw a court under the aegis of a judge willing to assume responsibilities not ordinarily exercised by traditional judges, a judge willing to bring all of the power and prestige of his office to bear in developing and coordinating a plan of services to help a child offender become a contributing member of society. What was truly novel in the juvenile court paradigm, in my view, was the expectation that a personal rapport between judge and child would develop. The promoters of the juvenile court anticipated that the courts would train judges to become experts in sifting out the motivational factors behind a juvenile's violations of law. The vision of a juvenile court under the command of an engaged interactive judge was realized at the dawn of the 20th century in the work of Judge Ben B. Lindsey of Denver, Colorado. Judge Lindsey was a charismatic, progressive, and somewhat controversial judge who transformed Colorado's system of adjudicating cases of delinquents.[3]

Although there were other judges of the era who also were instrumental in shaping the role of the juvenile court, Judge Ben Lindsey has come to be regarded as the quintessential judge of that genre.

Judge Lindsey believed that a judge should create a rapport with a young offender so that he could act as a catalyst for change in the child's behavior. He said, "This should be accomplished as a wise and loving parent would accomplish it, not with leniency on the one hand or brutality on the other, but with charity, patience, interest and, what is most important of all, a firmness that commands respect, love and obedience and does not produce hate or ill will."[4] He considered his work with children as a delicate artistry–"a human artistry."[5] His canvas was each child who came before him. He used dialogue to shape these children as Socrates did in his time to elucidate principles of living well. He used the occasion of a child's appearance before him to talk to the child, not at him, constantly searching for "hooks" to relate a moral to the child based on the child's experience. This required him to draw the child into conversation. The subject matter of these talks was sometimes suggested by the child after an inquiry by the judge. For example, if a child showed an interest in sports, Judge Lindsey used the game to show the value of rules, sportsmanship, practice, and discipline. Sometimes Judge Lindsey would suggest a topic if it appeared relevant to the case at hand, such as "our duties to each other"; "the absurdity of hate"; "truthfulness"; "about quarreling"; "money and manhood"; "evil association"; "the man who serves and the man who makes money"; "public service."[6] Under Judge Lindsey's leadership, the Denver court process embodied a deeply personal style of judicial involvement in the lives of the juvenile court children. It involved reaching out to foster a close relationship with each individual child. That was the essence of Lindsey's juvenile court. It was the principle that he believed provided the motivation for the child to improve his behavior, that is, the child's desire not to disappoint his judge. This was to be the starting point for the child's inculcation of virtue ultimately leading to constructive participation in society.[7]

Almost immediately from the inception of Judge Lindsey's practices, as well as that of other like-minded juvenile court judges, critics emerged locally and nationally. They contended that, in pursuing these methods, judges often had no specific statutory authority and that formal adjudication of guilt appeared to be secondary to providing the child with rehabilitative services. Indeed, the child's appearance before the juvenile court was looked on as an opportunity to rehabilitate the child whether the child was guilty or unjustly accused and formal adjudicatory procedures were not that crucial in the process. Critics envisioned dangerous repercussions in this approach: deprivation of a child's liberty without legal formalities or without due process, and undue reliance on the personality of a judge as the determining factor of the court's success. These critics contended that it was inappropriate and of flawed legality to substitute personal judicial involvement for formal trial procedures in the juvenile court. In many respects, these criticisms were and are well founded. In the Youth Part, we are conscious of these concerns and make every effort to insure the due process rights of a youth are not subrogated to rehabilitative efforts. If a child believes he has been deprived of his liberty unfairly, that very experience undermines respect for authority and the law. In contrast, the child who believes that he has been dealt with fairly will be a better prospect for rehabilitation.

By the middle of the 20th century, flaws in the juvenile court system were evident. In a series of cases, the U.S. Supreme Court[8] expressed dissatisfaction with the lack of due process in the procedures of that court. The Supreme Court, however, did not reject the premise of a separate juvenile court nor the vision of the appropriate role of a judge sitting in such a court. In *McKeiver v. Pennsylvania*,[9] the Supreme Court stated: "The court, although recognizing the higher hopes and aspirations of Judge Julian Mack, the leaders of the Jane Adams school, and the other supporters of the juvenile court concept, has also noted the disappointments of the system's performance and experience and the resulting widespread disaffection. There have been, at one and the same time, both an appreciation for the juvenile court judge who is devoted, sympathetic and conscientious, and a disturbed concern about the judge who is untrained and less than fully imbued with an understanding approach to the complex problems of childhood and adolescence."[10] The court continued, "… too often the juvenile court judge falls short of that stalwart, protective, and communicating figure the system envisaged."[11] Thus, the Supreme Court, albeit obliquely endorsed the concept of a communicative, that is, interactive juvenile court judge, embracing the rehabilitative potential of juvenile delinquents. A view reinforced by the former Chief Justice of the Supreme Court William Rehnquist in *Smith v. Daily Mail Publishing Company* when he stated: "[A]court concerned with juvenile affairs serves as a rehabilitative and protective agency of the state."[12] These pronouncements recognized the aspirational qualities of a judge having the responsibility of adjudicating cases involving children, characteristics that require more than dispassionate impartiality and knowledge of the law.

The idea of a judge who views the law as a social force and uses his authority to make a difference in people's lives is not a radical concept but is deeply rooted in legal principles and traditions. These characteristics have always been implicit in the concept of judging. When the biblical Solomon was said to have ordered the child before him to be split in two, was he merely acting as a dispassionate disinterested magistrate or was he creating a dynamic that would force the truth, a dynamic that flowed from awareness of the depth of feeling a mother would have for her child? In 1912, the legal scholar Rosco Pound spoke of "sociological jurisprudence," arguing that "the law must look to the relationship between itself and the societal facts it creates."[13] Oliver Wendell Holmes said that the life of the law has not been logic, it has been experience, and he believed that the practical necessities of the times have always shaped the rules of law and the legal procedures of a given age.[14] As noted, the traditional notion of a judge as a dispassionate fact-finder is difficult to reconcile with the expectations of society in dealing with delinquent children. Moreover, scientific and psychological advances have been incorporated into our criminal justice jurisprudence and judges are required to use all available means to deal effectively with offenders.

What does the law require of a judge who has the responsibility of dealing with the cases of 14- and 15-year-olds? Does it make any difference where the 14- and 15-year-old is prosecuted, that is, either in the juvenile court or the adult court? I submit that the situs of prosecution should not materially alter a judge's responsibility.

The essential characteristics of a child do not transform with the location of the courtroom or whether he is prosecuted as a juvenile or as an adult. When we acknowledge the grim reality that children prosecuted in the adult courts are more likely to reoffend than those prosecuted in the juvenile courts,[15] it is clear that adult court judges have a special obligation to protect society through an application of rehabilitative measures regardless of the situs of prosecution.

Recognition of this judicial obligation also may be found in laws that permit a judge to grant certain teenage offenders the legal equivalent of a second chance. For instance, New York's second chance statute is called the Youthful Offender Law.[16] The special status of children in the law is recognized in most states that have legislatively created ameliorative devices specifically designed to accommodate an offender's youth. Since 1945, the judges of New York have had the statutory authority to relieve offenders under 19 years of age of the consequences of their criminal behavior by granting them "Youthful Offender" treatment.[17] The procedure governing youthful offender adjudications is found in Article 720 of New York's Criminal Procedure Law. This procedure provides a mechanism by which the court may exercise discretion, on conviction of certain young offenders, in order to remove the permanent stigma of a felony conviction and provide an alternative sentence which may be a nonincarceratory sentence of probation. CPL Section 720.20 subdivision 1(a) provides: "If, in the opinion of the Court, the interest of justice would be served by relieving the eligible youth from the onus of a criminal record, and by not imposing an indeterminate term of imprisonment of more than four years, the court may, in its discretion, find the eligible youth is a youthful offender." Not all juveniles under 19 are eligible for this special treatment *and* even those who are eligible are not automatically entitled to such treatment. Only those who are eligible and in the discretion of the judge "deserving" are to be afforded this special treatment.[18]

The requirement that a judge exercise discretion in granting such treatment imposes a special responsibility. The judge must consider the individual circumstances of each eligible offender to determine whether he or she is suitable for a reduced sentence or probation, and whether the record of conviction should be sealed.

In *People v. Cruickshank*,[19] New York's Appellate Division stated: "Youthful Offender status permits the court to mete out fair punishment for a young adult's crimes and transgressions yet mitigates future consequences in recognition of *inter alia,* the youth's lack of experience and the court's hope for his future constructive life."[20]

A Youthful Offender finding is of great import for a child. If such a finding is made, the criminal conviction is vacated and is replaced by that finding. When a sentence is imposed, the finding and sentence merge into a youthful offender adjudication. There is no criminal conviction and the youth does not forfeit any civil rights. On entry of the youthful offender adjudication, all official records are sealed and deemed confidential.[21]

The determination of whether an eligible youth is either a youthful offender or a convicted felon has lifelong implications. If a youth is not otherwise precluded from eligibility by statutory criteria, such as age or a prior felony record, the court has an affirmative duty to exercise its discretion—that is, to proceed to a consideration of whether a youthful offender adjudication is appropriate in a given case and to announce that determination at the time of sentence.[22] Although there is no specific statutory formula that a judge must follow in exercising this discretion, case law has identified factors to be considered on an application for Youthful Offender treatment, which include: "the gravity of the crime and manner in which it was committed, mitigating circumstances, defendant's prior criminal record, prior acts of violence, recommendations in pre-sentence reports, defendant's reputation, the level of cooperation with authorities, *defendant's attitude towards society and respect for the law, and the prospects for rehabilitation and hope for a future constructive life"* (emphasis added).[23]

Thus, the YO law as an expression of public policy imposes an obligation on a judge to consider a youth's "prospects for rehabilitation and hope for a future constructive life" before determining an appropriate sentence. This requires more than a detached evaluation of the past behavior of the child; it requires the court to consider the impact of arrest and conviction on a youth. It also requires a judge to look forward, to anticipate future behavior, not just on the basis of what the child has done in the past but on what he appears willing to do in the future. How does one "judge" a youth's attitude toward society and his prospects for rehabilitation without talking to the youth, without communicating in some fashion? How does one appraise the potential of a young offender? The Youth Part process helps us to make that determination. An integral aspect of that process is the interaction between the judge and the offender. The entire process of trying children as adults is envisioned as a dynamic interactive process, a process that serves as a guide for a child's rehabilitation. It is an approach that looks on each appearance of a child before the court as an opportunity to educate and motivate, to help the young offender understand the behavior that brought him before the court.

The Interactive Technique

How can a judge use the process of adjudication in the adult court to assist a juvenile offender to gain insight into his or her behavior in a manner consistent with his constitutional responsibilities? Judge Lindsey believed that establishing a level of communication between the judge and offender was the essential requirement for dealing effectively with children.[24] In his *Treatise on Rhetoric*,[25] Aristotle taught that the art of persuasion begins with effective communication. People can be motivated to change their opinions and improve their lives through the power of speech. Aristotle's teachings can provide a method for judges who wish to communicate more effectively with child offenders. Modifying his principles of rhetoric to our purposes, a judge is in a special position to exercise influence over a young offender. The first precept of the Aristotelian method of persuasion is to learn everything possible about your audience. Knowledge of an audience's characteristics will help the speaker frame arguments drawn from the audience's own experience, using familiar examples or stories to teach a point. For instance, when a member of an older group attempts to influence or communicate with a member of a younger group, the older speaker should engage in a process of remembrance, of empathetic association with the person spoken to. With respect to the young, Aristotle taught that in order to influence their behavior you must be aware of their special characteristics and traits, their likes and dislikes. Thus, he provided his students with a detailed description of the special qualities of youth, quoted in Chapter 2.[26]

Specifically, Aristotle taught that the persuasive power of rhetoric depended on the ability of the speaker to communicate three things: truth, trust, and conviction—truth, the logical validity of what is stated; trust, the speaker's success in awakening in the person spoken to the state of assured reliance on the wisdom of the speaker; and conviction, the speaker's firm belief in the truth of what he or she is saying. The persuasive power of conviction is in its ability to project the conviction of the speaker onto the person spoken to—the ability to stir the emotions of the audience, creating a willingness to accept the views of the speaker and act in accordance therewith. The Greeks referred to this trilogy of rhetorical principles as *logos,* logical argument; *ethos,* the projection of the speaker's character; and *pathos,* awakening the emotions of the audience.

The purpose of applying these techniques is to motivate a child so that he or she will seek positive help when needed, resist negative peer pressure, and consider consequences before acting. Homer, a poet and philosopher, saw rhetoric as the ability to see the available means of persuasion and then to seize that moment. It is that dynamic that is of special import in the Youth Part. It instructs us to be alert for the teachable moments in a child's appearances before the court. In applying the Aristotelian method in this fashion, we are simply modifying and implementing the art of the orator—an art defined by John Stuart Mill in this way: "Everything important to his purpose was said at the exact moment when he had brought the minds of his audience into the state most fitted to receive it."[27]

Gaining insight into the culture of modern teenagers is, therefore, the first step in applying the Aristotelian method of persuasion. I once heard on a PBS radio program that the average adolescent listens to approximately three hours of music each day.[28] Perhaps music is the single most important cultural influence on the children I see. Rap music, for example, often depicts the dilemma and frustration of urban life in disadvantaged minority neighborhoods. It is a useful source of information about the way today's children are living and behaving, a source that can provide valuable insight into the current adolescent world. Of course, I'm not endorsing the veracity of some of the lyrics; however, they reflect a youth's perception of the world, rightly or wrongly. Consequently, a glimpse into the world of adolescence can be found through a familiarity with contemporary and popular music. Moreover, suggesting that we familiarize ourselves with the likes and dislikes of those with whom we are dealing does not mean going down to a child's level of perception but instead finding ways to communicate in a manner comprehensible to the child, so that the child's understanding and insight is actually elevated to the point where the child can envision and abide by a workable plan toward a promising future.

These theories are the basis for the method of adjudication that I call interactive justice. I define interactive justice as that dynamic, based on principles of rhetoric, that permits a judge to seize the opportunity to teach a child or to inspire or, when necessary, to impose appropriate constructive discipline. The task of an effective adult court judge presiding over cases of children prosecuted as adults thus requires the judge to be firm, yet, in an appropriate case to extend an invitation to the child offender to freely and willingly embrace the opportunity to change his behavior if he wants a second chance. This can be accomplished by gaining the trust and confidence of the child.

The interactive approach presupposes a certain amount of freedom or latitude because it requires a judge to directly address a young offender during court proceedings. A prerequisite to such interaction is the acquiescence of counsel for the youthful defendant. Before the entry of a plea of guilty or a conviction after trial, a judge is limited in his ability to sua sponte or directly communicate with an accused offender. This is because a conscientious lawyer would be concerned that his client might unwittingly make potentially incriminatory admissions. The responses to an inquiry by a judge, even an inquiry seemingly collateral and innocuous, may result in a damaging admission that could be used against an accused at a subsequent proceeding.

Consequently, it is imperative that a judge wishing to apply these techniques obtain the trust of the lawyers who appear before him. This trust can be developed only if all the parties recognize that the goal of the court's inquiries is to gather information about the character and prospects of a child to determine the pivotal issue in most child offender proceedings—whether to grant the child YO status— the legal equivalent of a second chance.

The basis for a defense counsel's concern is often unfounded in Youth Part cases. In most cases, there is often little dispute as to guilt or nonguilt. There are, of course, instances in which the degree of culpability is disputed, but by and large a child offender's lack of experience and sophistication is reflected in the manner and nature of the crime. Resolution of factual disputes or the interpretation or application of statutes is not usually in the forefront of the adjudication of most juvenile offender cases. But I wish to emphasize that no defendant or his counsel is required to waive any rights either to suppression hearings or the right to a jury trial in order to get the benefit of the court's attention. Furthermore, there are no penalties for insisting on these rights. The overwhelming majority of children appearing in the Youth Part plead guilty. The court then bears the weighty responsibility to devise an individualized sentencing plan for the defendant, which often hinges upon whether the court grants or denies Youthful Offender treatment to the juvenile. Nevertheless, one must be cautious and sensitive to the issue of self-incrimination when speaking to youthful offenders, especially at initial appearances before plea or conviction. The purpose behind the dialogue, after all, is to assess the child's ability and willingness to modify his behavior. After a conviction, whether by plea or trial, the issue of direct judicial interaction with an offender is of less concern because most federal and state statutes impose an affirmative duty on the sentencing judge to invite an offender to speak in mitigation of sentence.[29] In the Youth Part, we try to talk to every child, to get a sense of who they are. We want to know how the child responds to questions. What they say is often not as important as how they say it.

Assuming a judge is able to establish credibility and gain the confidence of defense counsel and the prosecutor, how does a judge, in the context of adjudicating a case involving children, establish truth, trust, and conviction in order to influence a child's behavior? In establishing truth, that is speaking the truth, a judge should attempt to connect a child's predicament to his behavior. For example, a child's failure to resist negative peer pressure is frequently the reason why he is before the court and facing imprisonment. In establishing trust, we can't expect children to readily and candidly respond to judicial inquiries. It may be argued that a juvenile under 16 years of age, for instance, may be so intimidated by court surroundings and the significance of the proceeding that he will be unable to speak coherently in his defense or in response to an inquiry by the court. It is the court's responsibility in such a situation to insure that the atmosphere of the proceeding is conducive to the child taking advantage of an opportunity to engage in a dialogue.

The synergy behind the persuasive power of the judge is the judge's conviction, the strength of belief in his work. When addressing juveniles, I am confronted with a societal dilemma that we all face in our families, our homes, our schools and our communities. How do we persuade children that they can achieve their goals without violence when they are living in a violent world? For example, how do we persuade a 14-year-old boy growing up in a tough neighborhood that he can gain respect without using violence? How can we teach that boy to act decently when he is surrounded by others, including adults, who are willing to act indecently to get what they want or what they believe they need? How do we persuade that child to live according to precepts that many adults don't even follow? For me, the answer begins with an intractable affirmation that you can achieve your goals and succeed in our democratic society without violence, fraud, cheating, or theft; that no matter who you are or where you come from, you have an equal opportunity to succeed. I am committed to these ideals and to insuring that I do all I can by my actions to demonstrate their soundness. The challenge for me is to persuade these children in our brief interactions to believe in their capacity to succeed, that they have the ability to overcome the circumstances into which they were born. This is a formidable task, one that is not always successful. In deciding whether to give a child accused of a violent

crime a second chance, I try to find a voice to speak to these children, to listen to them, to exploit the teachable moments in our interaction in an effort to determine who is amenable to counseling and
who is not. In my experience, the greatest alternative to detention is
paying attention to children.

As we enter the 21st century, these words and the sentiments
they represent may seem out of place when the brutality of juvenile
crime has shocked the nation. By contrast, the concept of a judge as
a formidable force in shaping the lives of juveniles appearing before
him is perhaps even more compelling now than it was a century ago.
The community brings its adolescent offenders to the courts and
expects that the court will deal with these children swiftly, effectively, and constructively.

CHAPTER 7

Fridays in the Youth Part :
How the Judicial Interactive
Process Works

Caroline Joy DeBrovner

I N THE FALL of 2000, I brought my Juvenile Delinquency class to observe the Youth Part.[1] Immediately, I was profoundly moved by what I saw as Judge Corriero's approach in dealing with this youth population that has been so often demonized by the media and politicians. The social scientist in me was inspired to learn and understand more. I was curious about the interaction between the judge and his defendants, as well as his courtroom at large. I have spent nearly four years attending Judge Corriero's Friday calendar and developing an understanding of his methods and philosophy of dealing with juvenile offenders. After a few weeks passed, what most interested me was how the judge's interaction with each defendant bespoke a personal relationship that had developed or was developing. I believe that my analysis of my field notes and observations dispels the notion that the Youth Part's success derives primarily from Judge Corriero's charisma and personality. His approach and methods can be adopted in other courts irrespective of the judge's personality.

As I was trying to develop an understanding of the judge's methods, four major categories emerged from my notes on his interactions with young defendants: character building, family involvement, mentoring and socialization, and forging a social bond.

Judicial Goals and Methods

Our current juvenile justice policy is heavily shaped by the assumption that swift and appropriately severe punishment deters crime in individuals and in general. The deeper assumption is that after weighing the risks and benefits of pursuing illegal activity, individuals will make rational choices. General or society-wide deterrence occurs as a result of public or publicized, punishment when law-abiding citizens and those contemplating crime learn vicariously that crime is not worth the risk of punishment.[2] We live in an age of *wars on drugs, getting tough on crime, super predators, three strikes you're out,* and *zero tolerance policies.* In the past 25 years, judges' discretion has been limited or eliminated by legislation that attempts to deal with juvenile delinquency by trying juveniles as adults.

In the Youth Part, Judge Corriero strikes a balance between reliance on "the carrot" and "the stick" in his efforts to rehabilitate the juvenile offenders before him and, at the same time, protecting public safety.

Young defendants who have been incarcerated soon realize that Judge Corriero's court is different. The judge wears a black robe but does not use a gavel. He conveys an unexpected degree of sensitivity to the indignities of incarceration and expresses his hope and belief that the defendant can be more than an inmate.

> JUDGE CORRIERO: Is it tough for you at Riker's?
> DEFENDANT: You get used to it.
> JUDGE CORRIERO: Don't ever get used to it. Riker's Island, you
>   can survive it, but don't get used to it.[3]

Another defendant, handcuffed to a leather strap around his waist and wearing leg irons, was led into the courtroom by an Office of Children and Family Services (OCFS) escort:[4]

JUDGE CORRIERO: You can unhandcuff him and everything else.
ESCORT OFFICER: We never take them [cuffs and leg irons] off.
JUDGE CORRIERO: You do in my courtroom.
(Escort Officer takes them off).[5]

The message is clear: Judge Corriero does not want his defendants, or their families, to be subjected to humiliation. Judge Corriero's humanity is also evident when he tells a defendant's mother,
"When they bring in the kids from upstate, it's not that they are particularly dangerous; that's the way they transport *all* of them."[6] Here
he shows a concern, not only for her reaction to viewing her son in
leg irons but also for this defendant's feelings about his mother seeing him that way. By enabling his defendants to maintain a modicum
of dignity in his court, he can begin the long-term work of character
building and involving their families in their rehabilitation. "You want
this experience to be part of rehabilitation. Here, I am society to
them; it should reflect the best of society."[7] Because of the judge's
concern with the impact of his procedural choices, he routinely takes
the guilty pleas for the most sensitive charges in a vacant jury room.
This choice protects the defendant's privacy and avoids needlessly
upsetting the members of the courtroom audience.

As part of Judge Corriero's innovative strategy of adjourning sentencing, placing appropriate candidates in alternative-to-incarceration (ATI) programs and closely monitoring their progress, he lays
down a list of expectations and conditions of release (e.g., regular
school and program attendance, obeying curfew, etc.). A child who
violates these conditions or does not meet expectations risks remand,
and, in the most serious of situations, jail/prison time, and loss of
Youthful Offender status. By contrast, the success of the Youth Part
is best seen by the transformation in young defendants that takes
place as a result of the judge's sincere praise and positive reinforcement for demonstrated progress and steady focus on the ultimate
reward of achieving success. The explicit goal of the Youth Part is to
use the authority and resources legally available in the most therapeutic fashion possible, to enhance a defendant's chances of ending
his or her criminal career.

Even when there is evidence of only small steps toward progress, Judge Corriero takes the time to acknowledge them and offer encouragement. Interacting with young defendants, the judge searches for signs of progress. He attempts to "read" the defendants and their attitude and to forge a social bond with them. In one situation, the ATI program representative said that the defendant "has become a role model for our newer members" and handed Judge Corriero an evaluation letter:

> JUDGE CORRIERO: I don't even need to read it. I see it in your face, your demeanor. I'm really proud of you. How do you like the people there?
>
> DEFENDANT: They're nice.
>
> JUDGE CORRIERO: You made me proud of you. You made my day.[8]

This sincere expression of pride allows the defendant to experience praise; it motivates him to earn more praise and continue to do well.

In another case, Judge Corriero gave a young defendant positive attention and showed appreciation for the effort that went into writing a book report. He focused more on process than product seeing the voluntary exercise as a sign of significant progress. He rewarded the defendant's efforts by offering him a book from the Youth Part Library:[9]

Judge Corriero (book report in hand): I'm going to have to read this, Carlos. It looks like you put a lot of effort in it. I appreciate it. Keep up the good work, I'm proud of you. (Turns to Caroline): I think it might be a good idea to read another book, one of our books.[10]

The Youth Part and Therapeutic Jurisprudence:

In the last decade, David B. Wexler and Bruce J. Winick developed the concept of therapeutic jurisprudence, which relies on ideas from the behavioral sciences:[11] "to analyze, implement and reform the law." Their fundamental contention is that "Legal rules, legal procedures, and the roles of legal actors (such as… judges) constitute social forces that, like it or not, often produce therapeutic or antitherapeutic consequences. Therapeutic jurisprudence proposes that we be sensitive to those consequences, and that we ask if the law's antitherapeutic consequences can be reduced, and its therapeutic consequences enhanced, without subordinating due process and other justice values."[12] The use of the term "therapeutic" has evolved within the therapeutic jurisprudence literature to be understood more broadly than the strictly psychological sense. In a criminal justice context, it is applied to the use of the court, any aspect of a defendant's experience in the court, and treatment programs to reduce recidivism as well as motivate positive changes in the defendant's life.

Judge Corriero's judicial interactive process demonstrates how the law can function therapeutically, although his interactions appear instinctive and spontaneous.

A guiding belief of therapeutic jurisprudence that is reflected in Judge Corriero's judicial character is that "everyone, no matter who has something positive within their make up that can be built upon."[13] In applying therapeutic jurisprudence, the authority and actions of the judge are of central importance in the process, providing fair and consistent sanctions for failure to engage in the required conditions (such as program attendance), and providing praise and reinforcement where any progress is made. Consistency is a critical factor;[14] each time a young person appears in court, he or she interacts with the same judge. Providing such consistency was one of the central goals for the Youth Part; only Judge Corriero would preside over the "treatment" and the cases of all the children in Manhattan tried as Juvenile Offenders. This enables him to develop detailed knowledge of each child before him and to build the rapport that will advance the rehabilitation process. My observations of the Youth Part led me to conclude that the children attach some significance to the fact that a single judge monitors their progress and performance, carefully reviews their cases on a continual basis, and knows about their circumstances (and even personal interests). I often have noted that the judge seems to be the first person in authority to demonstrate a consistent interest in a particular defendant. Perhaps this focus helps the child to appreciate the judge's praise and his responses to setbacks with fair and appropriate sanctions. This consistency and his "judicious use of colloquy"[15] are effective tools for achieving therapeutic ends and should be essential elements in any attempt to reform our juvenile justice system.

Judge Corriero's courtroom interactions with his defendants rely on various strategies to help them build character. To protect public safety when releasing (either on bail or on his/her own recognizance) a defendant into the community, and to determine whether a defendant has earned Youthful Offender treatment, the judge must assess a defendant's trustworthiness, and then continue to work to build trust in their relationship. Essentially applying a therapeutic jurisprudence approach, he helps the defendants strengthen their resources to deal with future challenging and potentially dangerous situations that may arise in their community (such as peer pressure, taunting, threats of violence). He attempts to redefine their previous understanding of manhood, bravery, strength, and respect, offering alternative conceptions. When discussing their criminal involvement, the judge asks the defendants questions in an effort to get them to feel empathy, remorse, and an appreciation for the seriousness of their crime. In shepherding these youngsters, the judge aims to trigger a sense of individual responsibility for their actions and their consequences.

Judge Corriero's interaction with defendants strongly suggests that he believes that the development of trust is a reciprocal process—a proverbial "two way street"—but particularly when adults are dealing with young people. For Judge Corriero to gain increasing confidence in the trustworthiness of his defendants, as consistently evidenced by their actions and attitude, he strives to show them, by his own actions, that he is fair, looking out for their interests, that they can trust him. This a very serious matter, and the judge demonstrates that he knows the stakes are high; for every defendant who is given the opportunity to earn a second chance (allowed to reside in the community, assigned to an ATI program, granted Youthful Offender treatment, etc.), public safety, the judge's reputation, the respect of the prosecutor, and future second chances for other young defendants all hang in the balance.

Although it may appear at first glance to be a distinction without a difference, functionally the judge's method of establishing trust differs depending on whether the defendant is *"out"* or *"in"* when he/she first appears in the Youth Part. An *"out"* defendant is one who has been released on his/her own recognizance by the initial arraigning judge in the lower court, or has made the bail set by that judge. Judge Corriero does not see that defendant when he or she first enters the system. A defendant comes to the Youth Part only after he or she is indicted, a process that may take 30 to 40 days. An *"in"* defendant is one who has been remanded or unable to make the bail set by the initial arraigning judge.

When a defendant is *"out"* the judge must make a judgment, after reviewing the evidence of the nature of the crime and the PPI report, whether to continue a defendant's "out" status and rely on frequent court appearances, communication, and reports from program representatives to measure the defendant's progress in meeting the court's expectations. Here, Judge Corriero's interactive method stresses progress, as opposed to perfection, to help the defendants feel comfortable enough to talk with him when they have problems. This makes it possible for the judge to redirect the defendants before small problems become bigger ones. This is a crucial safety valve when they are living in the community. The following interaction displays this defendant's surprising trust and candor, which then allows Judge Corriero to assume a colorful problem-solving role. In this case an "out" defendant who has been assigned to an ATI program has tested positive for marijuana use. Judge Corriero inquires about when she smoked:

DEFENDANT: I was with my friends and couldn't say no.

JUDGE CORRIERO: Do you think you can say no the next time when your friends pass you a joint?

DEFENDANT: I don't know, I'll try.

JUDGE CORRIERO: Say, "Judge Corriero says if I do, he's going to put me in jail," and when your friends say "Who's Judge Corriero?" you'll say, "You'll see."

(Laughter.)[16]

Recognizing the openness and act of trust inherent in this defendant's admission of self-doubt, the judge seizes this opportunity to coach and guide her. He turns the peer pressure situation on its head so that, in alliance with the judge, she can see that the joke is on her friends.

In contrast, when dealing with cases when the defendant is "in," the judge has to decide whether to let the defendant out of jail after a period of time has elapsed. In practice, these cases tend to be more serious cases, for example, postplea, where the defendant is promised a year "in" [jail], after which a chance to earn YO treatment would be considered. Here, the relationship and social bond between the judge and the defendant have had time to develop, as he sees all defendants, including those who are "in," on a monthly basis. Within this context, the judge's ability and willingness to trust the defendant appears to hinge on an understanding and recognition of what he/she did, and why, and on the defendant's progress while incarcerated. When pleading guilty, to satisfy the requirements of the charge, the defendant must answer the judge's question, "What did you do to be guilty of this crime?" The allocution requires the defendants to admit the specific details of their wrongdoing. This confessional experience is usually followed by the judge asking the defendant, "Why did you do this?" The waiving of the defendant's right to remain silent, and his/her admission of guilt, marks a new chapter in the interactive process between the judge and the defendant.

But how can the judge gauge whether a defendant will be a recidivist? In all relationships, trust must be earned, but when community trust has been violated by a defendant, how does the judge discern, and continue to reevaluate, the defendant's present trustworthiness? What would need to change for the judge to be able now to trust the defendant? The judge maintains that a defendant who doesn't know why he/she committed a crime cannot be trusted not to commit another one. This defendant had a prior record of delinquency in the Family Court:

JUDGE CORRIERO: Why didn't you learn your lesson?
DEFENDANT: Because I was young.

JUDGE CORRIERO: Why should I trust you [now]?
DEFENDANT: Because I'm willing to change myself as a person.
JUDGE CORRIERO: You don't have to change who you are, you
   just have to work on who you are.[17]

Ultimately, the methods of trust-building overlap and certain defendants who have spent significant time in jail are, at the appropriate time, released back into the community. On releasing this defendant from jail, Judge Corriero in essence tells him, "I don't expect perfection. I expect progress." Especially in these more serious cases, there is a looming risk of remand, which could inhibit the defendant from disclosing potentially self-incriminating "issues." But the judge helps to weave a fabric of long-term trust.

To be able to be most therapeutic in his role as judge, Judge Corriero must gain the defendants' trust. Only then can he attempt to overcome their deep-rooted conceptions that the justice system, indeed, society as a whole, is unfair. Unless the judge can accomplish this challenging task, there is little chance that the defendants will truly be able to work *with* him, believe in the possibility of a second chance, cooperate with the rules and conditions he imposes, and commit themselves to working with the ATI, psychological counseling, or substance abuse programs in which he places them to address their needs. Indeed, they may lose all hope and think "what's the point" of even trying.

We also must keep in mind the interactional context of the Youth Part courtroom. When Judge Corriero speaks with a defendant standing before him during allocution, he sends powerful messages about justice and fairness to the defendant before the bench, as well as to the other defendants on the calendar, watching and waiting for their names to be called. Defendants in the courtroom "audience" watching this dramatic exchange vicariously experience the judge's commitment to putting the promise of justice into action. "I represent society to them. If they think I'm biased, then that's their perception of society."[18]

For example, some young defendants try to plead guilty while maintaining their innocence, because they believe this will help them

secure a better outcome. Judge Corriero will, pointedly, communicate to them that he will not let them do this. Although all judges and
prosecutors assess allocutions, finding them *"acceptable"* or not, not
all judges interact inquisitively with each defendant. The law pre-
scribes no precise formula for the "factual basis inquiry," which in
practice means that judges have much discretion in terms of the style
of taking guilty pleas.[19]

Some judges find it sufficient to read off the charge(s) and require
only a "yes" or "no" answer from the defendant. Judge Corriero's
style of taking guilty pleas reflects the concern that, as a judge dealing with children, simply requiring a "yes" or "no" may communicate
that the "deal is done" and he doesn't really care to insure that he is
treating the defendant fairly and protecting the defendant's rights.

In contrast, during allocutions in the Youth Part, Judge Corriero
asks each defendant to explain, specifically, what he/she did to be
guilty of the alleged crime:

> JUDGE CORRIERO: What did you do to be guilty of this crime?
> (Defendant denies involvement.)
> JUDGE CORRIERO (FORCEFULLY): Juan, I said if you're not
> guilty, don't plead guilty, but don't lie to me. If you're not
> guilty, don't plead guilty, but don't lie to me either. You
> have an excellent lawyer.[20]

Judge Corriero tells this defendant that if he is truly innocent, he
should go to trial. Whatever notions the defendant has about the system being unjust may have convinced him that taking a plea will
lead to the best outcome. Although this might be true (for if he
goes to trial he may lose), Judge Corriero forces him to reexamine
these assumptions.

During allocution, Judge Corriero also questions defendants
about the social context leading up to the crime, their thoughts, feelings, and intentions, so that they seem to come to greater insight into
why they think they committed the crime. Judge Corriero uses allocution as a character-building interactive process. He maximizes this
opportunity to reach each child and leave a lasting imprint that will

hopefully allow that child to appreciate the seriousness of what he or she has done, and make better choices in the future.

How is a judge to demonstrate that he is acting fairly to a child in crisis who likely feels the world is unfair? In dealing with young defendants, especially males, Judge Corriero frequently employs sports analogies. Because young men accept the importance of rules and fair play in sports, these analogies are effective in helping young male defendants appreciate the fairness of Judge Corriero's decisions. For example, Judge Corriero often uses the term "foul up" this defendant, a basketball player, can relate to it:

> JUDGE CORRIERO: I could put you in jail for ten years. You play baseball?
>
> DEFENDANT: Basketball.
>
> JUDGE CORRIERO: How many fouls are you allowed?... My rules about fouling out are not the basketball rules. It's not five... [21]

When a defendant, given a second chance, violates the court's expectations, it is only fair and just that Judge Corriero keeps his word and sentences him/her as the law requires. These moments are sobering and dramatic and are an opportunity to demonstrate justice and fairness to the defendant and all the other defendants watching in the audience:

> JUDGE CORRIERO: The defendant was given a number of chances by me and was not able to stay out of trouble. He got rearrested on what Family Court considered a serious matter. I went out pretty much on a limb over the objection of the Corporation Counsel and DA... I have to keep my word... Defendant is sentenced to two and a third to seven years. He should get credit for time served. [22]

An essential part of the character development process involves teaching defendants that they should tell the truth and that they should understand why the truth is important. The judge emphasizes that he expects them to be truthful with him (as well as with others such as parents and program representatives) and that lying is risky. At the same time, he communicates empathically that he understands why they might try to deceive him. This is a fine balance, but what comes across is the judge's commitment to mentor them, and his concern for their well-being. In this dialogue, trust and respect are inextricably tied to the truth:

> DEFENDANT: I didn't do nothing [sic].
> JUDGE CORRIERO: You mean, you're innocent? I don't know whether you're telling the truth or not. I don't want you to lie to me, then I can't trust you. When you lie, it's really dumb because, usually, you're going to get found out. If you lie to someone, it's really like you don't respect them.
> DEFENDANT: Yeah.
> JUDGE CORRIERO: Yes.[23]

In the Youth Part, Judge Corriero attempts to offer suitable defendants the opportunity to earn a second chance, to achieve a more optimistic outcome for them than simply the end of their criminal careers. He capitalizes on the currency of trust; evidence of meeting his expectations in a trustworthy fashion earns the defendants incremental privileges (everything from an extended curfew to YO), and with the experience of earning his trust comes a boost to the defendant's self-esteem. Ultimately, Judge Corriero's investment in building mutual trust with his defendants is supported by his sincere hope for their future—hope that they can become trustworthy citizens and believe in themselves.

The majority of defendants in the Youth Part are male; the ratio is roughly 9 in 10. Young men tend to look for external validations of their manhood. Their peers, culture, and the media link what they understand as the defining qualities of manhood to violence, intimidation, fearlessness, and group validation. The judge attempts to guide them to a different understanding of manhood, searching for "teachable moments" to expand the young defendant's immature and undeveloped understanding of manhood and strength. Judge Corriero uses

his engaged interaction during allocution to attempt to awaken a
defendant's remorse and foster empathy development:

> JUDGE CORRIERO: What about the person? You put a gun to
> his head. What do you think he felt?
> DEFENDANT: (No response).
> (Later on in the interaction:)
> JUDGE CORRIERO: You can be smart and still be a criminal
> and still have no empathy.[24]

Questioning another defendant:

> JUDGE CORRIERO: You punched that person in the face. Have
> you ever been punched in the face? How does it feel?
> DEFENDANT: I guess I was being stupid.[25]

The defendant in the first interaction offers no response, and the
defendant in the second one doesn't answer Judge Corriero's question directly. Male defendants, who have been socialized not to express
fear, do not usually express empathy for their victims. The judge will
continue to work on this aspect of their character development.

Although Judge Corriero is optimistic enough to try to use his role
as a judge to help defendants work on their strength of character and
morals, he is also a realist. He knows, that not showing physical
strength or aggressiveness in violent neighborhoods, especially if the
defendant is associated with a gang can be dangerous. Much of the
judge's "judicious use of colloquy" with his male defendants is directed
at giving them tools to help them save face and avoid violence.

Judge Corriero sometimes uses books as a form of "bibliother-
apy" to aid him in this difficult task. For example, having assigned a
defendant to read *To Kill a Mockingbird,* the judge recounts a mem-
orable scene from the movie version of the book. In the scene, the
daughter Scout witnesses some racist townspeople taunt her father,
Atticus Finch, and one man spits in his face. The judge points out
that Atticus Finch *"didn't respond in kind."* This example illustrates
a man whose identity is internally, not externally, based, a concept

that is virtually incomprehensible to an adolescent. Nevertheless, the seed is planted in the defendant's mind. The judge also uses this compelling scene to convey the notion that external observers and influences may be ignorant. Ideally, the judge discussing the example of Atticus Finch will give the defendant a new way of seeing the strength it takes to be nonreactive to taunts, so that he can save face and be able to walk away from peer-pressure situations. Yet, when the defendant doesn't respond, Judge Corriero focuses on progress over time, and shows compassion for how difficult it is to deal with feeling disrespected.

> JUDGE CORRIERO: That was the measure of the man. That was just ignorance. You don't respond to ignorance with violence. Ignorance begets ignorance, like violence begets violence. Do you think you could do that if someone spit in your face?
>
> DEFENDANT: (No response.)
>
> JUDGE CORRIERO: I know it's difficult. It will take time.[26]

When the judge is deciding whether to release a defendant from jail, his interactions with this defendant afford him the opportunity to link freedom with characteristics that he expects of their future behavior. Given the incentive of gaining their freedom, Judge Corriero asks them if, despite their youthful mistakes, they are now capable of assuming mature responsibility. Tasting freedom, the defendant is likely to be at his most receptive for internalizing what it takes to be a *free man*. He would be most open to hearing the judge reconceptualize strength. This defendant is about to be released after four months in jail:

> JUDGE CORRIERO: You have learned your lesson?
>
> DEFENDANT: Yes.
>
> JUDGE CORRIERO: You think, or you're sure?
>
> DEFENDANT: Yes.
>
> JUDGE CORRIERO: You consider yourself a man?
>
> DEFENDANT: Yes.

JUDGE CORRIERO: Why? What does it mean?

DEFENDANT: [To] be responsible for what you do.

JUDGE CORRIERO: Not to hurt people. To help people, [to] be responsible to your family, and true to your word, most of all… Strong enough to walk away when someone on the street [disrespects you]. The strongest thing is to be able to walk away because a lot of people are depending on you. You can do that?[27]

To make the judge's reconceptualizations of manhood and strength more readily accessible to the defendants, Judge Corriero uses accessible terms (although never inappropriate ones) and frames of reference to which the defendants can relate, such as getting even, proving how strong you are, and being successful. The defendant in the following case discusses his progress and how the program is helping him to deal with his anger, and the judge responds:

JUDGE CORRIERO: I'm proud of you… If someone insults you, you could use violence, or this is a chance to prove how strong you are. The way to get even is making something with your life, using that energy to become the best you can be in life. Keep up the good work.[28]

Judge Corriero has to challenge the notion that it is not manly to discuss problems, ask for help from others, or be emotionally vulnerable. By ordering this defendant to cooperate, rather than asking him to, Judge Corriero permits the defendant to maintain the idea that he is not asking for help. At the same time, the Judge's colloquy tries to improve defendant's attitude by destigmatizing the concept of getting help:

JUDGE CORRIERO: You know this was a serious matter to begin with. The only reason you're out is I felt it was important to give you a chance to deal with your issues in a positive way. You must cooperate and get counseling. James, there's nothing wrong with talking to people and getting help.[29]

The following case provides an opportunity for Judge Corriero to positively reinforce a defendant's bravery in the wake of a crime he had committed with codefendants. The defendant and his friends stole property—food and money—from a delivery person. The defendant and his friends then ate the food, but subsequently the defendant must have stood up to his friends, because he returned the money to the victim. This colloquy, which took place during allocution, shed light on the meaning of true bravery. The defendant is pleading guilty, with the promise of getting five years' probation and YO (the defendant was at that time in the DOME project):

> JUDGE CORRIERO: What did you do to be guilty of this crime?
> DEFENDANT: I was with them, I took the money, but I gave it back.
> JUDGE CORRIERO: After you were arrested?
> DEFENDANT: No. I realized what I did was wrong and gave the money back to the man.
> JUDGE CORRIERO: Your conscience bothered you; I'm very impressed... I'm very moved to see that you could realize this on your own, Anthony. [This] makes a big difference.[30]

What emerges here is a kind of morality tale, perhaps, told primarily for the benefit of the other defendants watching the calendar proceedings. Using this defendant's decision to give back the money he had taken and, in so doing, risk the ridicule of his peers, Judge Corriero transforms this case into a story the conclusion of which debunks an adolescent notion of bravery, in which one is defined a "chicken" if one doesn't go along with the group. The brave man has a conscience, a sense of individual responsibility, and the ability to think for himself and oppose the group. The judge commends this defendant for doing this even at the risk of being called a "traitor," a "rat," a "sissy," that is, not a man.

Judge Corriero's interactive style is to engage the defendants and encourage them to tell him about their interests and subjects they are studying in school. He then uses these topics as part of his

application of the therapeutic jurisprudence model, to impart a con-
science-raising and character-building message. The therapeutic
impact of the judge's use of family involvement is also important in
the next example. In the following colloquy, notice how adroitly
Judge Corriero links the message of the Constitution as well as the
defendant's mother's reasons for coming to America, into guiding
this defendant to have the courage and motivation to withstand
peer pressure:

> JUDGE CORRIERO: What's you favorite subject?
> DEFENDANT: History.
> JUDGE CORRIERO: What are you studying?
> DEFENDANT: The Constitution.
> JUDGE CORRIERO: What do you like about it?
> DEFENDANT: (Silent.)
> JUDGE CORRIERO: Where were you born?
> DEFENDANT: [A location in Latin America.]
> JUDGE CORRIERO: (addresses the mother) Why did you come
>   here with your family?
> MOTHER: (via translator) I came in search of more opportu-
>   nities.
> JUDGE: (to defendant) Why? To make a better life for you, so
>   you could be somebody—no matter the color of your skin,
>   religion, where you were born—isn't that what the Con-
>   stitution says? It's not a crime to be born in a poor neigh-
>   borhood. But you have to have the strength, the courage
>   to tell your foolish friends you're not going to do [what they
>   want to do/something criminal]. You want to take care of
>   your mother. If you carry a gun again [in this instance, it
>   was a fake gun], you will jeopardize all of that.[31]

Respect is a powerful currency in the world of the adolescent male;
patiently and persistently, the judge attempts to empower the defendants to adopt a sense of self-respect that disregards the inconstant
reactions of peers. In this case, the judge acknowledges that the defendant had stabbed another young man in the back, "out of anger," being

"so overcome by these signs of disrespect." The judge then guides him to consider a more solid, reconceptualized, notion of self-respect:

> JUDGE CORRIERO: When we have to look for respect outside of ourselves, based on what others think, then we are not really talking about respect. Nobody can take away who you are by what they say or do.[32]

Although he understands the provocation, the judge's only option is to sentence the defendant to jail time because of his age and the extreme seriousness of the crime.

Some of the strategies that Judge Corriero implements draw on defendants' experiences in jail. Although you'd be hard-pressed to find a stronger advocate of ATI programs than Judge Corriero, he uses a defendant's own experience while incarcerated as a powerful resource in shattering preexisting conceptions of respect. Judge Corriero asks most defendants who are in detention facilities, "How long have you been in jail?" Because the defendants' records, which are before the judge, easily answer that question, the inquiry seems more of an attempt to discern their attitudes, searching for character-building teachable moments.[33] In the following colloquy, the defendant's response, an exact accounting of the number of days he has been incarcerated, appears to display a serious attitude and an appreciation of the fact that it is his actions that have resulted in his loss of freedom. Judge Corriero, attuned to this defendant's attitude, intervenes at a moment when the defendant is most likely to be able to *hear* him, to communicate the lesson that acting "tough" is not worth the price, that threatening someone with a weapon doesn't make a person powerful, that, on the contrary, criminal activity deprives one of freedom. The judge's query, *"Was it worth it?"* seems, therefore, to take on a rhetorical quality:

> JUDGE CORRIERO: How long have you been in jail?
> DEFENDANT: Ninety-seven days.
> JUDGE CORRIERO: You're counting. You don't like jail… Hands cuffed, behind your back… Your freedom is taken

away from you. You have no rights, no respect. You think you can get respect with a knife. You want to be a tough guy, a gangster, a wise guy. Why should I give you a second chance?

DEFENDANT: I thought it was cool because all of my friends were doing it. [I could] make a lot of money.

JUDGE CORRIERO: Was it worth it?[34]

Often, by the time the defendant has reached sentencing, and particularly if he or she has earned the second chance of probation and YO status, the concept of commanding respect takes on a new meaning: treating others with respect earns you respect. In the following parting interaction, Judge Corriero teaches the wisdom of "the golden rule." Before sentencing defendant to five years of probation and YO, they discuss defendant's plans of going to college:

JUDGE CORRIERO: Terrific, I just want you to be the best person you can be. Treat others how you would want to be treated. It's a very simple rule.[35]

In some of these dialogues the defendants demonstrate little sense of responsibility for their actions. In this they seem to be employing *techniques of neutralization,* that is, justifications/rationalizations that protect them from blame before and after the act.[36] One such technique of neutralization, "the denial of responsibility," is based on the assumption that "insofar as the delinquent can define himself as lacking responsibility for his deviant actions, the disapproval of self or others is sharply reduced in effectiveness as a restraining influence."[37] When denying responsibility, the delinquent sees him/herself as a "billiard ball," at the mercy of forces outside of his/her control.[38] When progress is made, defendants begin to assume responsibility for their wrongdoing and develop an empowering sense of agency.

Judge Corriero intervenes to provide a reality check and a sense of hope, stressing that a defendant shapes the future. The judge, recognizing that his previous strategies to communicate his expectations have not been internalized by the defendant, dismantles this defendant's resistance to authority by conferring a sense of control.

> JUDGE CORRIERO: The message is not being communicated. Why am I investing all this time in you, John? Why shouldn't I just put you in jail? If your next report is not positive, what's going to happen?
>
> DEFENDANT: You're going to put me in jail.
>
> JUDGE CORRIERO: So you're the judge. The key to your jail cell is in your pocket.[39]

Reconceptualizing manhood entails acquiring a new vision of the concept of responsibility: that men have a responsibility *to do* certain things, and a responsibility *not to do* certain things. Thus, when Judge Corriero is guiding the defendants' character-building process in this area, he addresses both of these dimensions:

> JUDGE CORRIERO: You understand it's your responsibility to educate yourself [and] your responsibility to take care of this child. If you want to act like a boy and bring a child into this world now, you have to be a man about it. A man doesn't respond to name calling, he doesn't have to. He knows who he is. I expect you to learn from this.[40]

Here, beyond the explicit responsibilities that Judge Corriero stresses this young father must take on, he also conveys that the defendant has a newfound responsibility to learn from his mistakes and to not lose his temper when provoked in the future.

As a strategy to activate a sense of individual responsibility in the defendants for their actions and their consequences, Judge Corriero empowers their sense of self-control, putting justice, so to speak, in their hands. This approach, fair in both its terms and consequences, seems tailored to fit the mindset of adolescents, who don't like to be told what to do, and are likely to feel defiant of authority. After clarifying his expectations, the judge tells the defendants that, from now on, they control their fate and have the power to stay out of jail.

"You're the judge!" he tells them, and makes it clear that they are the masters of their own destiny. Judge Corriero harnesses the defendant's desire for a sense of control, in a way that would appear to strengthen deterrence. The defendant's going on record as saying, *"Lock me up,"* and the judge stressing, *"You will sentence yourself,"* may promote an *"I'll show you I won't get in trouble"* response. This strategy artfully circumvents the self-defeating urge of adolescents to rebel against authority. To activate a sense of individual responsibility for the defendant's actions and their consequences, Judge Corriero asserts that he is sharing his judicial responsibilities and authority with the defendant:

> JUDGE CORRIERO: You will sentence yourself. The first time you take that joint and put it to your lips, you sentence yourself.[41]

A poignant aspect of Judge Corriero's character-building process involves supporting their development of self-respect and a sense of responsibility to themselves to realize their potential:

> JUDGE CORRIERO: You have great potential. (Defendant has been receiving "stellar reports" from a juvenile detention facility.)
> DEFENDANT: Thank you.
> JUDGE CORRIERO: I don't want you to waste it. I'm not just saying that. I have no reason to just say that.
> DEFENDANT: All right.
> JUDGE CORRIERO: It's not just "all right." It's: "of course I won't waste my life. I have no reason to waste my life."[42]

Judge Corriero's chief goal in the Youth Part appears to be to enable each defendant to make progress toward the best outcome, given his or her talents and circumstances. This can't happen unless the young person has a sense of self-respect and responsibility:

> JUDGE CORRIERO: You better understand this is not a game. If I am unfair to the prosecution the next child who

deserves a second chance won't get it... It's nothing personal. If I don't put you in jail, I won't be able to let another kid out of jail that deserves it.

(Discussion about outpatient programs.)

JUDGE CORRIERO: Over the objection of the people, I will give you a chance.[43]

Recognizing the adolescent concern with peer pressure, Judge Corriero frames the seriousness of the matter in a way the defendant is likely to appreciate. The judge tries to instill a sense of responsibility to other defendants who might deserve a second chance. Adolescent defendants in the Youth Part initially appear to not appreciate how their actions affect others. Judge Corriero challenges them to open their eyes and broaden their vision.

A hallmark of Judge Corriero's Youth Part is his extensive commitment to involve the defendants' families in court proceedings and in many important decisions. On meeting a defendant for the first time, he examines the family as a viable support network. When the judge decides to release a defendant into the community, he must involve the family. In often dramatic fashion, Judge Corriero skillfully uses the defendant's family to evoke a sense of remorse in the defendant.

This strategy is consistent with Wexler and Winick's use of behavioral science research on patient *"adherence"* and *"compliance"* (to the medical and psychological treatment process) to help judges improve the chances of this same type of outcome in defendants.[44] The analogy is not far-fetched because both patients and defendants are told by an authority figure to do certain things, whether they like it or not, to recover from their condition. Both groups also may show resistance to treatment programs and try to deny or minimize their situation.[45] Wexler and Winick report that "involving family members in the treatment process" served to "enhance patient adherence."[46]

Additionally, the literature supports the merits of Judge Corriero's strategy of asking a defendant to make a promise directly to his/her family in the courtroom, as to future behavior. "[P]ublic commitment," especially in the presence of family members,[47] was found to lead "to greater adherence than does private commitment..."[48]

Despite the fact that legislators have decided to try these young defendants as adults, Judge Corriero's judicial interactive process treats them as children belonging to a family, and actively involves the families in court proceedings. As an observer of the Youth Part, one senses a deep and genuine level of respect and compassion when Judge Corriero interacts with the families of defendants. The immediate effect, which would further accumulate over time, is to personalize, through role modeling, the kind of respect he expects the young people to have for their families. Additionally, this respect is established when Judge Corriero uses the family to awaken remorse in the defendant.

When Judge Corriero listens to the wishes and concerns of the families, he invests them with authority. Adopting the language of Mark H. Moore, Judge Corriero *deputizes the parent(s)*[49] when he returns young offenders to the custody of their families. He has a certain degree of confidence in the defendants' support network, and deputizing the parents is a key component of the Youth Part's innovative approach of adjourning the sentence, and giving defendants an opportunity to earn a second chance while living in the community. Because of the serious nature of their crimes, and the risk releasing them to the community may pose to the public, Judge Corriero must determine, using the PPI report, as well as his impression of the family before him, whether a family has the motivation and resources to help their child to succeed outside of jail.

The assessment of the extent to which Judge Corriero can involve the parent(s) begins at the defendants' first appearance. In questioning the parents or other significant relatives, the judge evaluates them as a part of the defendant's overall support network. With a respectful tone, he probes to examine various dimensions of capable guardianship. Almost every time the judge first meets a family, he begins by inquiring about the family composition and age distribution of children, what family members do for a living, sometimes also inquiring as to the hours that they work. This may raise questions as to whether this family has the time and resources to supervise their child's activity, to help him/her succeed.

Sometimes, when the defendants' siblings are older, Judge Corriero will ask whether any of the siblings have been in trouble with the law. By inquiring about the criminal history of the defendant's older siblings, Judge Corriero is establishing what kind of role models the defendant has. Younger brothers may look up to their older brothers and want to emulate them.

From the defendants' first appearance and continuing over the months or years of their involvement with the Youth Part, parental and extended families' presence on court dates demonstrates their fortitude and commitment. This sends a message that can sometimes make a decisive difference in Judge Corriero's willingness to take a risk on a defendant. Here, the defendant's family appears to have impressed Judge Corriero as being willing and able to join forces with him in a team effort. Judge Corriero's strategy of directing attention to the presence of the defendant's family may result in the defendant experiencing remorse for what he may have done, and feeling beholden to his family:

> JUDGE CORRIERO: You obviously have a family that cares about you and loves you…I'm not closing the door on this [giving the defendant Youthful Offender treatment].
> FATHER: How long is he going to be in?
> JUDGE CORRIERO: He could go to jail for ten years. If I decide to give him a second chance, it's on my shoulders.
> FEMALE RELATIVE: His whole family is here and we're willing to help him so it doesn't happen again.
> JUDGE CORRIERO: That's why I'm willing to consider giving him a second chance. I wouldn't otherwise.[50]

If the judge decides to release a defendant from custody, or he/she is placed in an ATI program following arraignment, the parent(s)/guardian(s) become(s) Judge Corriero's *deputies* on the front lines. Judge Corriero requires them to assume some responsibility for the defendant's attendance at school and programs. All too often, the defendants lack respect for their families. The judge then has the task of using his own authority to lend legitimacy to the authority of parents.

After Judge Corriero has assessed the defendant's support network, he turns his attention to clarifying that he expects parents/caretakers to exert adequate supervision:

> (The defendant's mother and father are in court).
> JUDGE CORRIERO (to mother and father): If I let him out, I don't want him out of the house [past curfew time]. We understand each other? If I give him this second chance, he has to stay out of trouble, go to school, go to [the] program, keep his curfew.[51]

Standing before the court, parents' initial impulse may be to give a false or overly positive report of how their child is doing at home, fearing the negative consequences of candor. Judge Corriero, therefore, has the challenge of gaining their trust and demonstrating his profound concern for their child's current and future well-being. To that end, Judge Corriero tries to impress on them the importance of reporting smaller problems before they turn into larger ones.

In many of the cases in which defendants ultimately demonstrate that they deserved the second chance, a parental alliance has been forged with Judge Corriero. They provide him with detailed reports, and he, in turn, respects their input. Parents often look to the judge for help. They feel they can't control their children, but they may think that the judge will be able to exert more power over them.

Although a judicial-parental alliance might make the defendant feel cornered, Judge Corriero actively attempts to bring the defendant into the problem-solving team. Before the following colloquy, the defendant's mother had expressed concern that her son was hanging out with the kids with whom he had gotten into trouble. The judge advises the defendant to tell his friends that he will go to jail if he associates with them.

> JUDGE CORRIERO (to defendant's mother): Is that all right with you?[52]

In asking if that was *"all right"* with the mother, the judge implicitly is deputizing her, giving her the authority to intervene and even report back to him if she finds that her son is hanging out with the old crowd. Judge Corriero expresses his commitment to ensuring a positive outcome for the defendant, and that such an outcome may depend, in large measure, on the mother's responsibility to monitor him and candidly report to the court.

One strategy that Judge Corriero uses to break through their developmental difficulties in this area is to have the defendants imagine themselves as the victim of their own crime. When the defendant's parent is in the audience, this dramatization, along with the recollection of any past event, appears particularly effective. By eliciting the admission of his having experienced pain when in the same situation as his victim, this *"show your mother"* reenactment strategy evokes a recognition of what the defendant's victim felt. Here, the judge wants the defendant to show his mother how he actually committed the crime in order to impress on him, and her, the seriousness of his behavior. The defendant is pleading guilty:

JUDGE CORRIERO: What did you do to be guilty of this crime?
DEFENDANT: I yoked him around the neck.
JUDGE CORRIERO: Show your mother how you did it.
DEFENDANT: (Imitates the yoking.)
JUDGE CORRIERO: Have you ever been yoked around the
    neck before?
DEFENDANT: Yes.
JUDGE CORRIERO: How does it feel?
DEFENDANT: [It] hurts.[53]

The judge's strategy here is clearly adoptive of the therapeutic jurisprudence model and supported by its research in several respects. In addition to using family involvement and a public declaration to enhance the defendant's compliance, Wexler and Winick argue that " the therapeutic potential of the role of the judge could be enhanced in guilty plea cases if the court engaged in detailed questioning of the defendant about the factual basis of the plea.

Specifically, the judge could address on the record some of the matters typically subject to cognitive distortion" to work "against denial and cognitive distortion and toward cognitive restructuring"[54] the allocution process functions so as to impart a therapeutic effect on the defendant.

When families of limited economic means post bail, they provide an opportunity for Judge Corriero to stress the sacrifices made on the defendants' behalf. A mother bailing her son out of jail enables Judge Corriero to emphasize to the defendant that he owes her respect and good behavior. This is the defendant's first appearance on a "Juvenile Offender" charge. His mother, a sewing machine operator, put up $5,000 bail.

> JUDGE CORRIERO (to defendant): How long were you in jail?
> DEFENDANT: Three days.
> JUDGE CORRIERO: You didn't put this money up, your mother did, her hard-earned savings.
> (There is a discussion of conflict in mother/son relationship.)
> JUDGE CORRIERO: Mothers always get the benefit of the doubt when their kids don't respect them. She works eight to nine hours a day, probably in a sweatshop. You think it's nice for her to have to come here and see you like this?

Judge Corriero required, as a condition of his continued release on bail, that this defendant be enrolled in Youth Advocacy Project.[55]

Humanizing the victim using the analogy of a family member is a strategy to help defendants develop empathy. After this next defendant served sufficient time, the judge was prepared to release him. Before taking a plea, Judge Corriero attempts to reach this defendant by having him imagine another criminal doing to his mother what he himself did to the elderly victim (and the defendant's mother suggests he think of his grandmother being victimized). This mental exercise puts the defendant in an indignant and protective frame of mind:

JUDGE CORRIERO: How would you feel if someone did this to your mother when she was sixty-three? What would you like me to do to them?

DEFENDANT: Lock them up.

JUDGE CORRIERO: Is that what I should do to you?

DEFENDANT: No. I want another chance.

JUDGE CORRIERO: What are you going to do for this older woman?

DEFENDANT: [Offer an] apology.

MOTHER: My mother is the same age. I told him, "How about if it was your grandma?"[56]

In examining these interactions between Judge Corriero and the defendants, as he attempts the challenging goal of fostering their development of empathy, we witness methods that have proven effective, within the limits of teenagers' developmental capacities. The compelling strategies of role-playing in front of their parents, and analogizing the victim to be a family member, appear to be particularly effective in instilling a spontaneous appreciation for the seriousness of the defendants' crimes.

When parents are present, Judge Corriero frequently will ask them how they are. This is a chance for him to awaken remorse in the defendants and a sense of responsibility for the problems they are causing their parents:

(The defendant is in a juvenile detention center).

JUDGE CORRIERO (to mother, via interpreter): How are you, mother?

MOTHER: I don't feel very well. I have a lot of worries. I don't sleep well.

JUDGE CORRIERO (to defendant): So, what are we going to do? Make your mother's life a little better.

(Judge Corriero reads off defendant's report card from the school at the juvenile detention center in which he's received 90s in all subjects).

JUDGE CORRIERO (to defendant): Very good. (To mother):
You should be proud of him. He's doing much better.
Soon he will be able to come home and help you.[57]

When Judge Corriero gives the defendant an opportunity to hear
his mother's physical and emotional distress, the defendant realizes
that his good behavior can really make a difference. Because Judge
Corriero has an excellent report of the defendant's progress and academic performance, he builds on this success. Additionally, part of
Judge Corriero's strategy of involving the parent appears to aim at
helping her to feel better, not to unduly blame him or herself, and
not to lose hope.

At the juncture when Judge Corriero is deciding whether to
release a defendant from jail, or is about to, his interaction with the
defendant seems to take on an increased intensity. This is a decision
that has serious potential consequences for public safety, as well as
for the defendant's future. In order to maximize the likelihood of the
defendant's success, Judge Corriero involves the family, strategizing
that perhaps the most effective way to reach the defendant is to have
him give his word publicly to his parents:

(Mother and father are present).
JUDGE CORRIERO: You care about your mother and father.
DEFENDANT: (Nods.)
JUDGE CORRIERO: You think it's nice for them to have to come
    down here like this? I want you to turn around and tell
    your mother and father you're never going to do this
    again. Tell them right now.
DEFENDANT (turns to parents and says in Spanish): I promise
    you... [58]

Although having one parent present at court appearances in the
Youth Part is the norm, some defendants have an extended family
support network present: siblings, grandmothers, aunts, cousins, and
so on. The benefit of having the defendant's extended family present
is maximized by Judge Corriero's frequently asking for their input.

He asks grandmothers, "How does he/she treat you?," "Does he/she listen to you?," "Does he/she obey your orders?," "Does he/she respect you?" He asks siblings, "What do you think of your brother/sister?" The more input, the better. Although negative reports provide important behind-the-scene evidence, positive reports and sentiments allow the defendant to feel loved, increasing his/her self-worth and sense of hope. There is a healing quality to defendants realizing that their worst actions do not define them in the eyes of those they love and on whom they depend.

Interaction with the family and their involvement at every stage of the rehabilitative process is extensive. The parental/judicial partnership is a fundamental component of the Youth Part, and serves to maximize Judge Corriero's impact on the defendants, and the likelihood of a successful outcome. There is an overwhelming emphasis on defendants' respect toward their caretakers. Judge Corriero role-models this by treating parents and guardians with respect and, when possible, he consults with the family, regarding their wishes (i.e., on a change of curfew). His strategy of empowering parents with authority and making them his allies in the defendants' support network not only rehabilitates the defendants; it rehabilitates the family as a whole.

When dealing with a juvenile population, teenage pregnancy often plays a part in building responsibility. Courtroom interactions about a defendant's unborn or newborn child focus on trying to impress on the defendant the seriousness of the matter, emphasizing his/her current and future responsibilities to the child. Note the shift now from teaching the defendant how to be a man to expecting him to be one. To awaken their conscience, Judge Corriero often conveys his expectations that they will assume their parental responsibilities and will take care of their baby, get a job, and pay child support:

> JUDGE CORRIERO: And how do you think you're going to take care of this baby from jail? That's where you'll be if you don't [meet conditional expectations]. You think you're a man because you can make a baby? You better start acting like one.[59]

The point here is to evoke a sense of responsibility.

When interacting with female defendants who are pregnant, one strategy that Judge Corriero adopts is a future-thinking approach. This asks the expectant mother/defendant to weigh her behavior in terms of its consequences not only for herself but also for her future child, to consider what would happen to her child if she ends up in jail. The judge also communicates his hope that the defendant will realize her own potential, and tries to help her believe in her capacity to achieve a positive future, through education and a career: Mentoring this young woman, Judge Corriero tries to prepare her for the challenges ahead. His concern seems to be to provide her with hope and to support her own development, never forgetting that, although she will soon have a child, she herself is a child. The defendant is two months' pregnant and taking college courses to become a nurse:

> JUDGE CORRIERO: Are you going to straighten everything out so that you can take care of this child? (He mentions family counseling.) You have a special responsibility for this baby. I can't not put you in jail because you're pregnant. You want to be a nurse; there's no reason you can't be.[60]

Judge Corriero holds firmly to the belief that "children are malleable, they can learn," that they are distinguished by their "willingness to be open and inspired, to be educated. If children can learn from their mistakes, [and be] influenced, [the] judge [serves] as [a] beacon of light, [to] show them where their errors are."[61] Within the limited time the calendar allows, Judge Corriero maximizes his interactions with young defendants, so as to impart important socialization lessons and practical tools for success, such as how to resist peer pressure.

On meeting new defendants, the socialization process begins. Judge Corriero gives them clear, firm, and reasonable guidelines regarding what he expects of them. As a relationship develops, he further socializes them as he role-models justice and fairness when making decisions big and small.

In his interactions with defendants, Judge Corriero adopts a holistic view of his role in ensuring their success. He takes on the responsibility of helping them understand how the world works and he gives them concrete ideas to help them succeed. In mentoring young defendants, he offers them practical tools and suggestions to help them navigate a society that is foreign to them in many ways.

In the following interaction, Judge Corriero mentors this defendant on how to make the best impression when applying for a job. Here, the judge's tone is not patronizing; he appears to appreciate that what might seem common sense is not obvious to young people lacking experience in professional situations:

> (Defendant is in an ATI program and is doing very well. He has an upcoming interview at a university in New York to do office work.)
> JUDGE CORRIERO: What time is the interview?
> DEFENDANT: Nine.
> JUDGE CORRIERO: What time are you going to get there?
> DEFENDANT: Nine.
> JUDGE CORRIERO: No, eight-thirty. What are you going to wear?
> DEFENDANT: (Shrugs).
> JUDGE CORRIERO: Wear your tie and your shirt. How about your earring? (Defendant has an earring).
> DEFENDANT: (Smiles).
> JUDGE CORRIERO: Be there early. (To program representative): And you are going to help him be prepared for the interview? Ask him questions?
> PROGRAM REPRESENTATIVE: Yes.[62]

Judge Corriero gives defendants clear, firm, and reasonable statements about what is expected of them: going to school every day, program participation, curfew, and so on. The importance of this is backed up by the therapeutic jurisprudence model's application of research on the psychology of compliance. This research suggests that judges must carefully and clearly instruct the defendant about the conditions of release, be engaged and pay attention to the defendant, take the time needed, ask them questions, let them speak in their own words, and use clear terms they can understand—avoid unexplained jargon.[63]

Additionally, when a defendant is not meeting Judge Corriero's expectations, he reemphasizes the consequences of not doing so. An important part of the defendants' socialization involves their internalizing what is at stake if they don't follow the judge's rules.

Whether coached or not, at some point defendants usually thank Judge Corriero. In what appears to be an almost reflexive response to a defendant's *"Thank you,"* the judge responds, *"Thank me by..."* This exchange occurs with such regularity that it takes on the status of a ritual in the Youth Part. The important message that Judge Corriero conveys in the following interaction is that actions speak louder than words:

DEFENDANT: Thank you.
JUDGE CORRIERO: Thank me by what? By doing your best.[64]

Judge Corriero's response to defendants' thanking him challenges them to mean something, crucially shifting the focus from what the judge did for them to what they will do with the second chance he has given them.

JUDGE CORRIERO: Are you just saying that to make me feel
better? You think I can tell just by looking at you by now?
DEFENDANT: Yes.[65]

Providing hope to defendants is especially important when Judge Corriero must incarcerate them, when they may feel their life is over. In the following interaction, the extent to which this care is internalized by a defendant is apparent. The judge once remanded the defendant to jail and then gave him another chance. This is a young man who has experienced what it feels like for someone to believe in him and his future, for someone to show care and concern for his feelings and well-being. His relationship with Judge Corriero has created a context for the development of empathy and compassion:

JUDGE CORRIERO: We want to see you become what you
    should become. Why? Why should I care?
DEFENDANT: Maybe you care about me.[66]

"I Think You Have a Gift"

Demonstrating belief in each child before him, and instilling hope
for his/her future, appears to be crucial—indeed, central—to Judge
Corriero's approach in the Youth Part. Placing defendants in programs to help them deal with their issues, and holding out a promise of YO status if they meet his expectations, demonstrates to the
defendants that the judge believes they deserve a second chance.
With a tone that is decidedly encouraging, he helps them to appreciate the potential that he sees in them.

In the interactions that follow, it is evident that Judge Corriero's
belief in these defendants has yielded a sense of belief in themselves.
In the first interaction, this young female defendant appears to
believe enough in herself to admit that she has a substance abuse
problem. She is determined to get the help she needs.

DEFENDANT: I really think I do have a problem. I will get the
    help I need.
JUDGE CORRIERO: How's school?
DEFENDANT: I like school.
JUDGE CORRIERO: I've always thought you were very bright,
    a young woman with great potential. I'm very moved by
    your insight into your own problems. All I want to see is
    you become the best woman you can be.[67]

I leave the reader with the words of a young defendant who developed the self-confidence and belief in the American dream to be
able to work toward and expect success as an entrepreneur. When
Judge Corriero asks him about his plans for continuing his education,
the defendant says he is planning on going to college to "study business management so [he] can own [his] own business":

JUDGE CORRIERO: What kind of business?

DEFENDANT: A restaurant.

JUDGE CORRIERO: What kind of restaurant?

DEFENDANT: Fast food.

JUDGE CORRIERO: What kind of fast food?

DEFENDANT: Soul food.

JUDGE CORRIERO: Are there any soul food fast food restaurants?

DEFENDANT: In a couple of years there will be.[68]

Appendix: Coding of Defendants

Sex
> M = male defendant
> F = female defendant

Detention Status
> I = "in"—defendant is currently in jail, either because he/she could not post bail, or was remanded.
> O = "out"—defendant is currently not in jail, out on bail, released on his/her own recognizance (ROR), on probation, back in the community, and so on.
> O/R = defendant is in a residential treatment facility (enters from "outside" and sits in audience)
> I/R = defendant is "in" a residential treatment facility (brought in from the back by corrections/court officers)

Race/Ethnicity
> AA = African American
> L = Latino/Latina
> W = White
> ME = Middle Eastern
> U = Unknown

CHAPTER 8

The Experiment that Failed

*It is one thing to teach a hard lesson, it is another to
learn the lesson taught.*
—CITIZEN'S COMMITTEE FOR CHILDREN

A T THE HEART of my issue with the Juvenile Offender Law
and similar laws across the nation that facilitate the prosecution of children in adult courts is their disregard of American
conceptions of the value and place of children in our society, as well
as their disregard of the scholarly research of behavioral scientists
establishing the developmental differences and needs of children.
Our nation's juvenile justice system was based on the premise that
juveniles can and should be rehabilitated. Indeed, the cornerstone of
this movement was that it is in the best interests of both juveniles and
society that young offenders be rehabilitated, insulated from public-
ity and the retributive atmosphere of adult courts.

The juvenile offender legislation of 1978 marked a significant
retreat from this goal. New York, the state in which most of our
nation's ancestors first disembarked, had a long tradition of protecting and treating with compassion the poor, weak, and vulnerable of
society, dating from the founding of the first House of Refuge for children of immigrants in 1824.[1] New York should have been at the forefront of protecting and dealing effectively with these children.
Instead, the JO legislation foreshadowed the dismantling of the entire

effort. When the JO law was first enacted, its mandatory nature was virtually unprecedented. Juveniles throughout the nation were generally subjected to prosecution in adult court only after a hearing in juvenile court, during which a juvenile court judge was required to examine factors enumerated in the Supreme Court case of *Kent v. United States*.[2] Such factors included the youth's age and social background, prior delinquency records, the nature of past treatment efforts and the availability of programs designed to treat the juvenile's behavioral problems. The JO law prevented judges from taking these critical individual factors into account before prosecution in the adult court and it did not provide adequate resources to deal with the special needs of young offenders. It represented a dramatic shift in policy from "individualized justice" to punishment and retribution as a first resort.

New York's Juvenile Offender Law presaged a growing American trend to criminalize juvenile delinquency. As a nation, we engaged in a collective regression that resulted in discarding or ignoring ancient assumptions, conventional wisdom and conscientious research concerning the nature of childhood and criminal responsibility. Many states, faced with what they believed was a wholly new kind of juvenile offender, began to view the principles at the core of the old system, the treatment orientation, the concern for offender privacy, as not merely outmoded but dangerous.[3] As violent crime continued to rise, other states began to mimic New York's rigid approach to juvenile offenders. From 1992 through 1997, all but three states changed laws to facilitate the prosecution of children in adult court.[4] Twenty-eight states now have statutes similar to that of New York, which remove certain offenders from the jurisdiction of the Juvenile Court simply on the basis of age and offense.[5] Currently, all states and the District of Columbia allow the adult prosecution of juveniles under some circumstances.[6] As a result, the pool of children eligible for prosecution as adults has expanded dramatically. Each year, approximately 200,000 juveniles under 18 are prosecuted in adult courts.[7] Although state laws requiring or allowing the prosecution of juveniles as adults are commonly thought to be legislative responses to increases in juvenile violence, a surprising number of such laws authorize criminal prosecution for nonviolent offenses. Twenty-one states require or allow adult prosecution of juveniles accused of certain property offenses. Statutes in 19 states authorize or mandate prosecution of juveniles accused of drug offenses in Criminal Court. Forty-six states allow waiver to Criminal Court for a range of offenses—personal and property, violent and nonviolent.[8]

Generally, the laws of these states simply exclude a child of a certain age facing a particular accusation from being defined as a "child" for juvenile court jurisdictional purposes. A juvenile accused of an excluded offense is treated as an adult from the beginning of the prosecution in the Criminal Court. A variety of new restrictions were imposed on a judge's discretion in terms of sentencing, often dictating outcomes based exclusively on the seriousness of the offense rather than the offender's individual culpability. Confidentiality protections, once considered vital to the juvenile justice system, have been eroded in favor of procedures contrary to those goals, such as open hearings and largely unrestricted exchange of information, thereby eclipsing a child's privacy. The traditional rehabilitative goal of juvenile sanctions has been "de-emphasized in favor of straightforward adult-style punishment and long-term incarceration with fewer allowances for individual circumstances and special needs of juveniles."[9] Glaringly absent from proposals to increase criminalization of youth by prosecution in adult courts is any consideration of whether juveniles are actually competent or fit for adult adjudication.[10]

Our nation's system of dealing with children who violate the law evolves around a statutory age at which adult criminal responsibility automatically begins.[11] Each state has established a threshold age of criminal responsibility. Individuals who reach the statutory age are placed under the jurisdiction of the adult Criminal Court while those who are younger fall under the jurisdiction of the juvenile court. "Mechanisms for taking 'hard cases' out of the juvenile justice system have been available for as long as there has been a juvenile court."[12] This was generally accomplished by states establishing a lower age threshold which marked the age at which a juvenile could be transferred to adult court for certain serious crimes. For example, a state could set an initial minimum age of criminal responsibility at 18 but permit juveniles under that age to be transferred to adult court provided certain criteria were met. Transfer mechanisms differed from one another primarily in where they vested authority for the transfer decision, that is, in the legislature, judiciary or prosecutorial (executive) branch. Most state laws authorizing the prosecution of juveniles in adult court contain at least a few features of New York's Juvenile Offender Law. The most common features are: prosecutions based on the offense rather than an individualized assessment of the offender; increased penalties and decreased judicial discretion in sentencing options. Thus, almost every statute that permits a state to prosecute children as adults is subject to the same analysis applicable to New York's Juvenile Offender law.

In 1978, when New York was exploring its legislative options to effectuate a change in the way violent juveniles were treated, three methods were available for transferring a child to Criminal Court. The most common method, referred to as "judicial" waiver, empowered a juvenile court judge to decide whether to transfer the youth to adult Criminal Court. The second, referred to as "prosecutorial waiver," circumvented the juvenile court judge by granting the prosecuting attorney discretion to file charges against the child in either juvenile or adult court.[13] The third statutory scheme, termed "legislative" or "automatic" waiver, also circumvented the juvenile court judge, as the state legislature determined and enumerated specific offenses for which a youth of a specified age could not be adjudicated in juvenile court. Thus, New York's legislature could have lowered the age of criminal responsibility, which at 16 was already one of the lowest in the nation, or adopted a judicial waiver or transfer up system, leaving the Family Court with original jurisdiction and giving the judges of the juvenile court the discretionary power to waive certain violent offenses to Criminal Court (the system most common in the United States at the time), or it could have wholly transferred original jurisdiction over certain violent offenses to the adult court. The legislature chose the third alternative. In so doing, New York became one of only four states that automatically prosecuted certain children in adult court.[14] It already was only one of four states where the statutory age for adult criminal jurisdiction was as low as 16 and it actually became the only state where 14- and 15-year-olds and some 13-year-olds could automatically be tried as adults.[15]

Underlying the choice of legislative transfer to Criminal Court, rather than judicial transfer from Juvenile (Family) Court, was the belief that the juvenile courts could no longer control or adequately address the problems of chronic delinquents. It was essentially a matter of trust and rearranging the balance of power. The Legislature chose not to repose authority for the transfer decision with the juvenile court judiciary. In a sense, the thinking behind the move to recriminalize children formerly considered juvenile delinquents was not that far removed from that underlying the creation of the Juvenile Court. Juvenile courts emerged at the beginning of the 20th century in response to the perceived failure of criminal courts to adequately address the delinquent behavior of adolescents. Now the juvenile courts were perceived as failing and the idea of returning these children to the criminal courts again gained favor.[16]

New York's Juvenile Offender Law fundamentally changed the way children who violated the law were viewed and treated. By adopting the mechanism of legislative transfer, an entire category of children were excluded from the juvenile court simply on the basis of reaching a threshold age and an accusation of culpability for a serious crime. New York defined childhood in exceedingly narrow chronological terms for purposes of original prosecution in the criminal court. In so doing, it marked the upper limit of childhood incapacity at 13 for intentional murder, 14 and 15 for other crimes. Children previously thought of as delinquents no longer fell within that classification for purposes of assigning criminal responsibility. The rationale for this approach has consistently been echoed in official policy statements contained in such gubernatorial pronouncements as: "We must come to grips with the harsh reality that violent juvenile offenders who prey on our society are no longer children and cannot be dealt with as such."[17] And "[a] vicious criminal should not be able to use their age to escape appropriate punishment."[18]

Children prosecuted pursuant to the JO Law are presumptively to be incarcerated. There is an inherent bias toward imprisonment drafted into the law. By requiring mandatory imprisonment and authorizing alternative sentences only to those eligible for YO treatment, a judge is required to make a decision based essentially on the past behavior of a juvenile rather than on his performance after arrest. Although transfer back to Family Court is statutorily permitted, as a practical matter once a juvenile has been indicted by a grand jury transfer back rarely occurs. Some children, of course, must be imprisoned, but the central issue is whether we are needlessly incarcerating children who could benefit from the more ameliorative resources of the juvenile court.

New York's Juvenile Offender Law has prevented individual assessment of each juvenile before exposure to adult procedures and penalties. The law has had a significant "net widening affect" that may not have been foreseen by its proponents. Because of its mandatory nature, the law does not take into consideration whether prosecution in the adult court is in the best interests of the juvenile or society, given the youth's psychological age, social background, prior delinquency record, nature of past treatment efforts, and availability of suitable programs designed to treat the child's behavioral problems. I have found no statistics recording the number of first-time offenders prosecuted in the adult court pursuant to the JO Law, but based on my experience approximately 50% of the juveniles who appear in the Youth Part have no prior delinquency record.

By restricting the sentences of juvenile offenders to institutional confinement in secure facilities, or probation through the granting of YO status, the JO Law adopted the adult penal scheme of indeterminate sentences and departed from the flexible array of dispositional alternatives that traditionally characterize juvenile dispositions.[19] A description of the essential problem posed by the enactment of the Juvenile Offender law is concisely captured by the authors of the Legal Aid Society's study of the Juvenile Offender Team:

Before the (JO) law, Family Court had jurisdiction over all 13- to 15-year-olds, regardless of the offense... The Family Court Act allows for different and more varied dispositional options than those available in Supreme Court. Juveniles can be transferred to a mental hospital, a treatment center, group home, or get placed in foster care or another Administration for Children's Services (ACS) placement; substance abuse and therapeutic interventions are also available for the juvenile and his family. ACS covers the costs of foster care placements, which includes residential therapeutic placements for emotionally disturbed juveniles; substance abuse programs get their own funding from a variety of federal, state and private sources. Many adolescents in the court system have substance abuse issues, mental health problems, have been victims of abuse, and have unstable home lives. These interventions provide the juveniles with the help they need and attempt to reform their behavior.

Family Court provides these interventions because the legislature recognized that decision makers would need flexibility to address the varied needs of court-involved youth. Unfortunately, the legislature did not extend these options to Supreme Court. Thus, if a court wishes to address the needs of JOs before it, it must seek options that provide funding streams independent of a court placement; the 1978 JO law did not include any provisions for the courts to address the specific issues that faced those now known as juvenile offenders and adjudicated through Supreme Court. As a result, JOs are not eligible for services through any statutory construct. Judges, defense counsel, and probation officers are left to their own devices to identify programs in the community and refer the youth charged with participation... Herein lies the problem: Adolescents are placed in an adult court system that is ill-equipped to manage their needs. Because of this lack of understanding and inappropriate treatment, factors (such as substance abuse or exposure to domestic violence) that often lead JOs to trouble with the law are not addressed. By imprisoning these juveniles and failing to provide the intervention necessary to tackle their issues, their problems are exacerbated, and thus many JOs become repeat offenders.[20]

Unlike judges of the Family Court, adult court judges are not authorized to sentence a juvenile offender to "placement" in a private voluntary agency or a residential treatment center, even though one of those agencies might better serve the youth's needs and further protect society. Judges cannot order convicted juvenile offenders as part of a JO sentence to be placed in a foster care setting even if they have been neglected or abused by parents or caregivers. Moreover, because of this lack of statutory authority, programs that offer these services and are willing to accept many of these children have no avenue of financial reimbursement. New York City's child welfare agency—the Administration for Children's Services—has often taken the position that once a child is arrested as a juvenile offender he is no longer the agency's responsibility but that of the adult criminal justice system. Children in foster care as a result of abuse, neglect, or abandonment and who are in the custody of the Administration for Children's Services at the time of an arrest for a JO offense, present special problems. When these children were placed under the authority of the adult court, I doubt whether legislators fully considered that the systems that affect the lives of these adolescents as they come in contact with criminal justice are extraordinarily complex and confusing even to those working in the courts and related social service programs. The system of serving this population represents a "maze of endless proportions."[21] As many as 12 different agencies can be involved in serving these adolescents including the Department of Juvenile Justice, the Administration for Children's Services and foster care agencies, Family Court, Criminal Court, mental health and substance abuse providers, the District Attorney's office, the Department of Probation, the Legal Aid Society, the Department of Correction, the Office of Family and Children Services, and the Department of Education.

In addition, the task of coordinating these agencies to provide an offender with necessary services is even more complicated when a juvenile is arrested and faces the consequences of prosecution in adult court. New York's Family Court Act specifically acknowledges the role of juvenile court judges in coordinating services on behalf of delinquents.[22] Section 255 of that Act imposes a duty on agencies providing services to children to cooperate with the court under the threat of contempt and, more significantly, gives the court the power to order cooperation, provided the agency is fiscally and structurally able to do so. The legislature, in enacting this provision recognized that from arrest to disposition the Family Court was dependent on the cooperation and assistance of other municipal agencies and private social agencies to accomplish its goals. This statutory authority is an impressive tool that enables the court to overcome lack of interagency coordination that often inhibits the provision of varied essential services for families and children. Remarkably, New York's adult court judges have no similar statutory authority.

Consequently, juvenile offenders are denied a broad array of resources that are available only through the Family Court. Judges having the responsibility of sentencing juvenile offenders are faced with two choices, neither of which may be totally satisfactory: mandatory imprisonment or Department of Probation supervision through a YO adjudication. Juveniles also present special issues for adult probation officers such as ineligibility for employment and inability to make decisions independent of their families on whom they have had to depend for financial support. As a result, probation is often an ineffectual option, given the lack of additional probation resources for special treatment of juveniles.[23]

Perhaps to the original supporters of the JO legislation, the idea of returning children to the jurisdiction of the criminal court seemed a convenient and uncomplicated way of dealing with complex issues of adolescence, failing families, failing schools, failing community standards of morality, and the perceived failures of the juvenile court. Ironically, they sought refuge in an archaic idea that did not distinguish between child and adult. If the goal of the legislature in enacting the JO Law was to identify, prosecute and punish dangerous juveniles for longer periods, the methodology selected for achieving this purpose was flawed. It was based on an assumption that youth involved in a serious offense also would likely be or become chronic offenders. However, "[m]any developmental theorists locate anti-social behavior as part of a normative developmental pattern that desists over time as adolescents enter adult developmental stages... Most juvenile offenders stop their pattern of offending, including most who engage in violence, during adolescence."[24]

The New York Penal Law defines serious offenses in the broadest way so as to encompass the multiple behaviors that can fall within the definition of a crime. Because the doctrine of accomplice liability plays a significant role in juvenile criminal responsibility, given the group context of most juvenile crimes, the law extended far beyond its intended purpose to target and identify the most dangerous and violent juvenile offenders. It also applied to many young offenders who could not fairly be classified in such a way. The legislature should have concentrated on both serious offenses and chronic offenders. The best way to accomplish that would have been through a hearing wherein a judge could discover and explore a defendant's background and prior delinquency record before determining whether to transfer a juvenile to adult court. As a result, the JO law swept many first-time offenders into the adult system, youth who were minimally or peripherally involved in a JO crime, as well as many youth who could benefit from the social service orientation of the juvenile court.

In 1984, six years after the enactment of New York's Juvenile Offender Law, the Citizen's Committee for Children conducted a study of the law's efficacy. In its report, the Committee concluded that the law was an experiment that failed: "Perhaps image, not actuality, is the point of it all. Perhaps the publicly announced legislative intransigence at the time of the law's passage was to be a warning to the young, with deterring consequences. It can only be said that nothing in our direct experience with the system, nor our interviews with juvenile offenders, nor any trend data support the view that the law has been an effective deterrent to youthful misconduct."[25]

The Citizen's Committee for Children was founded in 1945 by Eleanor Roosevelt and several other prominent New Yorkers who were interested in the welfare of children. It is an important voice for New York City's children and serves as an active guardian watching over systems such as child welfare, day care, education, mental and physical health, and juvenile justice.[26] At the time of the report, the Committee's membership stood at almost 200 and was composed of former mayors, judges, lawyers, educators, pediatricians, psychiatrists, psychologists, social workers, and business executives. As a watchdog for children, the Committee followed the course of the Juvenile Offender Law over the first five years of operation, especially in New York City where 88% of the arrests occurred during that period.[27] In preparing its report, the Committee had access to the files of New York State's Division of Criminal Justice Services (DCJS), the agency responsible for compiling data on juvenile offenders. These files covered the period from September 1, 1978, to January 1, 1983. The files contained information on each of 5,582 juvenile offender arrests that occurred in New York City during that period. The Citizen's Committee's second major source of information was the New York State Division for Youth (DFY), presently the Office of Children and Family Services, (OCFS), the agency which operates the secure facilities where children sentenced pursuant to the JO law are imprisoned.[28] To mark the complexities of the law and its implementation, volunteers were placed as observers at every step in the legal process. Hundreds of records were examined. Thousands of statistics were analyzed and dozens of people involved in the law's operation were interviewed. From that investigation, the Committee found that "the Juvenile Offender Law is punitive in intent, complicated, cumbersome, expensive and failing even on its own terms."[29]

The Committee recommended repeal of the Juvenile Offender Law and return of original jurisdiction over minors to the Juvenile Court along with an expansion of Juvenile Court sentencing authority. In 1983, shortly before the Citizen's Committee's report, the Association of the Bar of the City of New York also reviewed the impact of the Juvenile Offender law.[30] The Juvenile Justice Committee of the Association similarly concluded that the Juvenile Offender Law should be repealed and replaced with legislation providing Family Court judges with the authority to transfer certain juveniles to the adult court. Despite the criticism of the law by both the Citizen's Committee and the Association of The Bar of The City of New York, the law continued to have the support of successive governors and legislatures. As recently as 1998, it was amended to add two offenses to the original list of juvenile offender crimes, and in 2004 the legislature increased penalties for certain forms of murder.[31]

Virtually all laws that permit the prosecution of juveniles in adult court without a due process hearing concerning a child's fitness, competence, and capacity to be rehabilitated are subject to the same flaws as New York's Juvenile Offender Law. Transfer legislation rarely delivers the ancillary resources necessary to deal effectively with children tried in adult court such as mental health, education or employment counseling, or supplemental specialized probation services. State adult court systems are expected to make do with already limited existing resources.

Characteristically, laws that require automatic prosecution of youth in adult courts do not adequately address juveniles who exhibit mental health issues. In New York, these are some of the most difficult cases to handle. In 2001, it was reported that nearly 11,000 adolescents between the ages of 13 and 17 were arrested in New York City.[32] Data from New York's Legal Aid Society estimates that 20% of these adolescents are emotionally disturbed with cooccurring substance abuse disorders.[33] Gaining access to mental health services presents great difficulty for JOs either held in detention or, on conviction, committed to OFCS.

In this regard, consider the case of 14-year-old Louis, who was convicted before me of forcibly anally sodomizing his 11-year-old male neighbor in a staircase on the ground floor of the building in which they lived. Louis was sentenced to an indeterminate sentence that extended beyond his 16th birthday. Shortly after he turned 16, the Office of Children and Family Services filed a motion before me pursuant to the Executive Law to transfer Louis to an adult institution since he was not responding to psychiatric services. When questioned as to the nature of those services, the lawyers for the Office of Children and Family Services said he simply would not participate in their regularly scheduled group therapy sessions. I was astounded. How could that 14-year-old boy be expected to share his behavior with other teenagers in a group setting? When I made that point, the response was, "That's all we have. There is no psychiatrist permanently assigned to the institution." Group therapy was all that was available. In a 1995 report issued by the State Commission of Correction, which evaluated the secure centers operated by the

Office of Children and Family Services, it was observed that "counseling as a means of addressing the social and emotional problems of juvenile offenders was hindered by its excessive informality, poor record keeping and information exchange, a lack of fundamental counseling, competency, and the limited presence and support of central office management."[34] The Commission concluded that mental health services in most of the secure facilities was inadequate.[35]

Some time in September 1999, I received a letter from the mother of a youth I had sentenced. She eloquently and poignantly put into perspective the inadequacies of the Juvenile Offender Law in dealing with the special mental health needs of children. Her son Peter, who was 15 years old at the time he appeared in my court, was convicted after a jury trial of assault in the first degree for slashing the face of another teenager with a razor, causing the victim to receive over 150 stitches and leaving a scar that extended from his ear to his chin. The evidence revealed that the defendant committed this act because he believed that the boy had "disrespected" him.

"Dear Judge Corriero," his mother wrote, "I'm writing this letter to let you know how my son Peter is doing. He was convicted in your courtroom. Your Honor, this letter has been written in my mind for a very long time and I feel only obligated finally to putting it on paper. Sir, if you look through your records you will recall my son's case. He was arrested and convicted of assault in the first degree and you sentenced him to two to six years. At his sentencing I wrote you a letter asking your help. I explained that my son suffered from depression and he needed help, not jail. However, he was placed in a juvenile jail facility and his mental health was never an issue or addressed. Here we are, almost five years later, and my son is in a mental hospital and diagnosed with paranoid schizophrenia. Sir, he is in a mental hospital because he damaged my car and I had him arrested in hopes of getting him treatment which is exactly what happened. Two doctors had to sign the appropriate papers to have him committed for at least three months.

"Your Honor, my son will always be a burden to society for the rest of his life. I felt that if his illness was addressed at the time that he was in your courtroom and dealt with then he would have been diagnosed and forced to undergo treatment and medication. As it stands now, he is only in therapy and he is refusing medication. That is why he will be a burden on society. He will never get better, only worse. He will have relapses that will land him in jail first then the mental hospital.

"I wish that you would have understood the severity of his illness and his family's pleas for help. I wish that you would have had the time and opportunity to seek and read his school and medical records instead of thinking he was a hard-core criminal and that he needed to be put in jail instead of a mental institution. If after treatment, then he could have finished his imposed sentence in the correction facility of your choice. Sir, we weren't asking for the easy way out, just a chance for my son to get help. That was all. We weren't trying to "get over" on you or the system. For the rest of Peter's life he will be in torment and agony. He hears voices and at times hears his dead father talking to him. You cannot imagine the pain his family is going through and will be going through for the rest of his life, however long or short that is. If only you gave him a chance for treatment at the age of 15 then maybe he would have had a chance in life but now I guess we'll never know.

"Your Honor, I am just a mother, Peter's mother, and I'm begging you to please take into consideration my son's circumstances and hopefully the next time a young man or lady comes before you and it is pointed out to you that the juvenile may be suffering from a mental illness, please, please give them the opportunity of getting a mental health evaluation from a mental health professional before having them locked up. Jail is only a band-aid and they will not get the treatment they need there even if you order it. Sincerely, [Peter's mother.]"

How can I explain to that suffering mother that I did not have the statutory authority or discretion to sentence him to a mental health facility? Even if such authority existed, there simply were no secure mental health institutions for juvenile offenders like Peter in New York. Although I did prefer a mental health option for her son, a civil commitment would have required a dismissal of the charges or a lengthy postponement of the proceedings or a sentence of probation through the granting of Youthful Offender treatment, options that simply were not appropriate because of the circumstances of his case. The JO Law does not permit nor contemplate the "placement" of emotionally disturbed adolescents like Peter into residential treatment programs as an authorized sentence option. The "treatment" of choice is imprisonment. Unfortunately, as in Peter's case, a convicted adolescent can not only be an offender but often a victim as well as a result of being institutionalized without adequate care for extended periods of time.

Peter's case illustrates the frustration of working within a law that severely restricts discretion and opportunities to deal constructively with issues presented by young offenders a number of whom are more mentally ill perhaps than delinquent, yet delinquent enough to be dangerous. Had Peter's case been processed initially in New York's Family Court, however, he could have been remanded to a City psychiatric hospital or other diagnostic center for examination before or during a dispositional hearing. For youth subject to the jurisdiction of the Family Court who are changed with virtually the same crimes that qualify a juvenile for prosecution in the adult court, the juvenile court after a finding of guilt is required to order: "… a probation investigation and a diagnostic assessment. The probation investigation shall include but not be limited to the history of the juvenile, including previous conduct, the family situation, any previous psychological and psychiatric reports, school adjustment, previous social assistance provided by voluntary or public agencies and the response of the juvenile to such assistance. The diagnostic assessment shall include but not be limited to psychological tests and psychiatric interviews to determine mental capacity and achievement, emotional stability and mental disability. It shall include a clinical assessment of the situational facts that may have contributed to the act or acts; when feasible, expert opinion shall be rendered as to the risk presented by the juvenile to others or himself with a recommendation as to the need for a restrictive placement."[36] A Family Court diagnostic assessment may be conducted on an inpatient or outpatient basis. When found to be mentally ill, these youth are placed in civil hospitals and, if necessary, transferred to a state civil hospital for treatment, as opposed to imprisonment.

The nation has a significant interest in rehabilitating children not only for the sake of the individual child but also out of concern for public safety. However, the juvenile justice reforms of the latter part of the 20th century have been enacted with little empirical evidence of their effectiveness. Indeed, the "weight of empirical evidence strongly suggests that there are no general deterrent effects of increasing the scope of transfer on the incidents generally of serious juvenile crime."[37] Yet, despite this evidence, policy makers continue to support initiatives that facilitate the transfer of more juveniles into adult court, even though evidence suggests that such a policy is counterproductive and actually poses more of a threat to society than trying such children in juvenile court.

Columbia University professor Jeffrey Fagan astutely assesses this effect in his aptly titled article, "This Will Hurt Me More Than It Hurts You: Social and Legal Consequences of Criminalizing Delinquency."[38] He analyzes the effects of statutes that transfer juvenile offenders to adult court, concluding that "the policy goal of increasing punishment for adolescent offenders through transfer to the adult courts has generally been achieved. However, utilitarian goals for reducing juvenile crime rates have not been achieved."[39] Professor Fagan reviews several major studies analyzing the impact of these laws and makes the point that, rather than deter crime, transfer laws have the opposite effect. By punishing juveniles through extended incarceration, we are creating more violent criminals. He begins his thesis with the proposition that studies have demonstrated that most adolescents are unlikely to sustain juvenile crime beyond their teenage years, given opportunities for change via natural maturation or through the benefits of effective intervention programs. The impact of extended incarceration on adolescents through the process of transfer to adult court, which is generally accompanied by a potential increase in penalties, actually produces more crime. This is so, he contends, because incarceration interferes at a critical point in a child's normal developmental transition from adolescence to adulthood. It leads to the acclimation of a violent lifestyle, which reflects the culture of prison life and it culminates in long-term economic disenfranchisement through the stigma of felonization. Professor Fagan

asserts that "whatever the symbolic gains from sentencing adolescents as adults, these gains are discounted if not reversed by the
increased public safety risks of substantial punishment of juveniles
as adults."[40]

In sum, laws that provide for the automatic prosecution of juveniles in adult court fail because they are too broad in application,
encompassing many whose needs could be better met consistent with
public safety within the juvenile court—for example, children with
no significant prior delinquency record or who are on the periphery
of offenses and whose level of culpability rests solely on the law of
accomplice liability. For those children who are dangerous, these
laws also fail because they do not provide adequate sentencing flexibility or sufficient rehabilitative services while incarcerated.

The image of the juvenile delinquent has come a long way from
the Bowery Boys to the Bloods. However, we still have a responsibility to make an effort to separate and identify those children who are
brought into the adult system because of their peripheral or minor
involvement in serious crimes and those who may be more involved
but whose background and lack of significant prior delinquency indicate a reasonable likelihood of success in an alternative sentencing
program. The best way that we can do this is by consistent application of the Kent principles in a judicial due process hearing for every
child accused of a serious crime. Such a hearing should precede each
prosecution of a juvenile in adult court. Until the policy of trying
children as adults can be altered, I suggest that Youth Parts be established in all jurisdictions. A Youth Part can attempt to address the special needs of juveniles in a setting where a juvenile can be isolated
from adults and the limited resources of adult courts focused on
youths most likely to benefit from counseling.

CHAPTER 9

Creation of the Youth Part

*For every child let truth spring from earth and justice
and mercy look down from heaven.*
—Inscription on cornerstone of
New York's first Children's Court[1]

T HE ESTABLISHMENT of Manhattan's Youth Part was as much
a political process as it was a legal one. Policy makers within
the executive and judicial branches, as well as within the legal
community, had to be persuaded of its value. The idea of a special
court for youth tried in adult courts was not novel. Special courts for
young offenders above the age limit for juvenile court jurisdiction
were established as early as 1914 in Chicago and 1915 in Philadelphia.[2] In New York, the Wayward Minors Act of 1923 provided for
special treatment for offenders between the ages of 16 and 21. Pursuant to this act, adolescent courts were established in New York
City in 1935.[3] In 1943 Governor Thomas E. Dewey signed into law
comprehensive legislation providing for the separate and distinct
treatment of young offenders.[4]

This "Youthful Offender" legislation was designed to protect
youths ages 16 through 18 from the stigma of a criminal conviction
and it authorized sentencing alternatives not available to adult offenders.[5] The legislation specifically provided that proceedings involving
young offenders were to be held in special parts of the court: "All of
the proceedings and segregation had under the provisions of this title

may be private and shall be conducted in such parts of the court or judges' chambers as shall be separate and apart from the other parts of the court which are then being held for proceedings pertaining to adults charged with crimes."[6] As a result of that mandate, "youth parts" were established in the Courts of Special and General Sessions in New York City for processing cases of youths between 16 and 18 years of age.[7] The conventional wisdom of the time was that the court, with the aid of investigative resources, could identify and segregate a youth capable of reform from an incorrigible one. It was accepted as a sociological precept that adolescents had the capacity to change their behavior and that the court could develop a sentencing program that would serve not only to punish but also to rehabilitate.

In 1971, the original YO legislation was repealed and replaced by provisions that form the basis of New York's current YO law. The revisions to the YO law were designed to correct certain constitutional issues and to implement cost saving measures. The new legislation, unlike the original Youthful Offender statute, did not specifically provide for the procedural separation of youth. Nevertheless, despite this omission, the courts of criminal jurisdiction, pursuant to local court rules then in existence, continued to provide for separate Youth Parts.[8]

The enactment of the original YO legislation reflected the popular belief of the post–World War II era that various branches of government could effectively solve society's problems and that those adolescents who engaged in antisocial or criminal behavior could be rehabilitated. The best way of accomplishing this goal was believed to be through the establishment of separate court parts, where resources could be concentrated and youths would be insulated from more seasoned adult offenders. The procedural segregation of youths from adults was also believed to facilitate the identification of those most likely to benefit from the ameliorative provisions of the new YO Law, as it became known.

In the 1970s, however, government in general, and the courts in particular, lost a great deal of the public's confidence in its capacity to treat social ills. This pessimism was manifested in the public's hardening attitude toward young offenders and an increased demand for more severe treatment of all criminal offenders regardless of age.

The pendulum swung from the dominant rehabilitative goal of the 1940s, 1950s, and 1960s to a cry for "just desserts" for all criminal offenders. Many believed that the ameliorative treatment of adolescent offenders had outlived its usefulness; that the reason for the significant increase in youth crime was in large measure as a result of the "leniency" of the juvenile and criminal courts. Some commentators even questioned the continuing validity of the rehabilitative goal itself.[9] In 1978, the legislature, sensitive to the public outcry against juvenile crime as portrayed in the media, enacted the Juvenile Offender Law.[10] The Juvenile Offender Law, like the 1971 YO legislation, did not include any provision directing that proceedings involving juvenile offenders be conducted in separate parts. As a result, children as young as 13 were prosecuted in adult court along with other defendants regardless of age or charge.

Coinciding with the enactment of the Juvenile Offender Law came a shift in court administrative policy away from so-called specialized criminal parts to "all-purpose" parts. In the 1970s, consolidation of specialized courts into general all-purpose courts became the principal vehicle for court reform. It was believed that random assignment of cases among judges enabled the efficient monitoring of the progress of cases and insured the impartiality of individual judges. Thus began the gradual demise of separate youth parts maintained in New York's courts since 1943.

On January 6, 1986, with the promulgation of the Uniform Rules of the Courts of Criminal Jurisdiction, all preexisting court rules were rescinded, including those providing for separate Youth Parts.[11] The Uniform Rules did not specifically provide for the establishment of youth parts. The Chief Administrator of the courts was given authority under the Uniform Rules to establish whatever parts he or she deemed necessary to meet the goals of the court. Consequently, the existence of youth parts became a matter of discretion resting with the Chief Administrator.

By 1990, there were no special youth parts in the felony trial courts of New York City. In that year I wrote an article entitled "Youth Parts: A Constructive Response to the Challenge of Youth Crime."[12] The article traced the history of New York's special treatment of young offenders, describing the operation of the special Youth Parts that existed in the adult courts from 1942 to the early 1980s. I argued that the reestablishment of these special parts was even more crucial than before, as the jurisdiction of the adult criminal courts was expanded to include children as young as 13. I suggested that there were several advantages that could be realized in establishing such a Part: uniform treatment of teenage defendants; the concentration and integration of court and private agencies dealing with youths; a greater diversion of teenage offenders to private agencies for supervision and counseling, thereby supplementing an already overworked and overburdened Probation Department.

Shortly after its publication, Rose Washington, the New York City Commissioner of Juvenile Justice in the early 1990s, and her counsel, Kay Murray, expressed interest and support for the proposal of a separate youth part. As co-chair of the Committee on Criminal Justice Operations of the New York County Lawyers Association, I proposed that the Committee convene a forum on the topic of youth parts. The Committee agreed. The forum was held on October 10, 1991. I asked my Administrative Judge Peter J. McQuillan to join me as the forum's co-chair. The Committees on Juvenile Justice and Criminal Justice Operations of the Association of the Bar of the City of New York agreed to cosponsor the forum. It was attended by members of the judiciary, the legislature, lawyers, children's advocates, probation officials, and members of the alternative-to-incarceration program community. The question presented to the audience was: "At present, there are no separately maintained parts for juvenile or youthful offenders in the Criminal or Supreme Courts of New York City. Could separate 'Youth Parts' be a constructive response to the challenge of youth crime?"

Rose Washington agreed to be the keynote speaker at the forum. After pointing out several difficulties that the Department of Juvenile Justice encountered by not having a special part dedicated to handling juvenile offender cases, she stated, "I believe the development of a Youth Part might assist in a reduction of the length of stay in detention. As a result: one, we could use the money saved in a way which promotes more effective transition back to the community; two, it would focus the court's attention on the youth, providing an opportunity for the judges assigned to the cases, prosecutors and lawyers to get smarter concerning the law; three, it would provide an opportunity for the court to consider the alternative sentencing choices already existing... I urge that we at least begin a dialogue concerning the merits."[13]

Many of the lawyers and others attending the forum were familiar with the old youth parts, which were known as "Part 3." As defense lawyers, prosecutors and program representatives, they remembered the youth parts as places where they could get a child back on track. Part 3 was a place where they had an opportunity to use all of their skills and best efforts to advantage, working with kids who still had a chance. The response of those attending the forum was positive for the most part. The committees of both bar associations sponsoring the event passed resolutions in support of the reestablishment of a single part in both the Criminal and Supreme Courts designated for the processing of cases involving youths under 19 years of age. Judge McQuillan offered to establish a "Youth Part" in Manhattan Supreme Court subject to approval of the proposal by the Chief Administrator of the New York State Courts. Judge McQuillan's support was critical. He, too, was a former assistant district attorney in Frank Hogan's office and was familiar with the operation of such parts. He once stated: "I tried to simplify it (the JO law) for the judges and ended up writing a 30 page memo."[14]

Thereafter, with the assistance and support of Commissioner Washington and Kay Murray, several meetings were arranged with members of the Mayor's office, the New York County District Attorney's office, the Legal Aid Society, the Department of Juvenile Justice, the Probation Department, and the private bar. At these meetings, several concerns about the project were raised. Prosecutors were concerned that the Youth Part might simply be a device for treating offenders more leniently than they deserved. The Legal Aid Society, who represented most of the young offenders prosecuted in New York City courts, also had reservations. They believed that once attention was focused on these youthful offenders they might be subject to more restrictive sentences than they would otherwise have received. As the system functioned at that time, young offenders were randomly assigned among the judges of the Criminal Term, where they often appeared more vulnerable and sympathetic to judges whose calendars were composed primarily of adult cases. Moreover, the Legal Aid Society made it clear that their primary objective in representing juveniles in adult court was not social rehabilitation but legal defense. The Society needed to be assured that their lawyers would receive an opportunity to be heard fairly and fully. There was also opposition in the judiciary. At least one judicial administrator was critical of the proposal, expressing concern that a single judge presiding over the cases of an entire category of offender might affect the impartiality of the court. Moreover, creating a specialized part went against the predominant trend in court reform, which favored all-purpose Parts over specialization.

In 1992 David Dinkins was Mayor of New York City. He had appointed Fritz W. Alexander, a former judge of New York's Court of Appeals, as his Deputy Mayor for Criminal Justice. Rose Washington was able to persuade Judge Alexander of the merits of our proposal. In a letter to Matthew Crosson, the Chief Administrator of the courts, Martin Murphy, who was then on the staff of the Deputy Mayor for Criminal Justice, outlined several benefits that the City believed it could derive from the proposal: "As was discussed during our meeting with you, there are several benefits to reestablishing youth parts. Due in part to a more uniform treatment of teenage defendants, we anticipate a reduction in J.O. case processing time which has considerably increased in the past two years. The concentration of court personnel in parts specifically designated for juvenile and youthful offenders would result in these personnel becoming increasingly expert in handling such cases eliminating the errors in convictions [sic], sentencing and commitments that are currently experienced. These personnel would also be more familiar with treatment programs such as resident and nonresident rehabilitation regimens, employment training, drug treatment services and an array of other programs in public and private agencies available to the youthful offender. The net result would be a considerable reduction in the number of repeated adjournments and in the length of stay in detention."[15]

The Chief Administrator accepted Judge McQuillan's offer to establish a Youth Part in Manhattan Supreme Court. The support of the Mayor's office was instrumental in assuaging the concerns of the prosecutors, the defense bar, and ultimately the judicial administrators. Despite reservations, the prosecutors and defense attorneys were willing to cooperate with the project on an experimental basis.

Because I had campaigned for the return of the Part, Judge McQuillan asked me to be the presiding judge. On September 15, 1992, the Manhattan Youth Part began operation. No additional funding or resources were required to commence the functioning of the part. The courtroom over which I was then presiding was simply renamed the Youth Part or JO Part. Pursuant to a memorandum to the court clerks from Judge McQuillan, after arraignment on an indictment, all cases of children prosecuted as juvenile offenders were to be transferred to the Youth Part where the case would be adjudicated through sentence. The transfer of juvenile offender cases would include the transfer of all codefendants whether or not they were charged as juvenile offenders.

In order to fulfill the mission of the part and to coordinate treatment and disposition of juvenile offenders, I proposed that a Youth Part Advisory Board be established to give all of the agencies dealing with children prosecuted in adult courts a voice in the process. Ellen Schall,[16] a former Commissioner of the Department of Juvenile Justice with an excellent reputation in city government as a tough and independent administrator, agreed to chair the board. Representatives of the District Attorney's office, Legal Aid Society, Probation Department, Department of Juvenile Justice, Family Courts, child advocates, and representatives of alternative-to-incarceration programs were invited to participate. Regular monthly meetings were scheduled at which I presented periodic reports on the processing of cases, inviting suggestions for improvement and discussion of problem areas.[17] The Board proved to be a useful vehicle to facilitate discussion and coordination of various interests concerned with the operation of the part. One year following the inception of New York County's Youth Part, the counties of Kings, Queens, and the Bronx established similar Youth Parts.

During the administration of Mayor Dinkins, the City had invested significant resources in the development of "adult" alternatives to detention and incarceration pursuant to New York State's Classification Alternatives Act, which provided counties with financial incentives to develop programs and policies that reduced incarceration in "adult" facilities.[18] In December 1992, the Annie E. Casey Foundation launched a project known as the Juvenile Detention Alternatives Initiative (JDAI) to reduce the number of juveniles held in detention facilities pending trial and disposition when viable community-based supervisory options were available or could be developed.[19] New York City was selected as one of five sites to be awarded an initial planning grant and free technical assistance to develop a plan that would reduce the number of juveniles unnecessarily held in detention centers, including those prosecuted in adult courts. On completion of a suitable plan, the Foundation was prepared to award the City implementation grants of $750,000 per year for three years.

The Annie E. Casey Foundation Project required the City to bring together key participants in the juvenile justice system, including judges, policy makers, and advocates, to examine the ways in which detention was being utilized and to determine whether the current system could be improved to reduce reliance on secure confinement without compromising public safety. In February 1993, the Mayor's office created a task force chaired by Catherine McDonald, the Administrative Judge of the Family Court of the City of New York, to assist in the planning of the project. I was invited to participate as a member.[20]

The first step in the project was to develop a consensus among key policy makers to limit utilization of detention to its authorized purposes of assuring appearances in court and protecting the community through the prevention of delinquent acts during case processing. A key part of the JDAI project was to develop methods to substitute community-based alternatives in place of confinement in detention centers. The Youth Part was viewed as addressing this precise problem with some success and the concept of the Part was to be incorporated into the project.

The task force was unable to ultimately forge a consensus on a proposal that was acceptable to the Casey Foundation. During the planning period there was a change in City administration, a new mayor was elected and ultimately the City lost the opportunity to implement over $2 million in Casey grants to develop alternatives to juvenile detention.[21] The decision to discontinue the project had no immediate impact on the Youth Part. However, it highlighted the need for continued efforts at collaboration and involvement in the work of agencies addressing juvenile justice issues.

The proceedings of the Youth Part, because they take place in the adult court, are open to the public and therefore members of the press are free to observe and report on the sessions of the court. Since its inception, the Youth Part has attracted the attention of journalists who have visited the part to observe its proceedings and investigate its approach to juvenile crime. Approximately nine months after we began work in the Youth Part, Jan Hoffman, a reporter for the *New York Times,* spent several days in the part and set forth her observations in an article entitled "Punishing Youths without Throwing Away the Key."[22] The article was the first of many such articles published by New York City's newspapers.[23] In general, the reporting has been favorable. I point this out to emphasize the importance of the media, whose appraisal, if favorable, can generate understanding, interest, and support for the goals of a project. The Youth Part continues to function presently without any special funding, yet it has become the catalyst for many projects involving at-risk children. The jurisprudential basis for the part has proven to be more than merely pragmatic. The court has served as a model for the mobilization and coordination of treatment and social services for children prosecuted in adult courts.

CHAPTER 10

The Youth Part Model

It is the duty of a... man to teach others the good
which, because of the malignity of the times and of
fortune you could not achieve so that when some are
capable of it, one of them more loved by heaven may
be able to achieve it.

—MACHIAVELLI[1]

THE NEED FOR YOUTH PARTS in jurisdictions that prosecute children as adults is evident when we recognize the significant growth in the number of juveniles subject to the jurisdiction of adult courts. "Between 1992 and 1999, all but six states expanded their statutory provisions for transferring juveniles to criminal court, making it easier for more juveniles to be transferred. For example, states have added statutory exclusions, expanded the list of offenses eligible for transfer, and/or lowered the minimum age at which a juvenile may be transferred under one or more mechanisms."[2] The National Center for Juvenile Justice estimated that "in 1996 as many as 218,000 offenders younger than age 18 could have faced trial in criminal courts because State legislatures had set the age of adult criminal responsibility at 16 or 17. In comparison, juvenile court judges waived just 10,000 cases to criminal courts in 1996..."[3]

Once in adult court, regardless of the method of transfer, juveniles are subject to common principles of adjudication. Sentencing options may differ from state to state, but most states have second-chance legislation that acts as a safety valve for youths tried in adult courts. Implementation of this legislation is hindered to the extent that court systems do not provide for special treatment of youths tried in adult courts. A community seeking to establish a Youth Part can begin the process by identifying those judges within their adult court system who appear to possess the qualities they believe would be most useful in presiding over such a court. Judges can play a critical role in setting the stage for the creation of a Youth Part by making the case that such a court can facilitate the identification of those youthful offenders with good potential for supervision in the community from those more dangerous who require incarceration. By hearing the cases of juveniles tried in the adult court in one Part before one judge, a court system would be able to concentrate the resources of probation departments, treatment programs, and other counseling agencies in a single entity resulting in a more uniform treatment of teenage defendants and increasing the system's ability to divert young offenders from costly incarceration into less costly private programs.

Perhaps the most compelling reason for the establishment of such courts is their capacity to reduce future recidivism rates. The aim of a Youth Part is to develop a community-based early intervention response to juvenile offending within the framework of an adult legal system. In recent years, many jurisdictions have developed "problem-solving" courts specifically designed to address particular social issues such as drug abuse, domestic violence, and mental illness.[4] I believe similar institutional involvement on behalf of children tried in adult courts is equally important. By dealing effectively with children when they first enter the system, addressing issues of substance abuse, anger, and emotional instability, we can reduce the future caseloads of these very courts, as many young offenders without appropriate intervention would grow up to be drug abusers, domestic abusers, and sufferers of mental illness.

A Youth Part also can be a catalyst for the creative interplay between the court and social agencies. It can provide an opportunity to craft collaborative approaches to issues of juvenile offending. For example, in 1996, in collaboration with Big Brothers Big Sisters (BBBS) of New York City, I began a project to link a big brother or big sister with suitable young offenders who completed service in an ATI program and were about to be placed on probation. The idea for this project took shape when in 1995 I was invited to become a Trustee of Big Brothers Big Sisters. Traditionally at each board meeting a "big" (mentor) and his or her "little" (mentee) were invited to share their experience. I saw firsthand the impact that a positive role model could have on the lives of needy children. This partnership between the courts and the community was not unusual. The Big Brother movement began in 1904 when the Clerk of New York's Children's Court, Ernest K. Colter, saw the need for a mentoring program after witnessing thousands of children charged with myriad offenses passing before that tribunal. He assembled a group of civic-minded members of the community and persuaded them to take responsibility for children prosecuted in the court.

> [Colter] spoke of the thousands of boys each of whom needed a friend and who could be saved to useful citizenship by being made to feel that there was someone who really cared whether he got on or not and was willing to give him friendly help and advice.[5]

When the Youth Part was established, I believed that the Probation Department would need assistance in providing adequate supervision of young offenders especially as the Juvenile Offender law did not provide any additional funding or resources for the Department to handle this new category of offender who would now be under their supervision. Probation is not the mentoring program it once was. Because of its growth from the mere "whisper" of an idea in the early 20th century to the most frequently used sentence in New York's criminal justice system,[6] the stress on the probation system and its mentoring capacity has caused it to become more of a law enforcement rather than a human development agency. The shift in focus was understandable, considering the large number of defendants placed on probation during the course of a year. The mentoring aspect of probation, however, is especially important in juvenile cases because the overwhelming majority of young offenders come from single parent households. Rarely do we see intact families and even more rarely a father. The lack of a positive role model in the lives of many of these children contributes to their delinquency. Thus, linking an at-risk child with an adult mentor succeeding in the community could influence their lives and be a significant deterrent to recidivism.

Another initiative arising out of the centralization of court resources in the Youth Part focused on the improvement of legal representation of juvenile offenders prosecuted in adult court. In 1996, New York's Legal Aid Society created a pilot project to provide enhanced representation to juvenile offenders. "Project Turning Point" utilizes a team approach, integrating legal representation with forensic and therapeutic social work services. The goal of the project was to work in conjunction with the Youth Part and other courts trying juveniles to provide a credible alternative to incarceration. The project uses a team approach integrating legal representation with forensic and therapeutic social work services. A forensic social worker identifies each youth's needs by collecting social histories, school, foster care, and mental health records. The information is incorporated into reports submitted to the court which advocate for placement in appropriate community-based or therapeutic residential programs.

These are but two examples of how a youth part can serve as a stimulus for the creation of child-centered projects within the legal community.

State court systems differ from one another in organization, politics, customs, and legal culture. Although the particular events leading to the establishment of Manhattan's Youth Part were unique, the dynamics of the realization of an idea for such a specialized part are not: judicial leadership, collaborative partnerships, and support of key policy makers. Manhattan's Youth Part was created as a result of an administrative judge's order providing for the reassignment of juvenile offender cases. Other states or court systems may take a different approach. What is important, however, is that an adult court system provide a Part, an apparatus in which youths can be isolated and on the basis of available knowledge those most likely to benefit from counseling identified. In the Youth Part, we initiated a process to help us make this determination: First, we gather information about a youth; second, we assess the youth's background; third, we develop a plan to test the willingness of a youth to modify his behavior.

The process begins with the youth's first appearance in the part. An assessment is made of the seriousness of the charge, the extent of a youth's involvement, prior delinquency history, and suitability for placement in a program. The Probation Department conducts a prepleading investigation to document the youth's social history. The court has become a focal point for youth counseling and alternative-to-incarceration programs. Because juvenile offenders are now located in one part, many programs send representatives to the courtroom daily to help identify potentially suitable youths.

The court schedules an informal in-chambers conference subsequent to receiving a prepleading report. The conference is designed to explore issues in a relaxed setting, rather than during a hectic calendar call. In addition to the prosecutor and defense counsel, program representatives, and, when appropriate, social workers are asked to attend. At times, victims are seen at a separate conference (with counsel's approval) so that the judge can explain dispositional alternatives and hear the victim's position. The majority of cases are resolved at this conference. Where a guilty plea is to be entered and the defendant's background and involvement in the crime permit the court to consider an alternative to incarceration, a plea is structured to permit the child to demonstrate his willingness to cooperate.

Essential tools in this process are:

1. the postponement of sentence after plea;
2. the conditional nature of the sentence in order to permit a youth to "earn" probation and youthful offender treatment (nonconformance may result in an indeterminate sentence, which can be longer than that originally recommended by the prosecutor, and a felony record); and
3. validation. In order to validate the child's progress, the court closely monitors performance in the program—weekly, by calls from staff to the child's counselor, and every three weeks, when the child must appear in the Youth Part for a formal report. These contacts provide the

court with timely information on the child and convey the
court's concern and interest in the child to the child. If
the court learns a youth has violated the terms of the
deferred sentence, the case is immediately advanced and
the problem is addressed.

We have structured the Youth Part process as a system of reward
and punishment in the sense of providing encouragement and support when appropriate, as well as timely instilling discipline and
requiring the assumption of responsibility for misbehavior when necessary. We do this chiefly through the device of deferring a youth's
sentence for a sufficient period to enable the court to monitor a
youth's performance in a treatment program. This permits a proportionate response by the court to any misbehavior during the monitoring process rather than presenting a youth with simply a one-shot
opportunity for a second chance.

Manhattan's Youth Part has functioned without any special funding, technology, or additional support staff. Recognizing that each
state court system has its own fiscal limitations, I want to emphasize
that establishing a youth part need not require any additional budg-
etary expenditure. Assuming, however, a state has the fiscal capacity
to expand its approach to the resolution of juvenile offender cases, a
state might consider the following proposals: a model Youth Part
could utilize a new class of court personnel that emerged with the
development of problem-solving courts; individuals with titles such
as "resource coordinator," "monitor," and "court liaison."[7]

Resource Coordinator

The fragmentation of public, private, and nonprofit institutions and
organizations dealing with children is well documented. Children
appearing in adult courts are often involved in the foster care system,
the welfare system, or the juvenile justice system. Failure to locate
and utilize appropriate treatment options often results in a child being
held in detention. One of the principal objectives of the Youth Part

is to identify suitable juveniles who can be channeled out of detention into alternative-to-incarceration programs. To facilitate the identification of suitable ATI programs and placement of appropriate juveniles, a Youth Part could benefit from the appointment of a resource coordinator who would have the responsibility of exploring, reviewing, and cataloging all public and private programs serving delinquent youth in a community as well as information regarding admission criteria and the area of expertise or regimen of each program. This would speed placement of a youth from detention into an appropriate treatment program and address the youth's long-range rehabilitation needs. A coordinator also could assist the court in monitoring a child's progress in a program.

Court Liaisons

Child welfare and education systems rarely coordinate services and treatment with the adult criminal justice system, thus a great deal of time is spent trying to navigate bureaucratic barriers to resolving problems. Court liaisons from those agencies could help expedite appropriate dispositions. For example, when a juvenile offender is released from detention while his case is pending, it is our practice to condition that release upon regular school attendance. If the court learns that a youth has cut classes or has unexcused absences, the youth is considered in breach of the terms of his release and may be remanded.

In addition, a large number of school-aged youth when arrested and incarcerated, even for a short period of time, have great difficulty reregistering in the school they were attending prior to arrest. The importance of this issue led the Center for Alternative Sentencing and Employment Services (CASES) in 2002 to collaborate with the New York City Department of Education and City and State criminal justice agencies to create the "School Connection Center" project.[8] The Center serves as a school admissions office and social service referral center for students released from custody. The Center is designed to expedite the return of previously incarcerated youth to the school system. The displacement caused by arrest and custody has profound consequences for the continued education of court-involved youth. Education departments, by providing a youth part with a professional skilled in the readmission process, as well as with computer technology linking the court with appropriate Board of Education data, could facilitate the transition of youth from custodial to community schools.

The Probation Department, the social services arm of the family and criminal courts, has a special mission regarding juvenile offenders. It plays a crucial role in the information gathering process and is the agency that ultimately bears much of the responsibility for rehabilitation of juveniles sentenced to probation. Thus, probation officers should have an effective and integral presence in a Youth Part.

Cross-Agency Computer Links

A formal information-sharing system integrating data from schools, social services agencies, and the juvenile court should be available to the Youth Part. Immediate access to a juvenile's school, welfare agency, and juvenile court records is imperative to assist the court in making determinations concerning the nature of a disposition, plea negotiations, and detention status.

A Youth Part with Comprehensive Jurisdiction over Juvenile Offenders *(Ab Initio)*

In New York, juvenile offenders enter the system through case processing in the lower criminal courts. On indictment, the case is transferred to the Superior (Supreme) Court for arraignment. It is only at that point that the juvenile enters the Youth Part process. It takes on average 40 days following entry into the criminal justice system for a case to first appear in the Youth Part. A single Youth Part authorized to handle cases from the initial court appearance through final disposition could integrate and coordinate court diagnostic facilities such as forensic, psychiatric, and probation services at the earliest opportunity.

Psychiatric Facilities for Juvenile Offenders

New York State does not maintain a single secure juvenile facility the primary goal of which is to address the mental health needs of youth convicted and sentenced pursuant to the Juvenile Offender law. A number of the children who appear in court present with significant mental health issues. Some of these juveniles pose a threat to the community and require incarceration. The court must have the option to place these children in secure facilities whose primary orientation is to provide psychiatric services.

A psychiatric clinic is available to provide the court with diagnostic services but not treatment. If the clinic concludes that a youth requires treatment in a nonincarceratory setting, it can only be obtained through private psychiatrists, psychologists or community hospital clinics at the offender's own expense. A mental health clinic under the supervision of the court should be established for both the diagnosis and treatment of youth who are determined to be in need of outpatient services. This would improve the court's ability to insure that a youth's mental health needs are addressed.

Appropriate Court and Detention Facilities

In perhaps no other courtroom in the criminal term are so many interested parties—family members, alternative-to-incarceration program counselors, social workers, psychologists, teachers, and lawyers—assembled at times on a single case. When a youth's case is scheduled to be heard in the Youth Part, it is our practice to encourage the appearance of a parent, family member, and any other responsible adult who has information concerning the young defendant's background. It also is especially important that a juvenile be able to consult with a supportive adult, in addition to his counsel, at the time a plea is taken or during the course of a trial, and that an adult view and understand the process. The courtroom housing the youth part should be of adequate dimension to permit private, secure interaction among a youth, his family, and counsel.

Equally important is the separate treatment and detention of children housed in adult criminal court buildings while waiting for their cases to be heard by a judge. Federal law as well as state correctional policy require that young offenders be segregated and held out of "sight and sound" of adult offenders.[9] Ideally, a youth part should be situated in the juvenile court building where the services of that court would be readily available.

Juveniles who are prosecuted in adult courthouses and who are detained pending disposition in a juvenile detention center are often held in areas designed for adults. In New York, juveniles who are detained pending disposition in a juvenile detention center, such as New York's Horizon or Crossroads, are driven to court by van, which delivers them to the adult courthouse. They are transported to a holding area under the supervision of adult correctional officers to await their appearance in the part. The holding area consists of prison cells that were constructed for adults. They are locked behind iron doors with iron bars and no private toilet facilities. Attached to the Youth Part courtroom should be a holding facility designed to provide adequate security for detained juveniles and yet recognizes and respects their age and vulnerability.

Legislation Providing for a Model Youth Part

Some states may prefer statutory recognition of a judge's role in the coordination and provision of services for young offenders prosecuted in adult courts. In 1999, a bill was introduced into the New York State Legislature that would have created new statewide court parts devoted exclusively to the adjudication of serious offenses committed by persons under the age of 16.[10] It provided for the merging of the adult and Family Court systems for the purpose of resolving juvenile offender cases in a new juvenile-criminal part. Judges presiding over this new "hybrid" part would have been authorized to try cases in either a criminal proceeding or a juvenile delinquency proceeding. More significantly, all court-assisted services and programs available in the juvenile court would be equally available to the judge presiding over this new juvenile-criminal part. The bill was referred to the State Assembly's Committee on Children and Families and did not receive full consideration by the Legislature. Nevertheless, this proposed legislation provides an example of how the Youth Part concept can become an integral and permanent component of an adult court system.

All states that allow criminal prosecution of juveniles in adult courts could benefit from the establishment of a youth part. I believe I have presented a model for the effective treatment of these children in an atmosphere that permits a fair adjudication of their cases. Creation of a Youth Part, which in so many ways stands at the crossroads for these children, would be a constructive response to juvenile crime.

CHAPTER 11

A Model Juvenile Justice System

What is needed is a judicial and social welfare system able to operate with the maximum flexibility to determine cause as accurately as it deals with effect and empowered to intervene appropriately.
—MAIRE GEGHEGAN-QUINN, FORMER MINISTER OF
JUSTICE OF IRELAND

I N THIS CHAPTER, I present my proposals for a model juvenile justice system, one that recognizes children as children, tries them as children, and sentences them as such. In describing my proposal as a model "juvenile justice system," I do so in a broad sense that encompasses not only the juvenile courts but also adult criminal courts that are prosecuting children as adults. The model I offer serves to identify more precisely dangerous, violent, and chronic juvenile offenders, but it is also one that permits appropriate judicial responsiveness to the developmental needs of young offenders, providing suitable offenders with the opportunity to earn a second chance within the framework of a procedural and substantive partnership between the juvenile and adult courts. I am proposing a change to the predominant existing structure and procedure of the juvenile and adult criminal courts with respect to juvenile offenders. My vision of an effective juvenile justice system is premised on an accurate portrayal of the characteristics of youth. Appreciating the true nature of adolescence will help us develop appropriate laws, policies, and practices so that we can judge children more fairly.

Thousands of children are annually transferred automatically without judicial review from juvenile court jurisdiction to adult criminal court.[1] And, because of their immaturity, they are disadvantaged at every stage of the adult court process, a disadvantage that, in my view, amounts to injustice. This view is supported by the conclusions of behavioral scientists that, instead of deterring crime, transfer laws actually seem to produce an increase in criminal activity, in comparison to the behavior of those children retained in the juvenile justice system.[2]

How did this happen? How did we, a nation based on the promise of a better future for our children, justify criminalizing children as young as 13, 14, and 15 years of age for their behavior? I suggest that the answer lies in the phenomenon of disassociation—that is, viewing children who violate the law as falling outside the circle of the community. Thus, it becomes easier to view them not as "our" children. In the 1990s, this phenomenon of disassociation was fueled by certain myths and misconceptions that received widespread notoriety. One popular myth was that in the 21st-century society would witness an invasion of juvenile delinquents who were "qualitatively" different from delinquents of the past, and that the institution of the juvenile court would not be able to adequately deal with these offenders. Before we can consider effective strategies in dealing with adolescent offenders, we must first address these assumptions.

In 1998, I reviewed *American Youth Violence,* a book written by Professor Franklin E. Zimring.[3] The work was the product of a study conducted by the John D. and Catherine T. MacArthur Foundation and consisted of a series of essays written to examine specific current issues concerning the juvenile justice system. Zimring's analysis of the juvenile justice reforms of the 1990s resonated with my own experience. His work provided scientific affirmation for what we were attempting to accomplish in the Youth Part. He assembled the factual, statistical, and analytic information that effectively exposed the flaws and misperceptions that led to our current youth policy.

The Myth of the "Coming Storm"

In the 1990s, certain pundits foretold of a "coming storm," a new breed of vicious and violent juvenile delinquents, qualitatively different from juveniles who committed crimes in the past. The scenario forecast by these commentators was that of an army of "270,000 juvenile super-predators coming at us in waves" starting in 2010.[4] This prediction generally was accepted without careful analysis by politicians, legislators, as well as the media. It was based on interpretations of youth population projections, which predicted that there would be an approximate 19% increase in the number of children in their mid-teen years by the year 2010.[5] The inferences drawn from this population growth, however, did not withstand sociologic scrutiny.

According to Professor Zimring, these predictions were based on an "extreme version of a deterministic view of the causes of juvenile violence [that] [gave] support to the notion that homicide rates 15 years in the future can be predicted for a group of children that were between two and four years old"[6] and that there exists "fixed relationships between population characteristics and rates of serious violence."[7] In analyzing these projections, he asserted that these conclusions were "irrational to the point of superstition"[8] and that no such generalization about the behavior of such a cohort of youths could be supported by empirical evidence.

The Viability of the Juvenile Court

Integrated into the flawed scenario of a coming "blood bath" attributable to a malevolent breed of juveniles was the widespread perception that lenient treatment by the juvenile justice system caused the higher rates of youth crime. Thus, the most common proposal for reform by policy makers who shared such a perception was the transfer of more children out of the juvenile court into the adult criminal court where they presumably would be subject to and receive more severe punishment.[9] After analyzing the nature of cases in the juvenile court, Zimring concluded that: "Trends in the rate and character of youthful violence in the United States provide no reason for a shift in the operating philosophy of the juvenile court and delinquency cases."[10] "If the consequences of transfer to Criminal Court are to be consistent and severe," he asserted, "only a very few cases of juvenile robbery or assault will demand transfer and discretionary decisions will be necessary to select the one in 100 or the one in 25 cases from the others."[11] Instead of eliminating the juvenile court as an institution for addressing juvenile violence, Zimring proposed that a coordinated effort be developed that could effectively harness both institutions to a common strategy. He concluded that the juvenile court remained a viable institution, but that it must be viewed in a modern context as a partner with the adult criminal court in serving the needs of both juveniles and society.

Instead of choosing between these two court systems, the juvenile court and the adult criminal court must be coordinated into a complementary system of justice. The model juvenile justice system that I propose would accomplish this in a framework that recognizes the vulnerability and malleability of adolescents, without compromising public safety.

The model has four objectives:

First, the development and implementation of a statutory strategy of prosecution that serves to identify more precisely dangerous, violent and chronic juvenile offenders;

Second, the development of "punishments" that are primarily intended to educate an offender;

Third, a system of prosecution and punishment of juveniles that is flexible enough to recognize and accommodate juveniles who have the capacity to change their behavior by participating in alternative-to-incarceration programs;

Fourth, the development of mechanisms to remove the stigma of a felony conviction from those juveniles who have demonstrated that they have conformed their behavior to society's standards after having been convicted and imprisoned.

Targeting Dangerous Juveniles

The most critical decision in our present scheme of prosecuting children in the adult court is the transfer decision. Most states historically relied on transfer hearings conducted by juvenile court judges in order to make that determination. As previously noted, the reforms of the 1990s increasingly placed authority for that decision in the legislature or prosecutorial authority. I believe that the juvenile court judicial waiver or transfer up process is the most effective way of targeting dangerous juveniles. It is more precise than broad legislative determinations as to categories of offenders subject to prosecution in the adult court, less one-sided than prosecutorial determinations, and it takes advantage of the expertise of juvenile court judges. It also takes into account the malleability of children, the flexibility and specialization of the juvenile court, and provides a forum for examining a juvenile's developmental challenges. It permits a suitable child to remain in the family court setting where more social services are available and, at the same time, permits the adult court to focus on violent juveniles. If it is ultimately determined that a child is dangerous or that the charges are so serious that to prosecute in the juvenile court would undermine confidence in the administration of justice, then we must provide for transfer to the adult court where appropriate confinement would be available. The adult court could then focus on children who are chronic delinquents or children whose acts are so brutal, wanton, or reckless that prosecution in the juvenile court would be inappropriate.

Thus, a model juvenile justice system would provide a framework for practically applying advances in understanding adolescent behavior within the context of a judicial transfer hearing. Issues of maturity, competence, culpability, and amenability to treatment would be explored in a due process setting where research, practice, and policy can be integrated into a strategy that utilizes the juvenile and criminal court to benefit both the child and the community. The ultimate goal is to assure that no child is tried in the adult court without a hearing.

Punishment (Confinement) as an Educational Response to Juvenile Offending

Although incarceration may be unavoidable for certain young offenders, it should not be viewed as an end in itself. The Council of the City of New York, in a report assessing the City's response to juvenile crime, pointedly articulated the purpose of punishment for juveniles:

> During the time the state maintains custody of juvenile offenders, it must help redirect their lives. Punitive sanctions forcefully convey society's message of reprobation but they must also be viewed as important opportunities to deliver intensive treatment strategies that aggressively attempt to ameliorate individual dysfunctions. Those who wish to appease their justifiable frustration by simply locking up [juvenile offenders] often overlook the fact that most violent adolescent offenders will be released from incarceration as young adults and return to the communities from which they came. Depending upon the quality and scope of services provided during their stay, some will emerge as hardened, callous individuals destined to recidivate and enter the adult criminal system, while others will return to their neighborhoods having received the guidance, skills, and treatment they need to turn their young lives around. To accomplish the latter will take greatly improved intensive juvenile correction services which emphasize reintegration into the community. Thus, sentencing of violent adolescent offenders can and must be multifaceted–at once punitive, incapacitative and rehabilitative. Every component of the juvenile justice system must reflect these integrated goals.[12]

Punishment in a model juvenile/criminal justice system should be designed to educate and socialize children by insuring that a young offender receives academic assistance and therapeutic treatment while incarcerated. Such a system not only benefits the child but also society. It will require, however, "the redirection of resources, rein-vestment in reintegration and a reorientation of correctional interven-tion to stress social skills, competencies and behavior necessary for a successful return to the neighborhood."[13]

Systemic Flexibility

The hallmark of a fair and just system of identifying and separating dangerous youths from corrigible youths is flexibility. If we accept that a child, because of his immaturity, should not be deemed as blameworthy as an adult, we must translate that belief into proper sanctions. Adolescent crime involves several dynamics that power-fully make the case for judicial discretion, unhampered by uniform restrictions. Peer pressure and group standing often underlie the motivation for a juvenile's complicity in criminal behavior. As a result, adolescent offending is characterized by large variations in levels of involvement and individual culpability. A system that recognizes these variations in blameworthiness would provide for appropriate judicial discretion and dispositional alternatives. If the juvenile court is not used as a screening device, leaving only the most severe cases of juvenile violence to the jurisdiction of the adult criminal court, then the traditional flexibility of the juvenile court must be extended to the adult court.

The conventional belief is that once the decision to prosecute a case in the adult criminal court has been made, either by legislative fiat or unilateral prosecutorial discretion, the important decisions about punishment have also been made. However, given the devel-opmental differences in children, as well as the wide variations of involvement, this belief is flawed. Once in the criminal court, flexi-bility in decision making and dispositional alternatives is just as impor-tant as it is in the juvenile court because of the indelible repercus-sions of an adult court conviction. In the Youth Part, we have attempted to develop strategies to integrate the juvenile court and the adult criminal court process. Thus, in the model I propose, Youth Parts would exist in all adult criminal courts.

The method of prosecution and punishment adopted by a community must be flexible enough to recognize and accommodate juveniles who have the capacity to change their behavior. We can improve a juvenile justice system's response to delinquent offenders by providing judges in both the juvenile and criminal courts with authority to impose graduated sanctions through a continuum of treatment alternatives that include immediate intervention, intermediate sanctions, community-based alternatives as well as incarceration. Laws that require offense-based sanctioning mandating minimum periods of incarceration based on what the offender has done, rather than on what he is willing and capable of doing, emphasize punishment and incapacitation over rehabilitation. Such legislation is inconsistent with a system that requires flexibility to accommodate the individuality and potential of juvenile offenders.

Decriminalization of Young Offenders

It is estimated that approximately 600,000 inmates are released each year back into the community with no skills, no place to live, and few family ties.[14] In an editorial, the *New York Times* made the point that by ignoring the large number of former imprisoned felons reentering society, we were "creating the next crime wave."[15] Policy makers are beginning to recognize the enormous costs in ignoring the consequences of criminalization of so large a number of Americans. In New York, for instance, there is gathering support to revise the mandatory imprisonment provisions of its drug laws. In his 2004 State of the Union address, President George W. Bush proposed a four-year $300 million prison reentry initiative. In doing so he said, "America is the land of [the] second chance and when the gates of prison open, the path ahead should lead to a better life."[16] This was an important recognition of the value of reintegrating these individuals back into our society. The problem is even more acute in light of the fact that virtually all young offenders, many of whom are only 14 when sentenced to prison, will be returning to society in the prime of their youth and working years. Either we help them to get jobs or we will have to support them for the foreseeable future.

A criminal record presents an all but insurmountable bar to economic opportunity and might well prove a lifelong handicap. For instance, take the case of a 14-year-old youth who is convicted of robbery and sentenced to prison. After being released from prison he marries, has a child, and is looking for a job. He considers driving a taxi, working for the Transit Authority or the Sanitation Department. Except in very few instances, none of these opportunities are available to him because of his felony conviction. We must incorporate into our system of juvenile justice a process that provides such a youth with an opportunity to return to the court which sentenced him after an appropriate period of living without violating the law, to demonstrate that his conviction should be expunged.[17] We must be able to bring young offenders back into our society. The idea of forever defining an individual by acts committed at 14 or 15 years of age is at odds with everything we know about adolescence and what we expect from a just society. My vision of a model juvenile justice system is based on the belief that children ought to be given a second chance, after appropriate intervention, if to do so would not compromise public safety.

Many of the recommendations I have made will require enactment of legislation to replace current forms of juvenile prosecution. How this can be accomplished will be discussed in the final chapter. The long-term goal is to create a model juvenile justice system that unites the juvenile court and criminal court in a common strategy—the rehabilitation of juvenile offenders. This can be accomplished in a system that provides for the individualized treatment of all offenders under 18 years of age.

The American juvenile justice system is actually composed of 51 separate and distinct juvenile justice systems. Each state and the federal government has its own approach to prosecuting juvenile offenders. Different philosophies, practices, and customs exist throughout the nation. These differences are often represented in permissible terms of imprisonment for juveniles. For example, a 14-year-old arrested for a robbery involving the forcible taking of property by displaying and threatening the use of a knife could face a sentence of up to 10 years in New York;[18] in New Jersey up to 15 years;[19] and in California up to 5 years or 9 years, depending on the status of the victim.[20] In Texas, a 14-year-old found to have engaged in delinquent conduct may be incarcerated in the Texas Department of Criminal Justice, the adult penitentiary, for a period of up to 40 years, if the delinquent conduct constitutes a capital felony, a felony of the first degree, or an aggravated controlled substance felony.[21]

In constructing a model juvenile justice system, I view the central issue as judicial responsiveness rather than jurisdiction. In other words, the capacity of the judge presiding over a juvenile's case to craft dispositions designed to meet an offender's special needs is more important than whether jurisdiction over the young offender is in the juvenile or criminal court.[22] Several states have experimented with new approaches to sentencing youths eligible to be transferred to adult criminal court. New Mexico, for example, recognizing that the transfer decision is essentially a sentencing decision allowed juvenile court judges to sentence a certain category of juvenile offenders as adults, that is, to adult correctional sentences.[23] Minnesota chose to enact a blended or conditional form of sentencing that gave its judges an option to sentence a youth charged with serious felonies to a juvenile sanction with the threat of a more serious criminal sanction if the juvenile failed to meet the terms of the juvenile sentence.[24]

Regardless of the methodology a state chooses to prosecute and sentence juveniles, it should be one that allows the judicial decision maker access to all relevant background information on the offender before a decision is made to prosecute a youth in juvenile or criminal court or sentence such a youth as a juvenile or adult.

In the model system that I propose, all youth under 18 accused of a criminal offense would be referred initially to a juvenile or family court. A youth of a suitable age could be transferred to the adult court but only after a due process judicial hearing in which such a child was found not to be amenable to the programs or sanctions available in the juvenile court or that the public's interest would be best served by prosecution in the adult court. Youths transferred to adult court after such a hearing would have their cases referred to a special Youth

Part that could act as a further screening mechanism to help identify those children who, although charged with serious crimes and who may possess problematic backgrounds, can nevertheless be linked with appropriate educational and rehabilitative programs.

Although the judgments of legislatures have differed in distinguishing childhood and adulthood in terms of fixing criminal responsibility and determining appropriate sanctions, the model that I propose is intended to lend uniformity to that decision. Most states recognize the age of 18 as the age of majority in civil contexts. I would extend that recognition, in the first instance, to require all youth under 18 to be prosecuted in juvenile court. I would further recommend that no youth under 14 years of age be transferred to the adult court unless it can be established by clear and convincing evidence that such a youth is competent to understand and assist in the proceedings against him.[25] Such a system would be consistent with American Bar Association standards as well as national and international norms.[26]

The recent Supreme Court decision of *Roper v. Simmons*[27] provides a compelling brief for this position as it recognizes the need for the individualized treatment of juveniles under 18 years of age. Although the case dealt with the constitutionality of executing minors under 18 years of age, a majority of the Supreme Court justices recognized the developmental differences of such youth as an accepted societal factor in determining appropriate treatment of juvenile offenders. Specifically, the court stated, in an opinion written by Justice Anthony Kennedy joined by Justices Stevens, Souter, Ginsberg, and Breyer:

> Three general differences between juveniles under 18 and adults demonstrate that juvenile offenders cannot with reliability be classified among the worst offenders. First, as any parent knows and as the scientific and sociological studies respondent and his amici cite tend to confirm, "[a] lack of maturity and an underdeveloped sense of responsibility are found in youth more often than in adults and are more understandable among the young. These qualities often result in

impetuous and ill-considered actions and decisions." Johnson, supra, at 367; see also Eddings, supra, at 115–116 ("Even the normal 16-year-old customarily lacks the maturity of an adult"). It has been noted that "adolescents are overrepresented statistically in virtually every category of reckless behavior." Arnett, Reckless Behavior in Adolescence: A Developmental Perspective, 12 Developmental Review 339 (1992). In recognition of the comparative immaturity and irresponsibility of juveniles, almost every state prohibits those under 18 years of age from voting, serving on juries, or marrying without parental consent. See Appendixes B-D, infra.

The second area of difference is that juveniles are more vulnerable or susceptible to negative influences and outside pressures, including peer pressure. Eddings, supra, at 115 ("[Y]outh is more than a chronological fact. It is a time and condition of life when a person may be most susceptible to influence and to psychological damage"). This is explained in part by the prevailing circumstances that juveniles have less control, or less experience with control, over their own environment. See Steinberg & Scott, Less Guilty by Reason of Adolescence; Developmental Immaturity, Diminished Responsibility, and the Juvenile Death Penalty, 58 Am. Psychologist 1009, 1014 (2003) (hereinafter Steinberg & Scott) ("[A]s legal minors, [juveniles] lack the freedom that adults have to extricate themselves from a criminogenic setting").

The third broad difference is that the character of a juvenile is not as well formed as that of an adult. The personality traits of juveniles are more transitory, less fixed. See generally E. Erickson, Identity: Youth and Crisis (1968).

These differences render suspect any conclusion that a juvenile falls among the worst offenders. The susceptibility of juveniles to immature and irresponsible behavior means "their irresponsible conduct is not as morally reprehensible as that of an adult." Thompson, supra, at 835 (plurality opinion). Their own vulnerability and comparative lack of control over their immediate surroundings mean juveniles have a greater claim than adults to be forgiven for failing to escape negative influences in their whole environment. See Stanford, 492 U.S., at 395 (Brennan, J., dissenting). The reality that juveniles still struggle to define their identify means it is less supportable to conclude that even a heinous crime committed by a juvenile is evidence of irretrievably depraved character. From a moral standpoint it would be misguided to equate the failings of a minor with those of an adult, for a greater possibility exists that minor's character deficiencies will be reformed. Indeed, "[t]he relevance of youth as a mitigating factor derives from the fact that the signature qualities of youth are transient; as individuals mature, the impetuousness and recklessness that may dominate in younger years can subside. Johnson, supra, at 368; see also Steinberg & Scott 1014 ("For most teens, [risky or antisocial] behaviors are fleeting; they cease with maturity as individual identity becomes settled. Only a relatively small proportion of adolescents who experiment in risky or illegal activities develop entrenched patterns of problem behavior that persist into adulthood").[28]

Thus, the Supreme Court, in acknowledging the conclusions of behavioral scientists as to the diminished capacity and culpability of adolescents, presents a compelling argument for the adoption of a uniform standard of initial juvenile court jurisdiction.

In 1998, I participated in an American Bar Association task force that addressed the policy, procedural, and programmatic implications arising from the large number of juveniles being transferred to the adult criminal justice system. The work of the task force culminated in a publication entitled *Youth in the Criminal Justice System, Guidelines for Policymakers and Practitioners.* That publication provides a valuable framework that complements the proposed model juvenile justice system. The report presents a detailed response to the challenges presented to lawyers, judges, probation officers, correction officers, and social workers, by the prosecution of juveniles as adults. It calls for and outlines developmentally sensitive approaches to the issues presented by children at every stage of the adult court process from police investigatory issues and arrest, through sentencing and conditions of confinement.

The observation of Ireland's former Minister of Justice Marie Gehegan-Quinn, quoted at the beginning of this chapter, proposed two challenges—(1) dealing effectively with those accused of juvenile crime and (2) adequately addressing the causes of juvenile crime. Initiatives such as the Youth Part or even realization of the proposed model juvenile justice system are not going to solve or adequately address the juvenile crime problem unless they are part of a comprehensive strategy that addresses the societal environmental factors that affect crime. The goal of any comprehensive plan should be the prevention of juvenile crime. Courts only get involved with a juvenile after a crime has been committed. "Once a juvenile is apprehended by the police and referred to the juvenile court, the community has already failed; subsequent rehabilitative services, no matter how skilled, have far less potential for success than had they been applied before the youth's overt defiance of the law."[29] John A. F. Watson, a British magistrate who presided for many years over a tribunal dealing with young offenders, reflected on the limitations of his role in this fashion:

To purge this polluted atmosphere is beyond the scope of the courts. We who work there have only a minor role to play. It is not for us to treat the sickness of society at large. We must accept the damage done. Our task is to assess its diverse causes, seek to retrieve what has been lost, and to rebuild what has been destroyed; to instill discipline where there is no discipline; impose restraints where there is only license; evoke love and security where both have been denied.

Yet if the magistrates (judges) who form the juvenile courts are wisely chosen, if they are properly instructed, above all if they approach their task in the right spirit, they have the power to remake young lives.

There is tragedy in their work but also consolation; for there exists in these children so much sterling material only waiting to be brought to the surface...[30]

The model that I have suggested is judicially centered and requires a reinvestment in the juvenile courts in both conceptual and fiscal terms, but I submit it will lead to a more just system of adjudicating the offenses of juveniles. There are those who may be uncomfortable with a system that vests authority in the judiciary to determine who is able to be rehabilitated. However, the real issue that should be addressed is, as my British colleague pointed out, that judges selected to serve on the juvenile court should be wisely chosen, properly instructed and above all prepared to approach their task in the right spirit.

In the 1930s, a maverick congressman, Vito Marcantonio, described his responsibility to his constituency, the poor immigrant working class of East Harlem, as an interpreter of the "unrealized possibilities" of democracy.[31] In my role as judge, I, too, have tried to instill in young offenders a belief in their unrealized possibilities. I have encouraged young people to use their minds, develop their talents whether it is in the wizardry of words, the magic of music or the exhilaration of hard work. I have told them if they do this, we adults will make room for them in our society. The challenge of instilling that hope in these young offenders has proven to be considerable in a system that all too often indiscriminately prosecutes children as adults. The model that I have proposed respects the individuality of each child accused of a crime. I believe that our juvenile justice system should be a restorative process, a process of reconciliation of the child with society, a process of "soul awakening instead of soul debasing,"[32] a system that permits an assessment of a child's moral character, demonstrating by the fairness of its operation the value of truth, integrity and respect for the rights of others. Labeling children as some kind of "malevolent breed" who forfeit their right to childhood and in many instances a productive adulthood because of mistakes made at the beginning of their lives undermines the very foundation of our society. A democratic citizenry must demand much more of its juvenile justice system than "expedient" answers to highly complex problems. It must demand a juvenile justice system reflective and worthy of our democratic ideals.

Juvenile Justice Policy Reform

*If due process values are to be preserved in the bureau-
cratic state of the late 20th century, it may be essential
that officials possess passion, the passion that puts them
in touch with the dreams and disappointments of those
with whom they deal, the passion that understands the
pulse of life beneath the official version of events.*
—SUPREME COURT JUSTICE WILLIAM J. BRENNAN JR.

A N UNPRECEDENTED coalition of advocacy groups composed of physicians, behavioral scientists, child advocates, and lawyers came together to successfully challenge the juvenile death penalty statutes.[1] The same evidence that renders juveniles less culpable than adults in determining whether they can be constitutionally executed suggests as well that the majority of juveniles should not be tried as adults. Mobilization of a similar coalition could be effective in reversing the policy of trying children as adults.

America has a significant number of philanthropic foundations dedicated to improving the lives of children. These foundations have been instrumental in educating the public and providing the building blocks for reform through their support of adolescent research.[2] Foundations generally have acted independently of one another with respect to these projects—without substantial collaboration and coordination. Certainly, foundations may legitimately have different approaches to juvenile justice reform, but I believe that the model juvenile justice system I have proposed provides a framework for collaboration that can bring together foundations for the purpose of achieving the core objectives of that model. A consortium of like-minded foundations can pool resources and talent to create a formidable fund, which will in turn support a grassroots movement that will be influential enough to effect meaningful reform. I believe that such a unified consortium, speaking with one voice, one vision of social change, one framework for making judgments about projects will be a powerful force for reform, one that cannot be ignored by policy makers. Once such a consortium coalesces, the goal would be to form an alliance with government institutions having responsibility for developing and implementing statutory and policy changes in juvenile and criminal justice.

On a national level, the Office of Juvenile Justice and Delinquency Prevention (OJJDP) is the federal governmental agency primarily responsible for implementing juvenile justice policy. The office was established by the president and Congress through the Juvenile Justice and Delinquency Prevention Act of 1974.[3] It was intended to provide national leadership in addressing juvenile justice issues. Since its creation, OJJDP has reflected the changing views of government concerning the treatment of young offenders. For example, in 1998 federal policies encouraged states to "get tough" on juveniles. Congress authorized challenge grants, administered by OJJDP, which offered financial incentives to states that facilitated the prosecution of more children in the adult criminal courts.[4] Since that time, however, child advocates and behavioral scientists, with the support of foundations, have demonstrated that the policy of trying children as adults is misguided, shortsighted, and wasteful: misguided because it ignores essential differences between child and adult; shortsighted because it does not prevent juvenile crime or secure adequate protection of the public; and wasteful because it unnecessarily criminalizes children.

State and federal governmental leaders have come to recognize the destructive consequences of policies that unnecessarily expose young offenders to lifelong criminalization, not only in human terms but also in economic terms. As the direct impact of these policies on federal, state, and local budgets are calculated the increasing pressure to balance budgets is causing political leaders to rethink their approach to crime prevention.[5] Thus, I believe that the time is right for such a partnership between the federal government and foundations to initiate reform consistent with the objectives of the model juvenile justice system and that a true national commitment to address the systemic obstacles to such reform now exists.

Once such a private/public partnership is formed its goal would be twofold: first, to adopt a comprehensive plan for reform and, second, to create a superfund to finance it. Through the utilization of the grant process, local communities and governments can be encouraged to apply for funding of proposals consistent with the comprehensive plan. Government leaders will then be able to educate themselves concerning the merits of such a plan and in doing so take advantage of the resources made available by the partnership to initiate rational reform.

A model strategy for reform already exists. In 1995, OJJDP published the "Guide for Implementing the Comprehensive Strategy for Serious, Violent and Chronic Juvenile Offenders."[6] This manual contains a detailed proposal to enable local communities to mobilize support for a more effective juvenile justice system. It was designed by children's advocates, behavioral scientists, and youth program specialists brought together by the agency for the purpose of creating a comprehensive strategy to reduce juvenile violence. The plan called for a community-based preventive approach to juvenile offending coupled with a reorganization and revitalization of the juvenile justice system. It envisioned the expansion of the juvenile court's dispositional authority through a system of graduated sanctions designed to respond proportionately to the nature of the offender as well as to the offense. The plan's overall objective was to combine treatment and rehabilitation with reasonable, firm, humane, and appropriate sanctions primarily within the juvenile court setting. The Guide provides a clear and sound blueprint for reform that can be implemented at the community, city, state, and national level and it is consistent with the core principles of the proposed model juvenile justice system.

In the preceding chapters, I have presented my views on the nature of adolescence and juvenile crime and what I consider to be the flaws in our present policy of trying children as adults. I have set forth what I contend is a rational and just model for juvenile justice. One would like to think that the soundness of logic and analysis, as well as the empirical evidence provided by behavioral scientists, would lead to the adoption of the principles proffered. But the Justinian principle of justice, "giving each person his due," does not come easily in a modern competitive society, something more is needed.

Each generation must recognize the imperative for justice and must summon the passion to maintain a commitment to its principles. It is passion that converts good intention into commitment, commitment into perseverance, and perseverance into accomplishment. I speak of the passion that recognizes the human dimension in the problems presented by children who violate the law; the passion that the late Supreme Court Justice William J. Brennan so eloquently described in a speech before the Association of the Bar of the City of New York entitled "Reason, Passion and the Progress of the Law."[7]

His thesis was that passion, as well as reason, is a vital aspect of the judicial process. By passion he meant the passion born of a sensitive recognition of the human experience; the passion that gives rise to an instinct for justice. It is this concept of passion that ought to permeate our juvenile justice policy with respect for the individuality and potential of each child charged with criminal behavior. Justice Brennan asserted that nowhere is the necessity for passion more evident than in the interpretation of the constitutional concept of due process; a concept that defines the relationship between the governed and the government. He stated, "Perhaps more than any other provision of the Constitution, the due process clause requires reliance on both reason and passion for its interpretation. This is not simply because of the sweeping generality of its language. Other constitutional phrases—'equal protection of the laws' or 'cruel and unusual punishment'—are equally open-ended. Rather, it is because the due process clause commands that the government rely on both these basic human qualities in dealing with its citizens."[8]

I contend that the issue of trying children as adults is one of constitutional dimension. Our children are our most vulnerable citizens. Given the drastic consequences of prosecution as an adult, treating each child as an individual is a matter of due process.[9] In the past, America has protected our children from exploitation in the civil area and established a unique system to deal with their criminal behavior, the juvenile court, which was designed to nurture them into productive citizens. We were distracted from this tradition by sensational and extraordinary acts of violence by a few of our children. We can return to that rehabilitative tradition without compromising public safety by adopting the principles of a model juvenile justice system and the implementation of OJJDP's comprehensive strategy. Our nation deserves nothing less.

Notes

PROLOGUE

1. Language adopted from a decision of Michael Musmanno, former chief judge of the Pennsylvania Supreme Court in In Re Joseph Holmes, 379 Pa. 599 at p. 629 (1954).
2. New York courts are divided into "Parts." Each part is presided over by a judge sitting in a designated courtroom. Thus, the "Youth Part" is also known as Part 73.

CHAPTER 1: THE PROPOSITION

1. See, generally, Black's Law Dictionary, Seventh Edition, Bryan A. Garner, Editor-in-Chief, West Group, (St. Paul, Minn, 1999), p. 62, age of majority.
2. Elizabeth S. Scott, The Legal Construction of Adolescence, 29 Hofstra L. Rev. 547, p. 547.
3. Roper v. Simmons, 2005 WL 46 4890 (U.S. MO.); 125 S.Ct. 1183 (2005).
4. New York Law Journal, March 2, 2005, p. 1, In Brief.
5. U.S. Department of Justice; Office of Juvenile Justice Prevention; "Juvenile Offenders and Victims: A Focus on Violence," May 1995.
6. See Scott, supra Note 2.
7. James Hillman, The Soul's Code: In Search of Character and Calling (Warner Books, 1996).
8. N.Y. Criminal Procedure Law art. 720; see also Michael A. Corriero, Youth Parts: Constructive Response to the Challenge of Youth Crime, N.Y.L.J. Oct. 26, 1990, p. 1 col. 1 This article traces the development of Youthful Offender (YO) treatment and the historical context of separate youth parts.
9. On September 1, 1978, the Juvenile Offender Law, created as part of the omnibus crime control bill of 1978 (Laws of 1978, Chapter 48), was enacted in New York State.

This law created a new class of defendant called the "Juvenile Offender" to whom the statutory defense of infancy against criminal charges was no longer available. N.Y. Penal Law Section 30.00 (2). The new class was defined by the crime(s) the juvenile allegedly committed and the age of the individual at the time of the alleged commission of the offense. Thus, 13-, 14-, and 15-year-olds charged with the crime of murder, and 14- and 15-year olds accused of certain other serious crimes, including attempted murder and higher degrees of manslaughter, kidnapping, arson, assault, rape, sodomy, burglary, and robbery, were deemed criminally responsible for this conduct and were to be prosecuted in adult criminal courts. Since the initial enactment of the JO Law, additional crimes have been classified as JO offenses including criminal possession of a weapon in the second degree (Penal Law Section 265.03) and criminal possession of a weapon in the third degree (Penal Law Section 265.02), when such weapon is possessed on school grounds. See Eric Warner, *The Juvenile Offender Handbook* (Loose-leaf Publications, Inc., 1995); Penal law Section 10 (18).

10.   N.Y. Family Court Act, art. 3.

11.   For an excellent discussion of the Juvenile Offender law and its consequences, see Simon Singer, *Recriminalizing Delinquency* (Cambridge University Press, 1996).

12.   The Juvenile Offender Law was criticized by the Association of the Bar of the City of New York, as well as the Citizens Committee for Children. See The Majority and Minority Reports on the Juvenile Offender Law, Juvenile Justice Committee of the Association of the Bar of the City of New York (1983); see The Experiment That Failed: The New York State Juvenile Offender Law, Citizens Committee for Children of New York, Inc., Dec. 1984.

13.   Generally, in the Family Court a fact-finding hearing must be commenced within 30 days of the initial appearance and filing of the petition.

14.   A study of the Legal Aid Society's Juvenile Offender Team, Advanced Project In Public Policy Analysis, Prof. Charles Brecher, April 2004. Team Members: Melissa Auerbach; Jennifer Leung; Jessica Rosenzweig, and Sarah Sheffield.

15.   Id. at 21.

16.   Id. at 28.

17.   Offender Programs Report, Social and Behavioral Rehabilitation in Prisons, Jails and the Community, vol. 8, no. 2, July/August 2004: Community Based Sentencing Demonstrates Lower Recidivism among Felony-Level Offenders, Joel Copperman, Sarah Bryer, Hannah Gray, p. 17 at p. 29.

18.   E-mail on file in judge's chambers.

19.   Correctional Association of New York (2002), "Juvenile Detention in New York City Fact Sheet," <http://www.correctionalassociation.org/JJP_Detention_facts. htm#_ftn10>.

20.   Frederick Bruce (1999), "Factors Contributing to Recidivism Among Youth Placed with the New York State Division for Youth," DCJS, Bureau of Research and Evaluation.

21.   *The Changing Borders of Juvenile Justice*, edited by Jeffrey Fagan and Franklin E. Zimring (The University of Chicago Press, 2000), Chapter 10, The Reproduction of Juvenile Justice in Criminal Court: A Case Study of New York's Juvenile Offender Law, Simon I. Singer, Jeffrey Fagan, and Akiva Liberman, p. 353 at pp. 368–370.

22.   Id.

23.   This report was prepared by the New York City Criminal Justice Agency, a private not-for-profit corporation. It is titled *Adult Court Processing and Re-arrest of*

Juvenile Offenders in Manhattan and Queens. It compares and contrasts the Manhattan and Queens juvenile cases that entered the Supreme Court in those boroughs from 1997 through 2000. Rearrests were tracked through January 31, 2005. The research sample consisted of 304 Manhattan cases and 258 Queens cases.

24. Id. at p. 22.
25. Id. at p. 21.
26. See Responding to Juvenile Crime: Lessons Learned, Peter W. Greenwood, The Future of Children, The Juvenile Court, vol. 6, no. 3 (Winter 1996) (The David and Lucille Packard Foundation).
27. Report of Correctional Association, City of New York, Rethinking Juvenile Detention in New York City, p. 9.
28. Id.
29. See Franklin E. Zimring, *American Youth Violence* (Oxford University Press, 1998) at p. XI. See also Linda F. Giardino, Statutory Rhetoric: The Reality Behind Juvenile Justice Policies in America, Journal of Law and Policy, vol. V, no. 1; Juvenile Offenders and Victims, 1999 National Report Series, Juvenile Justice Bulletin, U.S. Department of Justice, Office of Justice Programs, Office of Juvenile Justice and Delinquency Prevention, Shay Bilchik, Administrator.
30. See *supra* note 29.

CHAPTER 2: THE NATURE OF ADOLESCENCE

1. Laurence Steinberg, Juveniles on Trial, MacArthur Foundation Calls Juvenile Competency Into Question, Juvenile Justice Update, vol. 9, no. 4, Aug./Sept. 2003, p. 3.
2. Wallace J. Mlyniec, A Judge's Ethical Dilemma: Assessing a Child's Capacity to Choose, 64 Fordham L. Rev. 1873, note 12. See G. Stanley Hall, *Adolescence,* first published in 1905 (Lawrence A. Cremin ed., Arno Press and the New York Times, 1969).
3. The discussion of the psychological effects of adolescence on criminal behavior is based on my analysis of material contained in the following sources: *Youth on Trial: A Developmental Perspective on Juvenile Justice,* edited by Thomas Grisso and Robert G. Schwartz (The University of Chicago Press, 2000); Laurence Steinberg and Elizabeth Cauffman, The Elephant in the Courtroom: A Developmental Perspective on the Adjudication of Youthful Offenders, 6 Va. J. Soc, Pol'y L. (1999); Elizabeth S. Scott and Thomas Grisso, The Evolution of Adolescence: A Developmental Perspective on Juvenile Justice Reform, The Journal of Criminal Law and Criminology, vol. 88, no. 1, Fall 1997, p. 137; Wallace Mlyniec *supra* note 2, as well as Professor Scott's article cited hereafter in note 4, provide an excellent review of current research data in the field.
4. I am indebted to Professor Elizabeth S. Scott's article for the crystallization of my thoughts concerning the classification of adolescence as a distinct legal category carrying its own implications for criminal liability. See Elizabeth S. Scott, The Legal Construction of Adolescence, 29 Hofstra L. Rev., 547.
5. Id. at pp. 573–574.
6. Wallace J. Mlyniec, A Judge's Ethical Dilemma: Assessing a Child's Capacity to Choose, 64 Fordham L.Rev. 1873, 1896.
7. *Supra* note 4 at n. 29 p. 554.
8. Aristotle, *On Rhetoric* (newly translated by George A. Kennedy, New York and Oxford [Oxford University Press 1991]), pp. 165–166.

9. Professor Franklin E. Zimring, *American Youth Violence* (Oxford University Press, 1998).
10. Id. at p. 78.
11. Michael Riera, *Uncommon Sense for Parents with Teenagers* (Celestial Arts, Berkeley, CA, 1995), p. 22.
12. *Supra* note 9 at p. 78.
13. For an excellent discussion on the competence of adolescents to understand legal proceedings and principles, see Laurence Steinberg, *Juveniles on Trial,* MacArthur Foundation Study Calls Juvenile Competency into Question, ABA Criminal Justice Magazine, Fall 2003, 21. The MacArthur juvenile competence study is a research project undertaken by the MacArthur Foundation Research Network on adolescent development and juvenile justice. The study focuses on two broad issues: the competence and culpability of adolescents, and the factors that influence their antisocial behavior. It should be noted that the author is a consultant to the MacArthur Project.
14. See Terrie E. Mofitt, Adolescence-Limited and Life-Course Persistent Antisocial Behavior: A Developmental Taxonomy, 100 Psychol. Rev. 674.
15. Aristotle, *supra* note 8, p. 166.
16. The concept of diminished capacity has been relied on to mitigate culpability. In the context of a criminal proceeding it permits evidence establishing that a defendant was less mentally capable than a normal person of having the requisite mental state for the offense charged. See <http://www.diminishedcapacity.com/sec2.htm>. The concept of proportionality requires the sentencing authority to impose a sentence that does not exceed the discernable degree of culpability of the individual offender. See Zimring, *supra* note 9, pp. 75–81.
17. Robert E. Shepherd Jr., Developmental Psychology and the Juvenile Justice Process, Criminal Justice Magazine, American Bar Association, Spring 1999, p. 43.

CHAPTER 3: THE CRIMINAL RESPONSIBILITY OF JUVENILES

1. Griffin, P., Torbet, P. M., and Szymanski, L. 1998, Trying Juveniles as Adults in Criminal Court: An Analysis of State Transfer Provisions. Report. Washington, DC: U.S. Department of Justice, Office of Justice Programs, Office of Juvenile Justice and Delinquency Prevention, p. 16.
2. See Laurence Steinberg, MacArthur Foundation Study Calls Competency into Question, Criminal Justice, ABA Crim. Just. Section Magazine, Fall 2003, p. 21.
3. See generally, Introduction to the Criminal Justice System, Second Edition, Hazel B. Kerper (West Publishing Co., 1979), p. 112; Criminal Law and Procedure, Perkins and Boyce (The Foundation Press, Inc., 1977), Chapter 8—Responsibility: Limitations on Criminal Capacity—Section 1 Immaturity (Infancy), pp. 508–539.
4. Aristotle, Politics, in Hall, *Readings in Jurisprudence* (Bobbs-Merrill Co., 1938), p. 5.
5. See *Criminal Justice, Cases and Comments, Inbau and Sowle* (The Foundation Press, Inc., 1964), pp. 383–384.
6. *State v. Monahan,* 15 N.J. 34, 104 A.2d 21, (Sup.Ct. 1954), dissent of J. Olphant, at 15 N.J. 65, A.2d 38.
7. All states have adopted the concept of a juvenile court with special authority over youths below a specified age. If a youth below a specified age committed an act that would otherwise be a crime, he would be subject to the jurisdiction of the

juvenile court. If a youth above that age committed a criminal act, he was deemed criminally responsible and prosecuted in the adult courts and subject to greater punishment. Although the commonlaw rule originally was adopted throughout the United States, most states today have discarded the rule in favor of an absolute statutory minimum age for criminal responsibility. See 1999 National Report, Juvenile Justice Bulletin, Office of Juvenile Justice and Delinquency Prevention (December 1999).

8.   Oliver Wendell Holmes, *The Common-Law* (Boston: Little Brown and Company, 1963), p. 42.

9.   New Jersey statutes annotated, N.J.S.A.2A: 4A-22(a).

10.   New York Penal Law Section 10.00 (18); Section 30.00 (2).

11.   See *supra* note 10.

12.   443 U.S. 622 (1979).

13.   Id. at pp. 633–636.

14.   455 U.S. 104 (1982).

15.   Id. at p. 115.

16.   Joan Jacobs Brumberg: Separate the Killers from the Boys, *New York Times*, December 18, 2003, p. A43. See generally, *Youth on Trial*, Thomas Grisso and Robert G. Schwartz, eds. (2000), a volume of research sponsored by the John D. and Catherine T. MacArthur Foundation, Research Network on Adolescent Development and Juvenile Justice.

17.   Elizabeth S. Scott, The Legal Construction of Adolescence, 29 Hostra L.Rev. 547, 591–592.

18.   Id. at 590.

19.   Id. at 593.

20.   Franklin E. Zimring, *American Youth Violence* (Oxford University Press, 1998), p. 75.

21.   William J. Winslade and Judith Wilson Ross, *The Insanity Plea* (Charles Scribner & Sons, 1983), pp. 12–13.

22.   Wallace J. Mlyniec, A Judge's Ethical Dilemma: Assessing a Child's Capacity to Choose, 64 Fordham L.Rev. 1873, 1896.

CHAPTER 4: SENTENCING CHILDREN TRIED IN ADULT COURTS

1.   The Juvenile Offender Law provides as a maximum sentence for most serious "JO" offenses, other than murder, an indeterminate sentence of a minimum of 3 years 4 months to a maximum term of 10 years. Fourteen- or 15-year olds convicted of manslaughter in the first degree or robbery in the first degree, and sentenced to a maximum term, can return to society as young as 18 years of age and generally no later than 21. Such an offender will "max" out of his sentence, after serving two-thirds of his term, assuming he does not lose good time credits (an offender earns good-time credit if he is well behaved in prison that usually amounts to one-third of the maximum sentence).

2.   See Responding to Juvenile Crime: Lessons Learned, Peter W. Greenwood, The Future of Children, The Juvenile Court, vol. 6, no. 3, Winter 1996 (The David and Lucille Packard Foundation). See also Report of Vera Institute of Justice by Rachel Kramer and Rachel Porter submitted to the New York City Office of the Criminal Justice Coordinator, June 2000, Alternative-to-Incarceration Programs for

Felony Offenders: Progress Report and Preliminary Findings From a Recidivism Analysis, p. 23.

3. *The World Almanac and Book of Facts 2004* (St. Martin's Press, 2004), p. 14. For the United States, the average life span is 77.14 years; the average for men is 74.37, and for women 80.05.

4. Fox Butterfield, Ideas and Trends; Prison: Where the Money Is, *New York Times*, Week in Review, June 2, 1996, sec. 4, p. 16, col. 1; but see Elliot Currie, *Crime and Punishment in America* (Owl Books, 1998), pp. 67–79, for a discussion of problems of analysis and interpretation raised by cost calculations of this nature.

5. *Supra* note 2.

6. See New York State Office of Justice Systems Analysis, Research Report 1999, New York State Division of Criminal Justice Services—Factors Contributing to Recidivism Among Youth Placed with the New York State Division for Youth, Bruce Frederick, Ph.D. See also New York State Program Abstract—Family Court Residential Placement Diversion Program, p. 1.

7. Rollin M. Perkins and Ronald N. Boyce, *Criminal Law and Procedure, Cases and Materials* (The Foundation Press, Inc., 1977), p. 538, quoting from the Introduction of the American Law Institute's Model Youth Correction Authority Act, John B. Waite, Reporter.

8. See *Invisible Punishment: The Collateral Consequences of Mass Imprisonment*, Marc Mauer and Meda Chesney-Lind, eds. (New York: New Press, 2002).

9. Franklin E. Zimring, *American Youth Violence* (Oxford University Press 1998), p. 144.

10. See Martin E. P. Seligman, Ph.D., Building Human Strengths: Psychology's Forgotten Mission, American Psychological Association, APA Monitor vol. 29, no. 1, 1998.

11. See Dr. Susan Linn, How Can I Raise a Moral Child? <http://www.familyeducation.com>.

12. See Section 340.1, N.Y. Family Court Act.

13. See Section 30.30, N.Y. Crim.Proc.Law.

14. Torbet, P., Griffin, P., Hurst, Jr., H., MacKenzie, L. R. (2000) Juveniles Facing Criminal Sanctions: Three States that Changed the Rules. Report. Washington, DC: U.S. Department of Justice, Office of Justice Programs, Office of Juvenile Justice and Delinquency Prevention. (The Justice Department Report refers to New Mexico and Minnesota) See also *Michigan v. Abraham*—File No. 9763787 FC— (Jan. 13, 2000). This case involved the sentencing of 11-year-old Nathaniel Abraham and referred to Michigan's blended sentencing statute.

15. Michel Foucault, *Discipline and Punish* (Vintage Books, 1979), p. 180.

16. Id. at 178.

17. Brent Staples, Prison Class: What Ma Barker Knew and Congress Didn't, editorial page, *New York Times*, Nov. 25, 2002, at A20.

18. Id.

19. Andre Compte-Sponville, *A Small Treatise on the Great Virtues* (New York: Metropolitan Books, Henry Holt & Company, 1996).

20. Id. at 10.

21. *Supra* note 9 at pp. 81–82.

22. Lauren Chambliss et al., Second Chances: 100 Years of the Children's Court: Giving Kids a Chance to Make a Better Choice (1999), a joint project of The Justice Policy Institute, Washington, DC, and Children and Family Justice Center, Northwestern University School of Law, Legal Clinic, Chicago, IL.

CHAPTER 5: OUR HARDEST-TO-LOVE CHILDREN

1. New York Penal Law Section 160.15(3).
2. John Lemmon, The Link Between Child Maltreatment and Delinquency: A Review of the Research and Literature, Juvenile Justice Update, October/November 1995, p. 7.
3. Id.
4. *The Challenge of Crime in a Free Society* (Avon Books, 1968), p. 130.
5. Ramsey Clark, *Crime in America* (Simon & Schuster, 1970), p. 242.
6. Nina Bernstein, Many More Children Calling New York City Shelters Home, *New York Times,* Feb. 13, 2002, p. B2.
7. Bob Herbert, Young, Jobless, Hopeless, *New York Times,* Feb. 6, 2003, p. A39.
8. Id.
9. Speech of Rev. Jesse Jackson before Governor Mario Cuomo's New York State Commission for the Study of Youth Crime, Violence and Reform of the Juvenile Justice System, 1994.
10. Shakespeare, *The Tempest,* Robert Longbaum, ed. (Signet Classics 1998), p. 71. Prospero describing the character Caliban. "Prospero: A devil, a born devil, on whose nature nurture can never stick; on whom my pains, humanely taken all, all lost, quite lost!..." Scene 4.1, lines 188–190.

CHAPTER 6: INTERACTIVE JUSTICE

1. Wu-Tang Clan, album *Enter the Wu-Tang, Shame On A Nigga* (Sony Records, Loud Label, December 2001).
2. Pink Floyd, album *The Wall,* "Hey, Teacher, Leave Those Kids Alone" (Columbia Records, December 1979).
3. See Charles Larsen, *The Good Fight: The Life and Times of Ben B. Lindsey* (Quadrangle Books 1972).
4. This quote has been attributed to Judge Ben B. Lindsey, although research has not revealed its source.
5. See Judge Ben B. Lindsey, *Wainwright Evans: The Revolt of Modern Youth* (University of Washington Press, 1925).
6. Id. at p. 85.
7. Id. at p. 45.
8. *Kent v. United States,* 383 U.S. 541 (1966); In Re Gault, 387 U.S. 1, (1967); In Re Winship 397 U.S. 358 (1970); *McKeiver v. Pennsylvania,* 403 U.S. 528 (1976).
9. McKeiver, *supra* note 8.
10. McKeiver, *supra* note 8 at 544.
11. McKeiver, *supra* note 8 at 544.
12. *Smith v. Daily Mail Pub. Co.,* 443 U.S. 9 (1979) at 107.
13. Roscoe Pound, The Scope and Purpose of Sociological Jurisprudance, 25 Harv. L. Rev. 140 (1912).
14. Oliver Wendell Holmes, The Sociology of Law 4.
15. Jeffrey Fagan, Franklin E. Zimring, *The Changing Borders of Juvenile Justice* (The University of Chicago Press, 2000), p. 261.
16. New York Criminal Procedure Law, Article 720.
17. See Michael A. Corriero, Youth Parts: A Constructive Response to the Challenge of Youth Crime, N.Y.L.J. Oct. 26, 1990.

18. Id.
19. Cruickshank, 105 App.Div.2d 325 (Third Dep't. 1985).
20. Id. at 334–335.
21. N.Y.CPL Sections 720.15, 720.35.
22. See *People v. Robinson,* 110 App.Div.2d 939 (Third Dep't. 1985); *People v. Mendoza,* 57 App.Div.2d 846 (Second Dep't. 1992); see also Preiser, Practice Commentaries, CPL Section 720.10 (McKinney's Consol. Laws 1995), p. 390.
23. Cruickshank, *supra* note 19 at p. 335.
24. *Supra* note 5 at p. 45.
25. Aristotle, *A Theory of Civic Discourse, On Rhetoric,* George A. Kennedy, trans. (Oxford University Press, 1941).
26. Id. at pp. 165–166.
27. Mill, John Stuart, *Autobiography,* vol. XXV, part 1 (The Harvard Classics, New York: P.F. Collier & Son, 1909–1914), Chapter 1—Childhood & Early Education, p. 13.
28. Group Magazine, September/October 1999, p. 57; see also Walt Mueller, *Understanding Today's Youth Culture* (Wheaton, IL: Tyndale House Publishers, 1999), pp. 80–88.
29. Section 32 (c)(3) of the Federal Rules of Criminal Procedure explicitly affords a convicted defendant two rights: (1) to make a statement on his own behalf and (2) to present any information in mitigation of punishment. The United States Supreme Court in *Green v. U.S.,* 365 U.S. 301 (1961) declared that before sentencing a defendant in a criminal case, trial judges should unambiguously address themselves to the defendant, leaving no room for doubt that the defendant has been issued a personal invitation to speak before sentence. Merely affording defendant's counsel an opportunity to speak does not meet the requirements of Federal procedure. New York's Criminal Procedure Law Section 380.50 codifies sentencing procedure as follows: At the time of pronouncing sentence, the Court must accord the prosecution an opportunity to make a statement with respect to any matter relevant to the question of sentence. The Court must then accord counsel for the defendant an opportunity to speak on behalf of the defendant. The defendant also has the right to make a statement personally on his behalf and before pronouncing sentence the Court must ask the defendant whether he or she wishes to make such a statement.

CHAPTER 7: FRIDAYS IN THE YOUTH PART

1. Caroline Joy DeBrovner, Ph.D., is an assistant professor at Pace University, New York, New York, with a joint appointment in the Department of Criminal Justice and Sociology. She has had extensive training as an academic sociologist and qualitative researcher. Her professional specialization is Sociology of Law, Juvenile Justice, Criminology, and Qualitative Methods.
2. See James Q. Wilson, *Crime and Human Nature* (New York: Simon & Schuster Adult Publishing Group, 1985); Cesare Beccaria, "On Crimes and Punishment," in *Classics of Criminology,* Joseph Jacoby, ed. (Prospect Heights: Waveland Press, 1988), 211–212; Jeremy Bentham, "An Introduction to the Principles of Morals and Legislation," in *Classics of Criminology,* Joseph Jacoby, ed. (Prospect Heights: Waveland Press, 1988), 61–63.
3. 12/12/03: M/I/AA (see the appendix to this chapter for all codes).

4. A number of defendants appearing in the Youth Part are serving sentences imposed for Family Court offenses that were pending when they were arrested on a subsequent Juvenile Offender offense. Often Judge Corriero will monitor their performance in the institution to which they were remanded pursuant to the Family Court sentence before making a final decision on the adult court sentence. These defendants are in the custody of the Office of Children and Family Services (OCFS) when they are transported to court.

5. 9/7/01: M/O/R/AA.

6. 5/24/02: M/O/R/AA.

7. Judge Corriero, speaking to a group of doctors visiting the Youth Part, 9/13/02.

8. 6/20/03: M/O/L.

9. For as long as I have observed Judge Corriero in the Youth Part, he has assigned books to his defendants, especially time-honored classics, such as *A Tale of Two Cities* by Charles Dickens. Initially, when I began my weekly observations of Judge Corriero's Youth Part, he assigned specific books, and the defense attorneys, most of them assigned public defenders, tried to come up with the funds, often paying for them out of pocket. Judge Corriero informed me that two of the facilities where New York City incarcerates our juvenile offenders, Crossroads and Horizons, did not have a library (or much of one beyond what books the Board of Education supplies for their regular school classes) or a full-time librarian.

    After over a year of observing his persistent efforts to incorporate bibliotherapy into his judicial interactive process, I proposed an idea to the judge: a Youth Part Library. Judge Corriero selected important and time-honored books that he knew and loved, and I was gratified to donate the initial collection. The Youth Part Library is housed in a beautiful bookshelf in Judge Corriero's chambers. The initial collection has grown as Judge Corriero has further assessed and responded to the varying needs and interests of his defendants. The judge came to realize that many of the wonderful books he assigned were just too dense and difficult for the many of his defendants to tackle, so we have added illustrated abridged editions of many classics such as *The Odyssey* and *Oliver Twist* to the Youth Part Library. Books with pictures are enticing to the imagination of children and they provide the defendants with weaker literacy skills the opportunity to gain confidence reading a book at their level. Judge Corriero screens all the books donated to ensure they are appropriate for an adolescent reader, and have the likelihood of being beneficial as bibliotherapy. Each book selected as part of the library is stamped "Property of the Youth Part Library," and when a book is loaned, it is noted in a defendant's court chart so that the judge (with the help of his clerk) can monitor the books. This ensures that a defendant, trusted by the judge to borrow one of his books, is accountable and responsible for its return. The act of the judge personally loaning his defendant a book, asking him or her to read it, and then clarifying that he expects its return to the court, affords Judge Corriero an opportunity to assess a defendant's commitment to working with him.

10. One of *"our books"* is a book from the Youth Part Library (see earlier). 12/13/02: M/O/L.

11. David B. Wexler and Bruce J. Winick, *Law in a Therapeutic Key: Developments in Therapeutic Jurisprudence* (Durham, NC: Carolina Academic Press, 1996), 157.

12. Id., xvii.

13. The "Vision Statement" of the District Court of the State of Washington for Clark County, Division of District Court, approved May 18, 2001, that specifically embraces the use of the principles of therapeutic jurisprudence; Judge Randall B. Frizler, a leading judicial voice in TJ is a judge in that judicial district.

14. A. J. Stephani, Symposium: Therapeutic Jurisprudence and Children, University of Cincinnati Law Review 71 (2002): 13–22.

15. Judge Corriero describing his own methodology in personal communication, comments on a rough draft of this chapter, in May 2004.

16. 12/12/03: F/O/AA.

17. 3/28/03: M/I/AA.

18. 4/21/03.

19. Susan U. Phillips, "Criminal Defendant's Resistance to Confession in the Guilty Plea," paper presented at Law and Society Association Meetings, Berkeley, CA (May 31–June 3, 1990), 162.

20. 6/6/03: M/O/L.

21. 2/22/02: M/I/AA.

22. 2/22/02: M/I/AA.

23. 3/14/03: M/I/L.

24. 5/30/03: M/I/AA.

25. 10/4/02: M/I/AA.

26. 4/4/03: M/O/L.

27. 6/20/03: M/I/L.

28. 7/6/01: M/O/AA.

29. 4/4/03: M/O/AA.

30. 9/21/01: M/O/AA.

31. 12/13/02: M/O/L.

32. 4/20/01: M/I/L.

33. Judge Corriero, speaking at the 2003 Friends of Island Academy's Youth Funding Conference.

34. 10/5/01: M/I/AA.

35. 5/9/03: M/O/AA.

36. Gresham Sykes and David Matza, "Techniques of Neutralization: A Theory of Delinquency," in Theories of Deviance, Stuart H. Traub and Craig B. Little, ed. (Itasca: Peacock Press, 1999): 207.

37. Id., 208.

38. Id.

39. 6/8/01: M/I/R/AA.

40. 5/3/02: M/U.

41. 9/12/03: M/I/AA.

42. 8/16/02: M/I/AA.

43. 12/13/02: M/O/ME.

44. David B. Wexler, "Therapeutic Jurisprudence and the Criminal Courts," in Law in a Therapeutic Key: Developments in Therapeutic Jurisprudence, David B. Wexler and Bruce J. Winick, eds. (Durham, NC: Carolina Academic Press, 1996): 165–167.

45. Id., 159–164.

46. Id., 166 [citing Donald Meichenbaum and Dennis C. Turk, Facilitating Treatment Adherence: A Practitioner's Handbook, 1987: 124].

47. Toni M. Massaro, Shame, Culture and American Criminal Law, Michigan Law Review 89 (1991): 1880.
48. David B. Wexler, Therapeutic Jurisprudence and the Criminal Courts, in *Law in a Therapeutic Key: Developments in Therapeutic Jurisprudence*, David B. Wexler and Bruce J. Winick, eds. (Durham, NC: Carolina Academic Press, 1996): 166 [citing Donald Meichenbaum and Dennis C. Turk, *Facilitating Treatment Adherence: A Practitioner's Handbook*, 1987: 174].
49. Michael H. Moore, *From Children to Citizens* (New York: Springer-Verlag, 1987); "The Future of the Juvenile Court," Children 6:3(1996): 142.
50. 6/6/03: M/I/L.
51. 7/3/03: M/I/L.
52. 2/22/02: M/O/AA.
53. May 2001: M/I/L.
54. David B. Wexler, Therapeutic Jurisprudence and the Criminal Courts, in *Law in a Therapeutic Key: Developments in Therapeutic Jurisprudence*, David B. Wexler and Bruce J. Winick, eds. (Durham, NC: Carolina Academic Press, 1996): 161 [citing H. Richard Uviller, Pleading Guilty: A Critique of Four Models, Law & Contemporary Problems 41 (1977): 102, 121].
55. 11/15/02: M/O/L.
56. April 2003: M/O/L.
57. 5/4/01: M/I/L.
58. 7/3/03: M/I/L.
59. 9/13/02: M/O/AA.
60. 12/13/02: F/O/AA.
61. Judge Corriero, speaking to a group of doctors visiting the Youth Part, 9/13/02.
62. 8/16/02: M/O/L.
63. David B. Wexler, Therapeutic Jurisprudence and the Criminal Courts, in *Law in a Therapeutic Key: Developments in Therapeutic Jurisprudence*, David B. Wexler and Bruce J. Winick, eds. (Durham, NC: Carolina Academic Press, 1996): 166 [citing Donald Meichenbaum and Dennis C. Turk, *Facilitating Treatment Adherence: A Practitioner's Handbook*, 1987, 71–229].
64. 4/27/01: M/O/AA.
65. 9/13/02: M/O/AA.
66. 09/19/03: M/I/L.
67. 11/15/02: F/O/AA.
68. 3/14/03: M/O/AA.

CHAPTER 8: THE EXPERIMENT THAT FAILED

1. See John N. Kane Jr., Dispositional Authority and Decision-Making in New York's Juvenile Justice System: Discretion at Risk, Syracuse Law Rev. vol. 45, pp. 925, 930, citing Whisenand and McLoughlin, Completing the Cycle: Realty and The Juvenile Justice System in New York State, 47 Alb.L.Rev.1 (1982).
2. The Kent factors or criteria have influenced statutes in states across the nation since the mid-1960s. The case of *Kent v. United States,* 583 U.S. 541 (1966) arose in the District of Columbia and involved the transfer of a 14-year-old boy to adult court without a hearing. The Supreme Court held that the circumstances of transfer were unconstitutional and required the lower court to conduct a hearing. In an appendix

to the decision, the court set forth the following criteria and principles concerning waiver of jurisdiction: "An offense falling within the statutory limitations... will be waived if it has prosecutive merit and if it is heinous or of an aggravated character, or—even though less serious—if it represents a pattern of repeated offenses which indicate that the juvenile may be beyond rehabilitation under Juvenile Court procedures, or if the public needs the protection afforded by such action. The determinative factors which will be considered by the judge in deciding whether the juvenile court's jurisdiction over such offenses will be waived are the following: 1. The seriousness of the alleged offense to the community and whether the protection of the community requires waiver; 2. Whether the alleged offense was committed in an aggressive, violent, premeditated or willful manner; 3. Whether the alleged offense was against persons or against property, greater weight being given to offenses against persons especially if personal injury resulted; 4. The prosecutive merit of the complaint, i.e., whether there is evidence upon which a grand jury may be expected to return an indictment (to be determined by consultation with the [prosecuting attorney]); 5. The desirability of trial and disposition of the entire offense in one court when the juvenile's associates in the alleged offense are adults who will be charged with a crime in [criminal court]; 6. The sophistication and maturity of the juvenile as determined by consideration of his home, environmental situation, emotional attitude, and pattern of living; 7. The record and previous history of the juvenile, including previous contacts with [social service agencies], other law enforcement agencies, juvenile courts and other jurisdictions, prior periods of probation to [the court], or prior commitments to juvenile institutions; 8. The prospects for adequate protection of the public and the likelihood of reasonable rehabilitation of the juvenile (if he is found to have committed the alleged offense) by the use of procedures, services and facilities currently available to the juvenile court."

3. See Franklin E. Zimring, *American Youth Violence* (1998); *Changing Borders of Juvenile Justice: Transfer of Adolescents to the Criminal Court*, Jeffrey Fagan and Franklin E. Zimring, eds. (2000); *Youth on Trial*, Thomas Grisso and Robert G. Schwartz, eds. (2000).

4. P. Torbet, P. Griffin, and H. Hunt, Jr., Juveniles Facing Criminal Sanctions: Three States That Changed The Rules, U.S. Department of Justice, Office of Justice Programs, Office of Juvenile Justice and Delinquency Prevention (2000), p. xi.

5. See P. Griffin, P. Torbet, and L. Szymanski, Trying Juveniles as Adults in Criminal Court: An Analysis of State Transfer Provisions. Report, Washington DC; U.S. Department of Justice, Office of Justice Programs, Office of Juvenile Justice and Delinquency Prevention (1998), at p. 8.

6. Id at p. 1.

7. Laurence Steinberg, Should Juvenile Offenders Be Tried as Adults? A Developmental Prospective on Changing Legal Policies, paper presented as a part of a Congressional research briefing entitled "Juvenile Crime: Causes and Consequences," Washington, DC, January 19, 2000. Although state laws requiring or allowing the prosecution of juveniles as adults are commonly thought to be legislative responses to increases in juvenile violence, a surprising number of such laws authorize criminal prosecution for nonviolent offenses. Twenty-one states require or allow adult prosecution of juveniles accused of certain property offenses—most often arson or burglary. Statutes in 19 states authorize or mandate prosecution of juveniles accused

of drug offenses in Criminal Court. Forty-six states allow waiver to Criminal Court for a range of offenses—personal and property, violent and nonviolent.

8. *Supra* note 5 at p. 13.

9. *Supra* note 5 at p. 1.

10. See Robert B. Acton, Gubernatorial Initiatives and Rhetoric of Justice Reform, Journal of Law and Policy, vol. 5, no. 1, 277, 291–292 (1996).

11. See *supra* note 5.

12. Patrick Griffin (2003) "Transfer Provisions," State Juvenile Justice Profiles. Pittsburgh, PA: National Center for Juvenile Justice. Available online: <http://www.ncjj.org/stateprofiles/>.

13. See *supra* note 10 at p. 284–287.

14. The Experiment that Failed: The New York State Juvenile Offender Law—A Study Report prepared by the Citizen's Committee for Children of New York (December 1984), p. 15; in 1978 the states with a 16-year age of criminal responsibility were Connecticut, North Carolina, and Vermont, in addition to New York. New York remains only one of three states—the other two are Connecticut and North Carolina—that continues to prosecute 16- and 17-year-olds as adults. Melanie Bozynski and Linda Szymanski, State Juvenile Justice Profiles (last modified Feb. 4, 2003) <http://www.ncjj.org/stateprofiles/overviews/upperage/asp>.

15. Id. at p. 7; see also Mara T. Thorp, "Juvenile Justice Reform," Trial, The National Legal News Magazine, Jan. 1979, Lucia B. Whisenand and Edward J. McLoughlin, Completing the Cycle: Reality and the Juvenile Justice System in New York State, 47 Alb.L.Rev. 1 (1982).

16. See Jeffrey Fagan and Franklin E. Zimring, eds., *The Changing Borders of Juvenile Justice,* Chapter 10—The Reproduction of Juvenile Justice in Criminal Court: A Case Study of New York's Juvenile Offender Law, S. I. Singer, J. Fagan, and A. Liberman, n. 4, p. 374 (University of Chicago Press, 2000).

17. Preamble to "Making Neighborhoods Safer," gubernatorial memorandum in support of amendments to Juvenile Offender Law, 1999, at <http://www.state.ny.us/renewdoc/final/renew-spirit.htm>.

18. *New York Times,* Metropolitan Section, p. B4, col. 6, August 19, 1998, Law Permits Trial of Youths As Adults For Guns At School, quoting Gov. George E. Pataki.

19. New York was already moving in this direction as early as 1976. See *supra* note 16 at pp. 258–259.

20. A Study of the Legal Aid Society's Juvenile Offender Team, Advanced Project in Public Policy Analysis, Professor Charles Brecher (April 2004), team members: Melissa Auerbach, Jennifer Leung, Jessica Rosenzweig, Sarah Sheffield, at pp. 6–7.

21. See document prepared in support of the sponsorship of a public forum on "Systems and Services Issues to Address the Needs of Emotionally Disturbed Substance Abusing Adolescents Involved in the Criminal Justice Systems in New York City" (Nov. 21, 2001), prepared by New York University's School of Social Work and the Wagner School of Public Service.

22. Section 255 of the Family Court Act provides: "It is hereby made the duty of, and the family court or a judge thereof may order, any state, county, municipal and school district, officer and employee to render such assistance and cooperation as shall be within his legal authority, as may be required, to further the objects of this act... It is hereby made the duty of and the family court or judge thereof may order, any agency or other institution to render such information, assistance and

cooperation as shall be within its legal authority concerning a child who is or shall be under its care, treatment, supervision or custody as may be required to further the objects of this act. The court is authorized to seek the cooperation of, and may use, within its authorized appropriation therefore, the services of all societies or organizations, public or private, having for their object the protection or aid of children or families, including family counseling services, to the end that the court may be assisted in every reasonable way to give the children and families within its jurisdiction such care, protection and assistance as will best enhance their welfare."

23. In April 2004 a pilot project was instituted by the Probation Department to address the special needs of juveniles tried in adult courts. As a result, a special team of probation officers was assigned to the Youth Part. This project was discontinued in 2005 because of a lack of funding.

24. See Jeffrey Fagan, This Will Hurt Me More Than It Hurts You: Social and Legal Consequences of Criminalizing Delinquency, Notre Dame Journal of Law, Ethics and Public Policy, vol. 16, no. 1, p. 1 (2002), p. 30, and n. 140.

25. *Supra* note 14 at p. 112.

26. It should be noted that the author is a member of the Citizen's Committee for Children's Advisory Board.

27. Supra Note 14 at pp. 1–3.

28. Supra Note 14 at pp. 29–33.

29. Supra Note 14 at p. 132.

30. Report of The Juvenile Justice Committee of the Association of the Bar of the City of New York (1983) recommending repeal of the Juvenile Offender Law and return of jurisdiction of juveniles to the Family Court and providing the Family Court judges with waiver-up authority; but see minority report.

31. As of November 1, 2003, juveniles convicted of intentional or depraved indifference murder must be sentenced to a minimum of 7.5 years to 15 years. For juveniles convicted of felony murder, the minimum remains 5 to 9 years, the maximum remains life. The crime of unlawful possession of a weapon defined in Penal Law Article 265, which makes a juvenile criminally responsible for possession of a weapon on school grounds, was made a juvenile offender offense by New York's Laws of 1998, Chapter 435, effective November 1, 1998. The Juvenile Offender Law is actually a series of amendments scattered throughout multiple sections of New York's Criminal Procedure Law, Penal and Executive laws and the Family Court Act of New York State. The Juvenile Offender Law was enacted as part of the omnibus crime control bill of 1978 (Laws of 1978, CH. 481). This law removed from the jurisdiction of the Family Court all 13-, 14-, and 15-year-olds accused of serious violent offenses. The JO offenses are: murder in the second degree (N.Y. Penal Law Sec. 125.25 (1)(2) [hereinafter PL]) committed by a 13-, 14-, or 15-year-old and, if committed by a 14- or 15-year-old, felony murder, provided that the underlying crime is one for which the defendant is criminally responsible (PL sec. 125.25(3)); arson in the first degree (PL sec. 150.20); kidnapping in the first degree (PL sec. 135.25); aggravated sexual abuse (PL sec. 130.70); arson in the second degree (PL sec. 150.15); assault in the first degree (PL sec. 120.10 (1)(2)); attempted kidnapping in the first degree (PL sec. 110/135.25); attempted murder in the second degree (PL sec. 110/125.25); burglary in the first degree (PL sec. 140.30); burglary in the second degree (PL sec. 140.25(1)(a),(b),(c),(d); manslaughter in the first degree (PL sec. 125.20); rape in the first degree (PL sec.

130.35(1)(2)); robbery in the first degree (PL sec. 160.15); robbery in the second degree (PL sec. 160.10 (2)(a)(b); sodomy in the first degree (PL sec. 130.50 (1)(2)); criminal possession of a weapon in the second degree (PL sec. 265.03) where such weapon is possessed on school grounds; criminal possession of a weapon in the third degree (PL sec. 265.02) where such weapon is possessed on school grounds. See PL sections 10.00 (18), 30.00; N.Y. Criminal Procedure Law section 1.20 (42) (hereinafter CPL). A juvenile offender who is not adjudicated a "youthful offender" must be sentenced to an indeterminate term of imprisonment. PL sections 60.10, 70.05. The sentencing parameters are as follows: For the class A felony of murder in the second degree (intentional and depraved), the minimum sentence is 7.5 to life; the maximum is 15 to life. For the class A felonies of arson in the first degree and kidnapping in the first degree, a juvenile offender may be sentenced to an indeterminate term with a minimum of 4 years and a maximum of 15 years, or a minimum of 6 years and a maximum of 12 years, or any combination in between. For class B felonies, the minimum sentence is an indeterminate term of imprisonment of 1 to 3 years and the maximum is 3 1/3 to 10 years; for class C felonies, the minimum sentence is an indeterminate term of imprisonment of 1 to 3 years and the maximum is 2 1/3 to 7 years. For class D felonies, the minimum sentence is an indeterminate term of 1 to 3 years and the maximum is 1 1/3 to 4 years. See Eric Warner, *The Juvenile Offender Handbook* (Looseleaf Publications, Inc., 2004).
32. *Supra* note 21.
33. Id.
34. An Evaluation of Secure Centers Operated by the New York State Division for Youth, foreword, p. VII, Jan. 1995.
35. Id.
36. New York Family Court Act, Art. 3, Sec. 351.1.
37. Fagan, *supra* note 24, p. 29. See also Simon Singer and David McDowall, *Criminalizing Delinquency: The Deterrent Effects of the New York Juvenile Offender Law* (University of New York at Buffalo and Albany, 1987). This study conducted by the State University of New York and funded by the National Institute of Justice evaluated the deterrent effect of the New York State Juvenile Offender Law. The study concluded that the law had no measurable effect on subsequent arrest of juveniles for serious crimes; Donna M. Bishop, Juvenile Offenders in the Adult Criminal Justice System, 27 Crime and Justice: A Review of Research 81, 85 (2000). Ms. Bishop reviewed two decades of research on transfer and concluded that the trend of criminalizing juvenile delinquents through the expansion of transfer mechanisms was not only ineffective but also harmful.
38. Fagan *supra* note 24.
39. Fagan *supra* note 24 at p. 42.
40. Fagan *supra* note 24 at p. 28; see also Laurence Steinberg et al., Reentry of Young Offenders from the Justice System: A Developmental Perspective, 2 Youth Violence & Juv. Just. 21 (2004), pp. 28–29.

CHAPTER 9: CREATION OF THE YOUTH PART

1. The Courthouse, which opened in 1916, is located at 137 East 22nd Street, New York. It is now part of Baruch College.

2. Johnson, *Introduction to the Juvenile Justice System* (West Publishing Co., 1975), p. 26.

3. Id. See generally Ludwig, *Youth and the Law* (1955), Chapter 2; this chapter is adapted, in part, from an article of the author entitled Youth Parts: A Constructive Response to the Challenge of Youth Crime, N.Y.L.J. Oct. 26, 1990, p. 1 col. 1. The article traced the development of Youthful Offender (YO) Treatment and the historical context of separate youth parts in New York.

4. L. 1943, CC549–551, eff. Sept. 1, 1943 became Sec. 31a to 31h N.Y. City Crim.Ct.Act, and Sec. 252a to 252h, Code Crim.Proc. Under L. 1944 Ch.632, Sec. 2, eff. April 7, 1944, the section numbers in the code became 913e to 913m; see Ludwig, *supra* note 3, p. 78, n. 7 for source of citation.

5. Waxner, New York Criminal Practice, vol. 2, Chapter 16, para. 16.1.

6. N.Y. Code Crim Proc. Sec. 913k; N.Y. Crim.Ct.Act Sec. 31g.

7. Court of Special Sessions, Youth Part Rules, adopted 1943, amend. 1945 Rules 1–4, Benders Rules of the Court (1st ed. 1947); see, Ludwig, *supra* note 3, p. 76, n. 12 for source of citation.

8. Rule 1 of the Rules of the Criminal Court, eff. as of Sept. 1, 1962, established a part in each county of the city, designated as Part Three for the: "Arraignment, pleadings, examination, trials and sentence of persons who have reached the age of 16 years but have not reached the age of 19 years..." McKinney's 1980 New York Rules of Court Sec. 2950.1 (22 NYCRR Sec. 2950.1). The Rules of the Supreme Court for each county in the City also provided for the separate treatment of youths between the ages of 16 and 19: New York and the Bronx, McKinney's 1980 edition, Rules of the Court, Sec. 666.3(c); Kings Sec. 751, Queens Sec. 796.8, and Richmond Sec. 755.27.

9. See generally Davis, *Rights of Juveniles* (1980), in particular Sec. 1.3.

10. N.Y. Crim.Proc.Law Sec. 1.20(42).

11. On the promulgation of the Uniform Rules of the Court, eff. Jan. 6, 1986, the rules providing for separate parts were rescinded. Research does not reveal any comparable rules in the Uniform Rules. Section 200.2(b) of the Uniform Rules for courts exercising criminal jurisdiction 22 NYCRR Sec. 200.2 (b) provides, however, "... there shall be such parts as may be authorized to be established from time to time by the chief administrator of the courts."

12. Michael A. Corriero, Youth Parts: A Constructive Response to the Challenge of Youth Crime, N.Y.L.J. Oct. 26, 1990, p. 1, col. 1.

13. Written remarks of Commissioner Rose Washington on file in chambers of Judge Michael A. Corriero.

14. Daniel Wise, New Part Set Up for Cases Against Violent Youths, N.Y.L.J., p. 1, col. 5, p. 38.

15. Letter of Martin P. Murphy dated July 30, 1992, on behalf of Fritz W. Alexander II, Deputy Mayor of New York City, on file in chambers of Judge Michael A. Corriero.

16. Ellen Schall is currently Dean of New York University's Wagner School of Public Affairs.

17. For example, in the case of Danny (Danny was used as a human holster by older youths), his case was resolved in 48 days from his arrest, as compared to an average of 110 days to resolution for similar youths previously prosecuted in adult court; see Wise article, *supra* note 14.

18. Memorandum from Deputy Mayor Fritz W. Alexander II dated February 22, 1993, to Judge Michael A. Corriero, on file in chambers of Judge Michael A. Corriero.
19. See David Steinhart, vol. 1, *Pathways to Juvenile Detention Reform* (Baltimore: The Annie E. Casey Foundation, 1999).
20. *Supra* note 18.
21. See Jack Kresnak, Modern Youth Jails Grow as Youth Advocates Try to Thin the Crowd, Youth Today, Sept. 1999, p. 28.
22. *New York Times,* Tues., May 25, 1993, p. B1.
23. For example, Larry Reibstein, Kids In The Dock: What Should A Judge Do With Underage Felons, *Newsweek,* May 26, 1997; William Murphy, Youth Crime No Kid Stuff: Judge Deals With Offenses On Adult Level, *Newsday,* April 17, 1994, at A 22; David Noonan, Young Ex-Cons Given Second Chance At Life, *N.Y. Daily News,* September 26, 1999, at 24; Ralph Gardener Jr., Friday Morning Breakfast Club: One Judge, 30 Teenagers and Me, *The New York Observer,* March 11, 2002.

CHAPTER 10: THE YOUTH PART MODEL

1. N. Machiavelli, Preface, *The Discourses.*
2. Snyder, H., Sickmund, M., and Poe-Yamagata, E. (2000) *Juvenile Transfers to Criminal Court in the 1990s: Lessons Learned From Four Studies* (Washington, DC: U.S. Department of Justice, Office of Justice Programs, Office of Juvenile Justice and Delinquency Prevention), p. xi.
3. Torbet, Patricia, et al. (2000) *Juveniles Facing Criminal Sanctions: Three States That Changed the Rules* (Washington, DC: U.S. Department of Justice, Office of Justice Programs, Office of Juvenile Justice and Delinquency Prevention), p. 3.
4. According to New York's Center for Court Innovation, more than 1,000 problem-solving courts are in existence. Every state has at least one in operation or in the planning stage. The Judges' Journal, American Bar Association, vol. 41, no. 1, Winter 2002, Greg Berman and John Feinblatt, *Beyond Process and Precedent: The Rise of Problem Solving Courts,* p. 6.
5. Eleventh Annual Report of the Big Brothers Movement, October 1916. Foreword, p. 7.
6. Elizabeth Stull, After a Century Probation Has Become New York's Most Frequent Sentence, (December 24, 2001), N.Y.L.J. 1 col. 3.
7. See report prepared for National Center for State Courts on Promising Components of Problem-Solving Courts: Pamela Casey and William E. Hewitt, Court Reponses to Individuals in Need of Services: Promising Components of Service Coordination Strategy for Courts, 2001.
8. In 2001 the Department of Education assigned an employee and a social worker to the Youth Part to speed readmission of students released from custody. When the School Connection Project was launched, this assignment was discontinued.
9. 42 U.S.C.A. Sec. 5633 (a)(12–13).
10. Assembly Bill No. 6975, 1999–2000, sponsored by Assemblyman Roger Green an act to amend the Family Court Act and the Criminal Procedure Law in creation of special juvenile-criminal parts, submitted March 17, 1999—read once and referred to the Committee on Children and Families.

CHAPTER 11: A MODEL JUVENILE JUSTICE SYSTEM

1. See Laurence Steinberg, MacArthur Foundation Study Calls Competency into Question, Criminal Justice (ABA Crim. Just. Section Magazine), Fall 2003, p. 20, at p. 21.

2. No Easy Answers: Juvenile Justice in a Climate of Fear, The Tenth Report to the President, The Congress, and the Administrator of the Office of Juvenile Justice and Delinquency Prevention, submitted by the Coalition for Juvenile Justice, 1995, pp. 28, 29. See also Jeffrey Fagan, This Will Hurt Me More Than It Hurts You: Social and Legal Consequences of Criminalizing Delinquency, Notre Dame Journal of Law, Ethics and Public Policy, vol. 16, no. 1, (2002), p. 28 (and studies cited therein).

3. Michael A. Corriero, A Democratic Society's Response to Juvenile Crime, Brooklyn Law Review, vol. 65, no. 3 (Fall 1999).

4. Franklin E. Zimring, *American Youth Violence,* at p. 11 (Oxford University Press, 1998).

5. Id.

6. Id.

7. Id.

8. Id. at 25.

9. Id. at 50, 63.

10. Id. at 174–175.

11. Id. at 125.

12. Violent Youth: A Call To Arms—The Need for Effective Treatment in the Juvenile Justice System, the Schools and the Community, A Report of the Committee on Youth Services, The Council of the City of New York (December 1990), pp. 20–21.

13. Id. at p. 73 quoting Jeffrey Fagan, Social and Legal Policy Dimensions of Violent Juveniles, 17 Crim. Justice and Behavior 93, 122 (March 1990).

14. Fox Butterfield, Repaving the Long Road Out of Prison, *New York Times,* May 4, 2004, A25.

15. Creating the Next Crime Wave, Editorial, *New York Times,* March 13, 2004, p. A16.

16. January 20, 2004, State of the Union Address, <http://www.whitehouse.gov/news/releases/2004/01/20040120–7.html>.

17. New York does provide for a "Certificate of Relief from Disabilities" for certain offenders. N.Y. Correction Law Article 23, Discretionary Relief from Forfeitures and Disabilities Automatically Imposed by Law. A certificate usually removes what are called "statutory bars" to employment or occupational licenses. This means that "instead of automatically being disqualified for a particular job or license because of your conviction(s), you have the right to be considered for the position on an individual basis." Certificates of Relief from Disability and Certificates of Good Conduct, a publication of the Legal Action Center, 2003, 153 Waverly Place, New York, New York 10014.

18. Penal Law sections 70.05 and 60.10.

19. New Jersey, N.J.S.A. 2C:15–1 (Robbery defined) and N.J.S.A. 2C:44–1f(b).

20. California, CA Penal Pt. 1, T.8, ch.4, section 212.5 (Robbery, Degrees defined) and section 213 (Robbery, Punishment).

21. Texas, V.T.C.A., Penal Code section 29.03 (aggravated robbery) and V.T.C.A., Penal Code section 12.32 (first degree felony punishment). See also Linda F. Giardino, Statutory Rhetoric: The Reality Behind Juvenile Justice Policies in America, 5 J.L. & Pol'y 203 (1996), 270 fn. 150. (Citing to Tex.Fam.Code Ann. Section 54.04 (d)(3)).

22. See Thomas A. Johnson, *Introduction to the Juvenile Justice System* (West Publishing Co., 1976), p. 31.

23. Patricia Torbet et al., *Juveniles Facing Criminal Sanctions: Three States That Changed the Rules* (Washington, DC: U.S. Department of Justice, Office of Justice Programs, Office of Juvenile Justice and Delinquency Prevention, 2000), p. iii.

24. Id.

25. Requiring that no juvenile under 14 years of age be transferred to adult court without a specific finding of competence is consistent with recommendations of experts in the field of child psychology who have found that "current knowledge about adolescent development raises strong doubts about the capacities of youths 13 and younger... to assist effectively in their own defense and to make self-interested decisions." Youth In The Criminal Justice System, ABA Task Force Publication, p. 15, n. 31. See Richard J. Bonnie and Thomas Grisso, Adjudicative Competence and Youth Offenders, in Thomas Grisso and Robert Schwartz, eds., Youth on Trial: A Developmental Perspective on Juvenile Justice 89 (2000).

26. See IJA-ABA Juvenile Justice Standards relating to transfer between courts, standard 1.1; see also United Nations Convention on the Rights of the Child.

27. *Roper v. Simmons*, 2005 WL 464890 (U.S.Mo.), 125 S.Ct. 1183 (2005).

28. Id. at 9–10; 125 S.Ct. at 1195–1196.

29. President's Commission on Crime in the District of Columbia, 1966, p. 733.

30. John A. F. Watson, *The Child and the Magistrate* (London: Jonathan Cape, 1965), p. 42.

31. See *I Vote My Conscience: Debates, Speeches and Writings of Vito Marcantonio,* selected and edited by Annette T. Rubeinstein and Associates (The Vito Marcantonio Memorial, 1956), reprinted by the Calandra Institute in 2002, p. 2.

32. This quote has been attributed to Judge Ben B. Lindsey, although my research has not revealed the source. For further information concerning Judge Lindsey, see Charles Larsen, *The Good Fight: The Life and Times of Ben B. Lindsey* (Quadrangle, 1972).

CHAPTER 12: JUVENILE JUSTICE POLICY REFORM

1. An alliance of approximately 50 child advocacy agencies representing physicians, behavioral scientists, and lawyers joined together to file an amicus brief in *Roper v. Simmons,* the Supreme Court case that banned the juvenile death penalty. See Patrick Boyle, Behind the Death Penalty Ban, Youth Today, vol. 14, no. 4 (April 2005), p. 1, at p. 37.

2. For example, the MacArthur Foundation through its development and support of The Research Network in Adolescent Development and Juvenile Justice has provided grants for research, model programs, and public education related to juvenile justice policy. It should be noted that I have served as a consultant to the Research Network Project.

3. The Juvenile Justice and Delinquency Act, 42 U.S.C. Section 5601.

4. The Juvenile Accountability Block Grants (JABG) program, established in 1998, is administered by the State Relations and Assistance Division of the Office of Juvenile Justice and Delinquency Prevention (OJJDP), Office of Justice Programs, U.S. Department of Justice. Through the JABG program, funds are provided as

block grants to states for programs promoting greater accountability in the juvenile justice system; see <http://www.ojjdp.ncjrs.org>.

5. See Michael Jacobson, *How to Reduce Crime and End Mass Incarceration, Downsizing Prisons* (New York University Press, 2005), Chapter 7.

6. *Guide For Implementing The Comprehensive Strategy For Serious, Violent and Chronic Juvenile Offenders,* James C. Howell, ed. (Office of Juvenile Justice and Delinquency Prevention, June 1995).

7. 42 The Record of the Association of the Bar of the City of New York 948 (1987), reprinted in 10 Cardozo L.Rev.3, 22 (1988).

8. Id. at 10 Cardozo L.Rev.3, p. 13.

9. It should be noted that although the Supreme Court has not definitively ruled that a judicial hearing before prosecution in an adult court is required by the due process clause, other courts have ruled that the placement of exclusive jurisdiction over a special class of juvenile offenders in the adult criminal courts by an "informed" legislature does not warrant a Kent-type hearing. See *United States v. Bland,* 472 F.2d 1329, cert. den. 412 U.S. 909; *Cox v. United States,* 473 F.2d 334, cert. den. 414 U.S. 869; *United States v. Alexander,* 333 F. Supp. 1213; *Woodward v. Wainright,* 556 F.2d 781, n. 10; *Broadway v. Beto,* 338 F. Supp. 827, aff'd. 459 F.2d 483, cert. den. 409 U.S. 1012; *United States v. Quinones,* 353 F. Supp. 1325, aff'd. 516 F.2d 1309, cert. den. 423 U.S. 852; *United States ex rel. Walker v. Maroney,* 444 F.2d 47.

Index